T0325432

THIS IS YOUR **PASSBOOK**® FOR ...

CLERICAL ASSOCIATE

NLC®

NATIONAL LEARNING CORPORATION®
passbooks.com

Copyright © 2018 by

National Learning Corporation

212 Michael Drive, Syosset, NY 11791
(516) 921-8888 • www.passbooks.com
E-mail: info@passbooks.com

PUBLISHED IN THE UNITED STATES OF AMERICA

PASSBOOK® SERIES

THE *PASSBOOK® SERIES* has been created to prepare applicants and candidates for the ultimate academic battlefield – the examination room.

At some time in our lives, each and every one of us may be required to take an examination – for validation, matriculation, admission, qualification, registration, certification, or licensure.

Based on the assumption that every applicant or candidate has met the basic formal educational standards, has taken the required number of courses, and read the necessary texts, the *PASSBOOK® SERIES* furnishes the one special preparation which may assure passing with confidence, instead of failing with insecurity. Examination questions – together with answers – are furnished as the basic vehicle for study so that the mysteries of the examination and its compounding difficulties may be eliminated or diminished by a sure method.

This book is meant to help you pass your examination provided that you qualify and are serious in your objective.

The entire field is reviewed through the huge store of content information which is succinctly presented through a provocative and challenging approach – the question-and-answer method.

A climate of success is established by furnishing the correct answers at the end of each test.

You soon learn to recognize types of questions, forms of questions, and patterns of questioning. You may even begin to anticipate expected outcomes.

You perceive that many questions are repeated or adapted so that you can gain acute insights, which may enable you to score many sure points.

You learn how to confront new questions, or types of questions, and to attack them confidently and work out the correct answers.

You note objectives and emphases, and recognize pitfalls and dangers, so that you may make positive educational adjustments.

Moreover, you are kept fully informed in relation to new concepts, methods, practices, and directions in the field.

You discover that you arre actually taking the examination all the time: you are preparing for the examination by "taking" an examination, not by reading extraneous and/or supererogatory textbooks.

In short, this PASSBOOK®, used directedly, should be an important factor in helping you to pass your test.

CLERICAL ASSOCIATE

DUTIES

Clerical Associates, under general supervision, with a limited latitude for independent judgment, perform clerical work in relation to records, files, invoices and reports using alphabetical and numerical procedures including data/control coding; perform ordinary mathematical calculations; operate a telephone call directory or switchboard; perform clerical operations in an assigned area, such as the filing of material and the searching of files for material difficult to locate; prepare reports requiring the selection of data from simple records or statistics; check records for accuracy of information and for conformity with established policy and procedures; perform data entry and retrieval using a video display terminal or other automated office systems; maintain related library files; may perform incidental typing.

SCOPE OF THE EXAMINATION

The multiple-choice test may include questions on standards of proper employee ethical conduct, and questions which require the use of any of the following abilities:

1. **Deductive Reasoning**: The ability to apply general rules to specific problems to come up with logical answers. It involves deciding if an answer makes sense. It is also defined as Alphabetical and Numerical Coding, or the ability to classify or code files, records, correspondence, and forms according to their contents using a standard/prescribed classification system;

2. **Information Ordering**: The ability to follow correctly a rule or set of rules or actions in a certain order. The rule or set of rules used must be given. The things or actions to be put in order can include numbers, letters, words, pictures, procedures, sentences and mathematical or logical operations. Specifically for Clerical Associate it includes the ability to file items in the proper alphabetical or numerical sequence;

3. **Number Facility**: The degree to which adding, subtracting, multiplying and dividing can be done quickly and correctly. This can be steps in other operations like finding percentages;

4. **Matching:** The degree to which one can compare letters, numbers, objects, pictures or patterns accurately. It includes the ability to detect errors, make the appropriate corrections, and recognize similarities in clerical materials; and

5. **Written Expression**: The ability to use English words or sentences in writing so that others will understand.

HOW TO TAKE A TEST

I. YOU MUST PASS AN EXAMINATION

A. WHAT EVERY CANDIDATE SHOULD KNOW

Examination applicants often ask us for help in preparing for the written test. What can I study in advance? What kinds of questions will be asked? How will the test be given? How will the papers be graded?

As an applicant for a civil service examination, you may be wondering about some of these things. Our purpose here is to suggest effective methods of advance study and to describe civil service examinations.

Your chances for success on this examination can be increased if you know how to prepare. Those "pre-examination jitters" can be reduced if you know what to expect. You can even experience an adventure in good citizenship if you know why civil service exams are given.

B. WHY ARE CIVIL SERVICE EXAMINATIONS GIVEN?

Civil service examinations are important to you in two ways. As a citizen, you want public jobs filled by employees who know how to do their work. As a job seeker, you want a fair chance to compete for that job on an equal footing with other candidates. The best-known means of accomplishing this two-fold goal is the competitive examination.

Exams are widely publicized throughout the nation. They may be administered for jobs in federal, state, city, municipal, town or village governments or agencies.

Any citizen may apply, with some limitations, such as the age or residence of applicants. Your experience and education may be reviewed to see whether you meet the requirements for the particular examination. When these requirements exist, they are reasonable and applied consistently to all applicants. Thus, a competitive examination may cause you some uneasiness now, but it is your privilege and safeguard.

C. HOW ARE CIVIL SERVICE EXAMS DEVELOPED?

Examinations are carefully written by trained technicians who are specialists in the field known as "psychological measurement," in consultation with recognized authorities in the field of work that the test will cover. These experts recommend the subject matter areas or skills to be tested; only those knowledges or skills important to your success on the job are included. The most reliable books and source materials available are used as references. Together, the experts and technicians judge the difficulty level of the questions.

Test technicians know how to phrase questions so that the problem is clearly stated. Their ethics do not permit "trick" or "catch" questions. Questions may have been tried out on sample groups, or subjected to statistical analysis, to determine their usefulness.

Written tests are often used in combination with performance tests, ratings of training and experience, and oral interviews. All of these measures combine to form the best-known means of finding the right person for the right job.

II. HOW TO PASS THE WRITTEN TEST

A. NATURE OF THE EXAMINATION

To prepare intelligently for civil service examinations, you should know how they differ from school examinations you have taken. In school you were assigned certain definite pages to read or subjects to cover. The examination questions were quite detailed and usually emphasized memory. Civil service exams, on the other hand, try to discover your present ability to perform the duties of a position, plus your potentiality to learn these duties. In other words, a civil service exam attempts to predict how successful you will be. Questions cover such a broad area that they cannot be as minute and detailed as school exam questions.

In the public service similar kinds of work, or positions, are grouped together in one "class." This process is known as *position-classification*. All the positions in a class are paid according to the salary range for that class. One class title covers all of these positions, and they are all tested by the same examination.

B. FOUR BASIC STEPS

1) Study the announcement

How, then, can you know what subjects to study? Our best answer is: "Learn as much as possible about the class of positions for which you've applied." The exam will test the knowledge, skills and abilities needed to do the work.

Your most valuable source of information about the position you want is the official exam announcement. This announcement lists the training and experience qualifications. Check these standards and apply only if you come reasonably close to meeting them.

The brief description of the position in the examination announcement offers some clues to the subjects which will be tested. Think about the job itself. Review the duties in your mind. Can you perform them, or are there some in which you are rusty? Fill in the blank spots in your preparation.

Many jurisdictions preview the written test in the exam announcement by including a section called "Knowledge and Abilities Required," "Scope of the Examination," or some similar heading. Here you will find out specifically what fields will be tested.

2) Review your own background

Once you learn in general what the position is all about, and what you need to know to do the work, ask yourself which subjects you already know fairly well and which need improvement. You may wonder whether to concentrate on improving your strong areas or on building some background in your fields of weakness. When the announcement has specified "some knowledge" or "considerable knowledge," or has used adjectives like "beginning principles of…" or "advanced … methods," you can get a clue as to the number and difficulty of questions to be asked in any given field. More questions, and hence broader coverage, would be included for those subjects which are more important in the work. Now weigh your strengths and weaknesses against the job requirements and prepare accordingly.

3) Determine the level of the position

Another way to tell how intensively you should prepare is to understand the level of the job for which you are applying. Is it the entering level? In other words, is this the position in which beginners in a field of work are hired? Or is it an intermediate or advanced level? Sometimes this is indicated by such words as "Junior" or "Senior" in the class title. Other jurisdictions use Roman numerals to designate the level – Clerk I, Clerk II, for example. The word "Supervisor" sometimes appears in the title. If the level is not indicated by the title, check the description of duties. Will you be working under very close supervision, or will you have responsibility for independent decisions in this work?

4) Choose appropriate study materials

Now that you know the subjects to be examined and the relative amount of each subject to be covered, you can choose suitable study materials. For beginning level jobs, or even advanced ones, if you have a pronounced weakness in some aspect of your training, read a modern, standard textbook in that field. Be sure it is up to date and has general coverage. Such books are normally available at your library, and the librarian will be glad to help you locate one. For entry-level positions, questions of appropriate difficulty are chosen – neither highly advanced questions, nor those too simple. Such questions require careful thought but not advanced training.

If the position for which you are applying is technical or advanced, you will read more advanced, specialized material. If you are already familiar with the basic principles of your field, elementary textbooks would waste your time. Concentrate on advanced textbooks and technical periodicals. Think through the concepts and review difficult problems in your field.

These are all general sources. You can get more ideas on your own initiative, following these leads. For example, training manuals and publications of the government agency which employs workers in your field can be useful, particularly for technical and professional positions. A letter or visit to the government department involved may result in more specific study suggestions, and certainly will provide you with a more definite idea of the exact nature of the position you are seeking.

III. KINDS OF TESTS

Tests are used for purposes other than measuring knowledge and ability to perform specified duties. For some positions, it is equally important to test ability to make adjustments to new situations or to profit from training. In others, basic mental abilities not dependent on information are essential. Questions which test these things may not appear as pertinent to the duties of the position as those which test for knowledge and information. Yet they are often highly important parts of a fair examination. For very general questions, it is almost impossible to help you direct your study efforts. What we can do is to point out some of the more common of these general abilities needed in public service positions and describe some typical questions.

1) General information

Broad, general information has been found useful for predicting job success in some kinds of work. This is tested in a variety of ways, from vocabulary lists to questions about current events. Basic background in some field of work, such as sociology or economics, may be sampled in a group of questions. Often these are principles which have become familiar to most persons through exposure rather than through formal training. It is difficult to advise you how to study for these questions; being alert to the world around you is our best suggestion.

2) Verbal ability

An example of an ability needed in many positions is verbal or language ability. Verbal ability is, in brief, the ability to use and understand words. Vocabulary and grammar tests are typical measures of this ability. Reading comprehension or paragraph interpretation questions are common in many kinds of civil service tests. You are given a paragraph of written material and asked to find its central meaning.

3) Numerical ability

Number skills can be tested by the familiar arithmetic problem, by checking paired lists of numbers to see which are alike and which are different, or by interpreting charts and graphs. In the latter test, a graph may be printed in the test booklet which you are asked to use as the basis for answering questions.

4) Observation

A popular test for law-enforcement positions is the observation test. A picture is shown to you for several minutes, then taken away. Questions about the picture test your ability to observe both details and larger elements.

5) Following directions

In many positions in the public service, the employee must be able to carry out written instructions dependably and accurately. You may be given a chart with several columns, each column listing a variety of information. The questions require you to carry out directions involving the information given in the chart.

6) Skills and aptitudes

Performance tests effectively measure some manual skills and aptitudes. When the skill is one in which you are trained, such as typing or shorthand, you can practice. These tests are often very much like those given in business school or high school courses. For many of the other skills and aptitudes, however, no short-time preparation can be made. Skills and abilities natural to you or that you have developed throughout your lifetime are being tested.

Many of the general questions just described provide all the data needed to answer the questions and ask you to use your reasoning ability to find the answers. Your best preparation for these tests, as well as for tests of facts and ideas, is to be at your physical and mental best. You, no doubt, have your own methods of getting into an exam-taking mood and keeping "in shape." The next section lists some ideas on this subject.

IV. KINDS OF QUESTIONS

Only rarely is the "essay" question, which you answer in narrative form, used in civil service tests. Civil service tests are usually of the short-answer type. Full instructions for answering these questions will be given to you at the examination. But in case this is your first experience with short-answer questions and separate answer sheets, here is what you need to know:

1) Multiple-choice Questions

Most popular of the short-answer questions is the "multiple choice" or "best answer" question. It can be used, for example, to test for factual knowledge, ability to solve problems or judgment in meeting situations found at work.

A multiple-choice question is normally one of three types—

- It can begin with an incomplete statement followed by several possible endings. You are to find the one ending which *best* completes the statement, although some of the others may not be entirely wrong.
- It can also be a complete statement in the form of a question which is answered by choosing one of the statements listed.
- It can be in the form of a problem – again you select the best answer.

Here is an example of a multiple-choice question with a discussion which should give you some clues as to the method for choosing the right answer:

When an employee has a complaint about his assignment, the action which will *best* help him overcome his difficulty is to
- A. discuss his difficulty with his coworkers
- B. take the problem to the head of the organization
- C. take the problem to the person who gave him the assignment
- D. say nothing to anyone about his complaint

In answering this question, you should study each of the choices to find which is best. Consider choice "A" – Certainly an employee may discuss his complaint with fellow employees, but no change or improvement can result, and the complaint remains unresolved. Choice "B" is a poor choice since the head of the organization probably does not know what assignment you have been given, and taking your problem to him is known as "going over the head" of the supervisor. The supervisor, or person who made the assignment, is the person who can clarify it or correct any injustice. Choice "C" is, therefore, correct. To say nothing, as in choice "D," is unwise. Supervisors have and interest in knowing the problems employees are facing, and the employee is seeking a solution to his problem.

2) True/False Questions

The "true/false" or "right/wrong" form of question is sometimes used. Here a complete statement is given. Your job is to decide whether the statement is right or wrong.

SAMPLE: A roaming cell-phone call to a nearby city costs less than a non-roaming call to a distant city.

This statement is wrong, or false, since roaming calls are more expensive.
This is not a complete list of all possible question forms, although most of the others are variations of these common types. You will always get complete directions for

answering questions. Be sure you understand *how* to mark your answers – ask questions until you do.

V. RECORDING YOUR ANSWERS

Computer terminals are used more and more today for many different kinds of exams.

For an examination with very few applicants, you may be told to record your answers in the test booklet itself. Separate answer sheets are much more common. If this separate answer sheet is to be scored by machine – and this is often the case – it is highly important that you mark your answers correctly in order to get credit.

An electronic scoring machine is often used in civil service offices because of the speed with which papers can be scored. Machine-scored answer sheets must be marked with a pencil, which will be given to you. This pencil has a high graphite content which responds to the electronic scoring machine. As a matter of fact, stray dots may register as answers, so do not let your pencil rest on the answer sheet while you are pondering the correct answer. Also, if your pencil lead breaks or is otherwise defective, ask for another.

Since the answer sheet will be dropped in a slot in the scoring machine, be careful not to bend the corners or get the paper crumpled.

The answer sheet normally has five vertical columns of numbers, with 30 numbers to a column. These numbers correspond to the question numbers in your test booklet. After each number, going across the page are four or five pairs of dotted lines. These short dotted lines have small letters or numbers above them. The first two pairs may also have a "T" or "F" above the letters. This indicates that the first two pairs only are to be used if the questions are of the true-false type. If the questions are multiple choice, disregard the "T" and "F" and pay attention only to the small letters or numbers.

Answer your questions in the manner of the sample that follows:

32. The largest city in the United States is
    A. Washington, D.C.
    B. New York City
    C. Chicago
    D. Detroit
    E. San Francisco

1) Choose the answer you think is best. (New York City is the largest, so "B" is correct.)
2) Find the row of dotted lines numbered the same as the question you are answering. (Find row number 32)
3) Find the pair of dotted lines corresponding to the answer. (Find the pair of lines under the mark "B.")
4) Make a solid black mark between the dotted lines.

VI. BEFORE THE TEST

Common sense will help you find procedures to follow to get ready for an examination. Too many of us, however, overlook these sensible measures. Indeed, nervousness and fatigue have been found to be the most serious reasons why applicants fail to do their best on civil service tests. Here is a list of reminders:

- Begin your preparation early – Don't wait until the last minute to go scurrying around for books and materials or to find out what the position is all about.
- Prepare continuously – An hour a night for a week is better than an all-night cram session. This has been definitely established. What is more, a night a week for a month will return better dividends than crowding your study into a shorter period of time.
- Locate the place of the exam – You have been sent a notice telling you when and where to report for the examination. If the location is in a different town or otherwise unfamiliar to you, it would be well to inquire the best route and learn something about the building.
- Relax the night before the test – Allow your mind to rest. Do not study at all that night. Plan some mild recreation or diversion; then go to bed early and get a good night's sleep.
- Get up early enough to make a leisurely trip to the place for the test – This way unforeseen events, traffic snarls, unfamiliar buildings, etc. will not upset you.
- Dress comfortably – A written test is not a fashion show. You will be known by number and not by name, so wear something comfortable.
- Leave excess paraphernalia at home – Shopping bags and odd bundles will get in your way. You need bring only the items mentioned in the official notice you received; usually everything you need is provided. Do not bring reference books to the exam. They will only confuse those last minutes and be taken away from you when in the test room.
- Arrive somewhat ahead of time – If because of transportation schedules you must get there very early, bring a newspaper or magazine to take your mind off yourself while waiting.
- Locate the examination room – When you have found the proper room, you will be directed to the seat or part of the room where you will sit. Sometimes you are given a sheet of instructions to read while you are waiting. Do not fill out any forms until you are told to do so; just read them and be prepared.
- Relax and prepare to listen to the instructions
- If you have any physical problem that may keep you from doing your best, be sure to tell the test administrator. If you are sick or in poor health, you really cannot do your best on the exam. You can come back and take the test some other time.

VII. AT THE TEST

The day of the test is here and you have the test booklet in your hand. The temptation to get going is very strong. Caution! There is more to success than knowing the right answers. You must know how to identify your papers and understand variations in the type of short-answer question used in this particular examination. Follow these suggestions for maximum results from your efforts:

1) Cooperate with the monitor

The test administrator has a duty to create a situation in which you can be as much at ease as possible. He will give instructions, tell you when to begin, check to see that you are marking your answer sheet correctly, and so on. He is not there to guard you, although he will see that your competitors do not take unfair advantage. He wants to help you do your best.

2) Listen to all instructions

Don't jump the gun! Wait until you understand all directions. In most civil service tests you get more time than you need to answer the questions. So don't be in a hurry. Read each word of instructions until you clearly understand the meaning. Study the examples, listen to all announcements and follow directions. Ask questions if you do not understand what to do.

3) Identify your papers

Civil service exams are usually identified by number only. You will be assigned a number; you must not put your name on your test papers. Be sure to copy your number correctly. Since more than one exam may be given, copy your exact examination title.

4) Plan your time

Unless you are told that a test is a "speed" or "rate of work" test, speed itself is usually not important. Time enough to answer all the questions will be provided, but this does not mean that you have all day. An overall time limit has been set. Divide the total time (in minutes) by the number of questions to determine the approximate time you have for each question.

5) Do not linger over difficult questions

If you come across a difficult question, mark it with a paper clip (useful to have along) and come back to it when you have been through the booklet. One caution if you do this – be sure to skip a number on your answer sheet as well. Check often to be sure that you have not lost your place and that you are marking in the row numbered the same as the question you are answering.

6) Read the questions

Be sure you know what the question asks! Many capable people are unsuccessful because they failed to *read* the questions correctly.

7) Answer all questions

Unless you have been instructed that a penalty will be deducted for incorrect answers, it is better to guess than to omit a question.

8) Speed tests

It is often better NOT to guess on speed tests. It has been found that on timed tests people are tempted to spend the last few seconds before time is called in marking answers at random – without even reading them – in the hope of picking up a few extra points. To discourage this practice, the instructions may warn you that your score will be "corrected" for guessing. That is, a penalty will be applied. The incorrect answers will be deducted from the correct ones, or some other penalty formula will be used.

9) Review your answers

If you finish before time is called, go back to the questions you guessed or omitted to give them further thought. Review other answers if you have time.

10) Return your test materials

If you are ready to leave before others have finished or time is called, take ALL your materials to the monitor and leave quietly. Never take any test material with you. The monitor can discover whose papers are not complete, and taking a test booklet may be grounds for disqualification.

VIII. EXAMINATION TECHNIQUES

1) Read the general instructions carefully. These are usually printed on the first page of the exam booklet. As a rule, these instructions refer to the timing of the examination; the fact that you should not start work until the signal and must stop work at a signal, etc. If there are any *special* instructions, such as a choice of questions to be answered, make sure that you note this instruction carefully.

2) When you are ready to start work on the examination, that is as soon as the signal has been given, read the instructions to each question booklet, underline any key words or phrases, such as *least, best, outline, describe* and the like. In this way you will tend to answer as requested rather than discover on reviewing your paper that you *listed without describing*, that you selected the *worst* choice rather than the *best* choice, etc.

3) If the examination is of the objective or multiple-choice type – that is, each question will also give a series of possible answers: A, B, C or D, and you are called upon to select the best answer and write the letter next to that answer on your answer paper – it is advisable to start answering each question in turn. There may be anywhere from 50 to 100 such questions in the three or four hours allotted and you can see how much time would be taken if you read through all the questions before beginning to answer any. Furthermore, if you come across a question or group of questions which you know would be difficult to answer, it would undoubtedly affect your handling of all the other questions.

4) If the examination is of the essay type and contains but a few questions, it is a moot point as to whether you should read all the questions before starting to answer any one. Of course, if you are given a choice – say five out of seven and the like – then it is essential to read all the questions so you can eliminate the two that are most difficult. If, however, you are asked to answer all the questions, there may be danger in trying to answer the easiest one first because you may find that you will spend too much time on it. The best technique is to answer the first question, then proceed to the second, etc.

5) Time your answers. Before the exam begins, write down the time it started, then add the time allowed for the examination and write down the time it must be completed, then divide the time available somewhat as follows:

- If 3-1/2 hours are allowed, that would be 210 minutes. If you have 80 objective-type questions, that would be an average of 2-1/2 minutes per question. Allow yourself no more than 2 minutes per question, or a total of 160 minutes, which will permit about 50 minutes to review.
- If for the time allotment of 210 minutes there are 7 essay questions to answer, that would average about 30 minutes a question. Give yourself only 25 minutes per question so that you have about 35 minutes to review.

6) The most important instruction is to *read each question* and make sure you know what is wanted. The second most important instruction is to *time yourself properly* so that you answer every question. The third most important instruction is to *answer every question.* Guess if you have to but include something for each question. Remember that you will receive no credit for a blank and will probably receive some credit if you write something in answer to an essay question. If you guess a letter – say "B" for a multiple-choice question – you may have guessed right. If you leave a blank as an answer to a multiple-choice question, the examiners may respect your feelings but it will not add a point to your score. Some exams may penalize you for wrong answers, so in such cases *only*, you may not want to guess unless you have some basis for your answer.

7) Suggestions
   a. Objective-type questions
      1. Examine the question booklet for proper sequence of pages and questions
      2. Read all instructions carefully
      3. Skip any question which seems too difficult; return to it after all other questions have been answered
      4. Apportion your time properly; do not spend too much time on any single question or group of questions
      5. Note and underline key words – *all, most, fewest, least, best, worst, same, opposite,* etc.
      6. Pay particular attention to negatives
      7. Note unusual option, e.g., unduly long, short, complex, different or similar in content to the body of the question
      8. Observe the use of "hedging" words – *probably, may, most likely,* etc.
      9. Make sure that your answer is put next to the same number as the question
      10. Do not second-guess unless you have good reason to believe the second answer is definitely more correct
      11. Cross out original answer if you decide another answer is more accurate; do not erase until you are ready to hand your paper in
      12. Answer all questions; guess unless instructed otherwise
      13. Leave time for review

   b. Essay questions
      1. Read each question carefully
      2. Determine exactly what is wanted. Underline key words or phrases.
      3. Decide on outline or paragraph answer

4. Include many different points and elements unless asked to develop any one or two points or elements
5. Show impartiality by giving pros and cons unless directed to select one side only
6. Make and write down any assumptions you find necessary to answer the questions
7. Watch your English, grammar, punctuation and choice of words
8. Time your answers; don't crowd material

8) Answering the essay question

Most essay questions can be answered by framing the specific response around several key words or ideas. Here are a few such key words or ideas:

M's: manpower, materials, methods, money, management
P's: purpose, program, policy, plan, procedure, practice, problems, pitfalls, personnel, public relations
  a. Six basic steps in handling problems:
     1. Preliminary plan and background development
     2. Collect information, data and facts
     3. Analyze and interpret information, data and facts
     4. Analyze and develop solutions as well as make recommendations
     5. Prepare report and sell recommendations
     6. Install recommendations and follow up effectiveness

  b. Pitfalls to avoid
     1. *Taking things for granted* – A statement of the situation does not necessarily imply that each of the elements is necessarily true; for example, a complaint may be invalid and biased so that all that can be taken for granted is that a complaint has been registered
     2. *Considering only one side of a situation* – Wherever possible, indicate several alternatives and then point out the reasons you selected the best one
     3. *Failing to indicate follow up* – Whenever your answer indicates action on your part, make certain that you will take proper follow-up action to see how successful your recommendations, procedures or actions turn out to be
     4. *Taking too long in answering any single question* – Remember to time your answers properly

IX. AFTER THE TEST

Scoring procedures differ in detail among civil service jurisdictions although the general principles are the same. Whether the papers are hand-scored or graded by machine we have described, they are nearly always graded by number. That is, the person who marks the paper knows only the number – never the name – of the applicant. Not until all the papers have been graded will they be matched with names. If other tests, such as training and experience or oral interview ratings have been given, scores will be combined. Different parts of the examination usually have different weights. For example, the written test might count 60 percent of the final grade, and a rating of training and experience 40 percent. In many jurisdictions, veterans will have a certain number of points added to their grades.

After the final grade has been determined, the names are placed in grade order and an eligible list is established. There are various methods for resolving ties between those who get the same final grade – probably the most common is to place first the name of the person whose application was received first. Job offers are made from the eligible list in the order the names appear on it. You will be notified of your grade and your rank as soon as all these computations have been made. This will be done as rapidly as possible.

People who are found to meet the requirements in the announcement are called "eligibles." Their names are put on a list of eligible candidates. An eligible's chances of getting a job depend on how high he stands on this list and how fast agencies are filling jobs from the list.

When a job is to be filled from a list of eligibles, the agency asks for the names of people on the list of eligibles for that job. When the civil service commission receives this request, it sends to the agency the names of the three people highest on this list. Or, if the job to be filled has specialized requirements, the office sends the agency the names of the top three persons who meet these requirements from the general list.

The appointing officer makes a choice from among the three people whose names were sent to him. If the selected person accepts the appointment, the names of the others are put back on the list to be considered for future openings.

That is the rule in hiring from all kinds of eligible lists, whether they are for typist, carpenter, chemist, or something else. For every vacancy, the appointing officer has his choice of any one of the top three eligibles on the list. This explains why the person whose name is on top of the list sometimes does not get an appointment when some of the persons lower on the list do. If the appointing officer chooses the second or third eligible, the No. 1 eligible does not get a job at once, but stays on the list until he is appointed or the list is terminated.

X. HOW TO PASS THE INTERVIEW TEST

The examination for which you applied requires an oral interview test. You have already taken the written test and you are now being called for the interview test – the final part of the formal examination.

You may think that it is not possible to prepare for an interview test and that there are no procedures to follow during an interview. Our purpose is to point out some things you can do in advance that will help you and some good rules to follow and pitfalls to avoid while you are being interviewed.

What is an interview supposed to test?

The written examination is designed to test the technical knowledge and competence of the candidate; the oral is designed to evaluate intangible qualities, not readily measured otherwise, and to establish a list showing the relative fitness of each candidate – as measured against his competitors – for the position sought. Scoring is not on the basis of "right" and "wrong," but on a sliding scale of values ranging from "not passable" to "outstanding." As a matter of fact, it is possible to achieve a relatively low score without a single "incorrect" answer because of evident weakness in the qualities being measured.

Occasionally, an examination may consist entirely of an oral test – either an individual or a group oral. In such cases, information is sought concerning the technical knowledges and abilities of the candidate, since there has been no written examination for this purpose. More commonly, however, an oral test is used to supplement a written examination.

Who conducts interviews?

The composition of oral boards varies among different jurisdictions. In nearly all, a representative of the personnel department serves as chairman. One of the members of the board may be a representative of the department in which the candidate would work. In some cases, "outside experts" are used, and, frequently, a businessman or some other representative of the general public is asked to serve. Labor and management or other special groups may be represented. The aim is to secure the services of experts in the appropriate field.

However the board is composed, it is a good idea (and not at all improper or unethical) to ascertain in advance of the interview who the members are and what groups they represent. When you are introduced to them, you will have some idea of their backgrounds and interests, and at least you will not stutter and stammer over their names.

What should be done before the interview?

While knowledge about the board members is useful and takes some of the surprise element out of the interview, there is other preparation which is more substantive. It *is* possible to prepare for an oral interview – in several ways:

1) Keep a copy of your application and review it carefully before the interview

This may be the only document before the oral board, and the starting point of the interview. Know what education and experience you have listed there, and the sequence and dates of all of it. Sometimes the board will ask you to review the highlights of your experience for them; you should not have to hem and haw doing it.

2) Study the class specification and the examination announcement

Usually, the oral board has one or both of these to guide them. The qualities, characteristics or knowledges required by the position sought are stated in these documents. They offer valuable clues as to the nature of the oral interview. For example, if the job involves supervisory responsibilities, the announcement will usually indicate that knowledge of modern supervisory methods and the qualifications of the candidate as a supervisor will be tested. If so, you can expect such questions, frequently in the form of a hypothetical situation which you are expected to solve. NEVER go into an oral without knowledge of the duties and responsibilities of the job you seek.

3) Think through each qualification required

Try to visualize the kind of questions you would ask if you were a board member. How well could you answer them? Try especially to appraise your own knowledge and background in each area, *measured against the job sought*, and identify any areas in which you are weak. Be critical and realistic – do not flatter yourself.

4) Do some general reading in areas in which you feel you may be weak

For example, if the job involves supervision and your past experience has NOT, some general reading in supervisory methods and practices, particularly in the field of human relations, might be useful. Do NOT study agency procedures or detailed manuals. The oral board will be testing your understanding and capacity, not your memory.

5) Get a good night's sleep and watch your general health and mental attitude

You will want a clear head at the interview. Take care of a cold or any other minor ailment, and of course, no hangovers.

What should be done on the day of the interview?

Now comes the day of the interview itself. Give yourself plenty of time to get there. Plan to arrive somewhat ahead of the scheduled time, particularly if your appointment is in the fore part of the day. If a previous candidate fails to appear, the board might be ready for you a bit early. By early afternoon an oral board is almost invariably behind schedule if there are many candidates, and you may have to wait. Take along a book or magazine to read, or your application to review, but leave any extraneous material in the waiting room when you go in for your interview. In any event, relax and compose yourself.

The matter of dress is important. The board is forming impressions about you – from your experience, your manners, your attitude, and your appearance. Give your personal appearance careful attention. Dress your best, but not your flashiest. Choose conservative, appropriate clothing, and be sure it is immaculate. This is a business interview, and your appearance should indicate that you regard it as such. Besides, being well groomed and properly dressed will help boost your confidence.

Sooner or later, someone will call your name and escort you into the interview room. *This is it.* From here on you are on your own. It is too late for any more preparation. But remember, you asked for this opportunity to prove your fitness, and you are here because your request was granted.

What happens when you go in?

The usual sequence of events will be as follows: The clerk (who is often the board stenographer) will introduce you to the chairman of the oral board, who will introduce you to the other members of the board. Acknowledge the introductions before you sit down. Do not be surprised if you find a microphone facing you or a stenotypist sitting by. Oral interviews are usually recorded in the event of an appeal or other review.

Usually the chairman of the board will open the interview by reviewing the highlights of your education and work experience from your application – primarily for the benefit of the other members of the board, as well as to get the material into the record. Do not interrupt or comment unless there is an error or significant misinterpretation; if that is the case, do not hesitate. But do not quibble about insignificant matters. Also, he will usually ask you some question about your education, experience or your present job – partly to get you to start talking and to establish the interviewing "rapport." He may start the actual questioning, or turn it over to one of the other members. Frequently, each member undertakes the questioning on a particular area, one in which he is perhaps most competent, so you can expect each member to participate in the examination. Because time is limited, you may also expect some rather abrupt switches in the direction the questioning takes, so do not be upset by it. Normally, a board member will not pursue a single line of questioning unless he discovers a particular strength or weakness.

After each member has participated, the chairman will usually ask whether any member has any further questions, then will ask you if you have anything you wish to add. Unless you are expecting this question, it may floor you. Worse, it may start you off on an extended, extemporaneous speech. The board is not usually seeking more information. The question is principally to offer you a last opportunity to present further qualifications or to indicate that you have nothing to add. So, if you feel that a significant qualification or characteristic has been overlooked, it is proper to point it out in a sentence or so. Do not compliment the board on the thoroughness of their examination – they have been sketchy, and you know it. If you wish, merely say, "No thank you, I have nothing further to add." This is a point where you can "talk yourself out" of a good impression or fail to present an important bit of information. Remember, *you close the interview yourself.*

The chairman will then say, "That is all, Mr. _____, thank you." Do not be startled; the interview is over, and quicker than you think. Thank him, gather your belongings and take your leave. Save your sigh of relief for the other side of the door.

How to put your best foot forward

Throughout this entire process, you may feel that the board individually and collectively is trying to pierce your defenses, seek out your hidden weaknesses and embarrass and confuse you. Actually, this is not true. They are obliged to make an appraisal of your qualifications for the job you are seeking, and they want to see you in your best light. Remember, they must interview all candidates and a non-cooperative candidate may become a failure in spite of their best efforts to bring out his qualifications. Here are 15 suggestions that will help you:

1) Be natural – Keep your attitude confident, not cocky

If you are not confident that you can do the job, do not expect the board to be. Do not apologize for your weaknesses, try to bring out your strong points. The board is interested in a positive, not negative, presentation. Cockiness will antagonize any board member and make him wonder if you are covering up a weakness by a false show of strength.

2) Get comfortable, but don't lounge or sprawl

Sit erectly but not stiffly. A careless posture may lead the board to conclude that you are careless in other things, or at least that you are not impressed by the importance of the occasion. Either conclusion is natural, even if incorrect. Do not fuss with your clothing, a pencil or an ashtray. Your hands may occasionally be useful to emphasize a point; do not let them become a point of distraction.

3) Do not wisecrack or make small talk

This is a serious situation, and your attitude should show that you consider it as such. Further, the time of the board is limited – they do not want to waste it, and neither should you.

4) Do not exaggerate your experience or abilities

In the first place, from information in the application or other interviews and sources, the board may know more about you than you think. Secondly, you probably will not get away with it. An experienced board is rather adept at spotting such a situation, so do not take the chance.

5) If you know a board member, do not make a point of it, yet do not hide it

Certainly you are not fooling him, and probably not the other members of the board. Do not try to take advantage of your acquaintanceship – it will probably do you little good.

6) Do not dominate the interview

Let the board do that. They will give you the clues – do not assume that you have to do all the talking. Realize that the board has a number of questions to ask you, and do not try to take up all the interview time by showing off your extensive knowledge of the answer to the first one.

7) Be attentive

You only have 20 minutes or so, and you should keep your attention at its sharpest throughout. When a member is addressing a problem or question to you, give him your undivided attention. Address your reply principally to him, but do not exclude the other board members.

8) Do not interrupt

A board member may be stating a problem for you to analyze. He will ask you a question when the time comes. Let him state the problem, and wait for the question.

9) Make sure you understand the question

Do not try to answer until you are sure what the question is. If it is not clear, restate it in your own words or ask the board member to clarify it for you. However, do not haggle about minor elements.

10) Reply promptly but not hastily

A common entry on oral board rating sheets is "candidate responded readily," or "candidate hesitated in replies." Respond as promptly and quickly as you can, but do not jump to a hasty, ill-considered answer.

11) Do not be peremptory in your answers

A brief answer is proper – but do not fire your answer back. That is a losing game from your point of view. The board member can probably ask questions much faster than you can answer them.

12) Do not try to create the answer you think the board member wants

He is interested in what kind of mind you have and how it works – not in playing games. Furthermore, he can usually spot this practice and will actually grade you down on it.

13) Do not switch sides in your reply merely to agree with a board member

Frequently, a member will take a contrary position merely to draw you out and to see if you are willing and able to defend your point of view. Do not start a debate, yet do not surrender a good position. If a position is worth taking, it is worth defending.

14) Do not be afraid to admit an error in judgment if you are shown to be wrong

  The board knows that you are forced to reply without any opportunity for careful consideration. Your answer may be demonstrably wrong. If so, admit it and get on with the interview.

15) Do not dwell at length on your present job

  The opening question may relate to your present assignment. Answer the question but do not go into an extended discussion. You are being examined for a *new* job, not your present one. As a matter of fact, try to phrase ALL your answers in terms of the job for which you are being examined.

Basis of Rating

  Probably you will forget most of these "do's" and "don'ts" when you walk into the oral interview room. Even remembering them all will not ensure you a passing grade. Perhaps you did not have the qualifications in the first place. But remembering them will help you to put your best foot forward, without treading on the toes of the board members.

  Rumor and popular opinion to the contrary notwithstanding, an oral board wants you to make the best appearance possible. They know you are under pressure – but they also want to see how you respond to it as a guide to what your reaction would be under the pressures of the job you seek. They will be influenced by the degree of poise you display, the personal traits you show and the manner in which you respond.

ABOUT THIS BOOK

  This book contains tests divided into Examination Sections. Go through each test, answering every question in the margin. At the end of each test look at the answer key and check your answers. On the ones you got wrong, look at the right answer choice and learn. Do not fill in the answers first. Do not memorize the questions and answers, but understand the answer and principles involved. On your test, the questions will likely be different from the samples. Questions are changed and new ones added. If you understand these past questions you should have success with any changes that arise. Tests may consist of several types of questions. We have additional books on each subject should more study be advisable or necessary for you. Finally, the more you study, the better prepared you will be. This book is intended to be the last thing you study before you walk into the examination room. Prior study of relevant texts is also recommended. NLC publishes some of these in our Fundamental Series. Knowledge and good sense are important factors in passing your exam. Good luck also helps. So now study this Passbook, absorb the material contained within and take that knowledge into the examination. Then do your best to pass that exam.

————

EXAMINATION SECTION

EXAMINATION SECTION
TEST 1

DIRECTIONS: Each question or incomplete statement is followed by several suggested answers or completions. Select the one that *BEST* answers the question or completes the statement. *PRINT THE LETTER OF THE CORRECT ANSWER IN THE SPACE AT THE RIGHT.*

Questions 1-5.

DIRECTIONS: Each question from 1 to 5 consists of a sentence with an underlined word. For each question, select the choice that is *CLOSEST* in meaning to the underlined word.

EXAMPLE

This division reviews the <u>fiscal</u> reports of the agency.
In this sentence the word *fiscal* means most nearly
   A. financial   B. critical   C. basic   D. personnel
The correct answer is A. "financial" because "financial" is closest to *fiscal.* Therefore, the answer is A.

1. Every good office worker needs <u>basic</u> skills.   1.____
    The word *basic* in this sentence means

    A. fundamental   B. advanced   C. unusual   D. outstanding

2. He turned out to be a good <u>instructor</u>.   2.____
    The word *instructor* in this sentence means

    A. student   B. worker   C. typist   D. teacher

3. The <u>quantity</u> of work in the office was under study.   3.____
    In this sentence, the word *quantity* means

    A. amount   B. flow   C. supervision   D. type

4. The morning was spent <u>examining</u> the time records.   4.____
    In this sentence, the word *examining* means

    A. distributing   B. collecting   C. checking   D. filing

5. The candidate filled in the <u>proper</u> spaces on the form.   5.____
    In this sentence, the word *proper* means

    A. blank   B. appropriate   C. many   D. remaining

Questions 6-8.

DIRECTIONS: You are to answer Questions 6 through 8 *SOLELY* on the basis of the information contained in the following paragraph:

The increase in the number of public documents in the last two centuries closely matches the increase in population in the United States. The great number of public documents has become a serious threat to their usefulness. It is necessary to have programs which will reduce the number of public documents that are kept and which will, at the same time, assure keeping those that have value. Such programs need a great deal of thought to have any success.

6. According to the above paragraph, public documents may be less useful if 6.____

    A. the files are open to the public
    B. the record room is too small
    C. the copying machine is operated only during normal working hours
    D. too many records are being kept

7. According to the above paragraph, the growth of the population in the United States has matched the growth in the quantity of public documents for a period of, most nearly, 7.____

    A. 50 years   B. 100 years   C. 200 years   D. 300 years

8. According to the above paragraph, the increased number of public documents has made it necessary to 8.____

    A. find out which public documents are worth keeping
    B. reduce the great number of public documents by decreasing government services
    C. eliminate the copying of all original public documents
    D. avoid all new copying devices.

Questions 9-10.

DIRECTIONS: You are to answer Questions 9 and 10 *SOLELY* on the basis of the information contained in the following paragraph:

The work goals of an agency can best be reached if the employees understand and agree with these goals. One way to gain such understanding and agreement is for management to encourage and seriously consider suggestions from employees in the setting of agency goals.

9. On the basis of the paragraph above, the *BEST* way to achieve the work goals of an agency is to 9.____

    A. make certain that employees work as hard as possible
    B. study the organizational structure of the agency
    C. encourage employees to think seriously about the agency's problems
    D. stimulate employee understanding of the work goals

10. On the basis of the paragraph above, understanding and agreement with agency goals can be gained by 10.____

    A. allowing the employees to set agency goals
    B. reaching agency goals quickly
    C. legislative review of agency operations
    D. employee participation in setting agency goals

Questions 11-15.

DIRECTIONS: Each of Questions 11 through 15 consists of a group of four words. One word in each group is *INCORRECTLY* spelled. For each question, print the letter of the correct answer in the space at the right that is the same as the letter next to the word which is *INCORRECTLY* spelled.

EXAMPLE

    A. housing   B. certain   C. budgit   D. money

The word "budgit" is incorrectly spelled, because the correct spelling should be "budget." Therefore, the correct answer is C.

11.	A.	sentince	B.	bulletin	C.	notice	D.	definition	11.____
12.	A.	appointment	B.	exactly	C.	typest	D.	light	12.____
13.	A.	penalty	B.	suparvise	C.	consider	D.	division	13.____
14.	A.	schedule	B.	accurate	C.	corect	D.	simple	14.____
15.	A.	suggestion	B.	installed	C.	proper	D.	agincy	15.____

Questions 16-20.

DIRECTIONS: Each question from 16 through 20 consists of a sentence which may be
  A.   incorrect because of bad word usage, or
  B.   incorrect because of bad punctuation, or
  C.   incorrect because of bad spelling, or
  D.   correct

Read each sentence carefully. Then print in the proper space at the right A, B, C, or D, according to the answer you choose from the four choices listed above. There is only one type of error in each incorrect sentence. If there is no error, the sentence is correct.

EXAMPLE

George Washington was the father of his contry.
This sentence is incorrect because of bad spelling ("contry" instead of "country"). Therefore, the answer is C.

16. The assignment was completed in record time but the payroll for it has not yet been pre-   16.____
parid.

17. The operator, on the other hand, is willing to learn me how to use the mimeograph.   17.____

18. She is the prettiest of the three sisters.   18.____

19. She doesn't know; if the mail has arrived.   19.____

20. The doorknob of the office door is broke.   20.____

21. A clerk can process a form in 15 minutes. How many forms can that clerk process in six   21.____
hours?

  A.   10   B.   21   C.   24   D.   90

22. An office staff consists of 120 people. Sixty of them have been assigned to a special   22.____
project. Of the remaining staff, 20 answer the mail, 10-handle phone calls, and the rest
operate the office machines. The number of people operating the office machines is

  A.   20   B.   30   C.   40   D.   45

23. An office worker received 65 applications but on the first day had to return 26 of them for   23.____
being incomplete and on the second day 25 had to be returned for being incomplete.
How many applications did <u>not</u> have to be returned?

  A.   10   B.   12   C.   14   D.   16

24. An office worker answered 63 phone calls in one day and 91 phone calls the next day. For these 2 days, what was the average number of phone calls he answered per day?

    A. 77   B. 28   C. 82   D. 93

24.____

25. An office worker processed 12 vouchers of $8.75 each, 3 vouchers of $3.68 each, and 2 vouchers of $1.29 each. The total dollar amount of these vouchers is

    A. $116.04   B. $117.52   C. $118.62   D. $119.04

25.____

KEY (CORRECT ANSWERS)

1.	A		11.	A
2.	D		12.	C
3.	A		13.	B
4.	C		14.	C
5.	B		15.	D
6.	D		16.	C
7.	C		17.	A
8.	A		18.	D
9.	D		19.	B
10.	D		20.	A

21.	C
22.	B
23.	C
24.	A
25.	C

TEST 2

DIRECTIONS: Each question or incomplete statement is followed by several suggested answers or completions. Select the one that *BEST* answers the question or completes the statement. *PRINT THE LETTER OF THE CORRECT ANSWER IN THE SPACE AT THE RIGHT.*

Questions 1-5.

DIRECTIONS: Each question from 1 to 5 lists four names. The names may or may not be exactly the same. Compare the names in each question and mark your answer as follows:

Mark your answer A if all the names are different
Mark your answer B if only two names are exactly the same
Mark your answer C if only three names are exactly the same
Mark your answer D if all four names are exactly the same

EXAMPLE

Jensen, Alfred E.
Jensen, Alfred E.
Jensan, Alfred E.
Jensen, Fred E.

Since the name Jensen, Alfred E. appears twice and is exactly the same in both places, the correct answer is B.

1. Riviera, Pedro S.   1.____
   Rivers, Pedro S.
   Riviera, Pedro N.
   Riviera, Juan S.

2. Guider, Albert   2.____
   Guidar, Albert
   Giuder, Alfred
   Guider, Albert

3. Blum, Rona   3.____
   Blum, Rona
   Blum, Rona
   Blum, Rona

4. Raugh, John   4.____
   Raugh, James
   Raughe, John
   Raugh, John

5. Katz, Stanley   5.____
   Katz, Stanley
   Katze, Stanley
   Katz, Stanley

Questions 6-10.

DIRECTIONS: Each Question 6 through 10 consists of numbers or letters in Columns I and II. For each question, compare each line of Column I with its corresponding line in Column II and decide how many lines in Column I are *EXACTLY* the same as their corresponding lines in Column II. In your answer space, mark your answer as follows:

Mark your answer A if only *ONE* line in Column I is exactly the same as its corresponding line in Column II
Mark your answer B if only *TWO* lines in Column I are exactly the same as their corresponding lines in Column II
Mark your answer C if only *THREE* lines in Column I are exactly the same as their corresponding lines in Column II
Mark your answer D if all *FOUR* lines in Column I are exactly the same as their corresponding lines in Column II

EXAMPLE

Column I	Column II
1776	1776
1865	1865
1945	1945
1976	1978

Only three lines in Column I are exactly the same as their corresponding lines in Column II. Therefore, the correct answer is C.

	Column I	Column II	
6.	5653 8727 ZPSS 4952	5653 8728 ZPSS 9453	6._____
7.	PNJP NJPJ JNPN PNJP	PNPJ NJPJ JNPN PNPJ	7._____
8.	effe uWvw KpGj vmnv	eFfe uWvw KpGg vmnv	8._____
9.	5232 PfrC zssz rwwr	5232 PfrN zzss rwww	9._____
10.	czws cecc thrm lwtz	czws cece thrm lwtz	10._____

6

Questions 11-15.

DIRECTIONS: Questions 11 through 15 have lines of letters and numbers. Each letter should be matched with its number in accordance with the following table:

Letter	F	R	C	A	W	L	E	N	B	T
Matching Number	0	1	2	3	4	5	6	7	8	9

From the table you can determine that the letter F has the matching number 0 below it, the letter R has the matching number 1 below it, etc.

For each question, compare each line of letters and numbers carefully to see if each letter has its correct matching number. If all the letters and numbers are matched correctly in
none of the lines of the question, mark your answer A
only one of the lines of the question, mark your answer B
only two of the lines of the question, mark your answer C
all three lines of the question, mark your answer D

EXAMPLE

WBCR   4826
TLBF   9580
ATNE   3986

There is a mistake in the first line because the letter R should have its matching number 1 instead of the number 6.

The second line is correct because each letter shown has the correct matching number.

There is a mistake in the third line because the letter N should have the matching number 7 instead of the number 8,

Since all the letters and numbers are matched correctly in only one of the lines in the sample, the correct answer is B.

11.   EBCT   6829   11._____
         ATWR   3961
         NLBW   7584

12.   RNCT   1729   12._____
         LNCR   5728
         WAEB   5368

13.   NTWB   7948   13._____
         RABL   1385
         TAEF   9360

14.   LWRB   5417   14._____
         RLWN   1647
         CBWA   2843

15.   ABTC   3792   15._____
         WCER   5261
         AWCN   3417

16. Your job often brings you into contact with the public. Of the following, it would be *MOST*   16._____
desirable to explain the reasons for official actions to people coming into your office for
assistance because such explanations

    A.   help build greater understanding between the public and your agency
    B.   help build greater self-confidence in city employees
    C.   convince the public that nothing they do can upset a city employee
    D.   show the public that city employees are intelligent

17. Assume that you strongly dislike one of your co-workers.   17._____
You should *FIRST*

    A.   discuss your feeling with the co-worker
    B.   demand a transfer to another office
    C.   suggest to your supervisor that the co-worker should be observed carefully
    D.   try to figure out the reason for this dislike before you say or do anything

18. An office worker who has problems accepting authority is *MOST* likely to find it difficult to   18._____

    A.   obey rules   B.   understand people
    C.   assist other employees   D.   follow complex instructions

19. The employees in your office have taken a dislike to one person and frequently annoy   19._____
her. Your supervisor *should*

    A.   transfer this person to another unit at the first opportunity
    B.   try to find out the reason for the staff's attitude before doing anything about it
    C.   threaten to transfer the first person observed bothering this person
    D.   ignore the situation

20. Assume that your supervisor has asked a worker in your office to get a copy of a report   20._____
out of the files. You notice the worker has accidentally pulled out the wrong report.
Of the following, the *BEST* way for you to handle this situation is to tell

    A.   the worker about all the difficulties that will result from this error
    B.   the worker about her mistake in a nice way
    C.   the worker to ignore this error
    D.   your supervisor that this worker needs more training in how to use the files

21. Filing systems differ in their efficiency. Which of the following is the *BEST* way to evaluate   21._____
the efficiency of a filing system?
The

    A.   number of times used per day
    B.   amount of material that is received each day for filing
    C.   amount of time it takes to locate material
    D.   type of locking system used

22. In planning ahead so that a sufficient amount of general office supplies is always avail-   22._____
able, it would be *LEAST* important to find out the

    A.   current office supply needs of the staff
    B.   amount of office supplies used last year
    C.   days and times that office supplies can be ordered
    D.   agency goals and objectives

23. The *MAIN* reason for establishing routine office work procedures is that once a routine is established

    A. work need not be checked for accuracy
    B. all steps in the routine will take an equal amount of time to perform
    C. each time the job is repeated it will take less time to perform
    D. each step in the routine will not have to be planned all over again each time

23.____

24. When an office machine centrally located in an agency must be shut down for repairs, the bureaus and divisions using this machine should be informed of the

    A. expected length of time before the machine will be in operation again
    B. estimated cost of repairs
    C. efforts being made to avoid future repairs
    D. type of new equipment which the agency may buy in the future to replace the machine being repaired

24.____

25. If the day's work is properly scheduled, the *MOST* important result would be that the

    A. supervisor will not have to do much supervision
    B. employee will know what to do next
    C. employee will show greater initiative
    D. job will become routine

25.____

KEY (CORRECT ANSWERS)

1.	A		11.	C
2.	B		12.	B
3.	D		13.	D
4.	B		14.	B
5.	C		15.	A
6.	B		16.	A
7.	B		17.	D
8.	B		18.	A
9.	A		19.	B
10.	C		20.	B

21.	C
22.	D
23.	D
24.	A
25.	B

EXAMINATION SECTION
TEST 1

DIRECTIONS: Each question or incomplete statement is followed by several suggested
answers or completions. Select the one that BEST answers the question or
completes the statement. *PRINT THE LETTER OF THE CORRECT ANSWER
IN THE SPACE AT THE RIGHT.*

1. Assume that a few co-workers meet near your desk and talk about personal matters dur-   1._____
    ing working hours. Lately, this practice has interfered with your work.
    In order to stop this practice, the BEST action for you to take FIRST is to

    A.   ask your supervisor to put a stop to the co-workers' meeting near your desk
    B.   discontinue any friendship with this group
    C.   ask your co-workers not to meet near your desk
    D.   request that your desk be moved to another location

2. In order to maintain office coverage during working hours, your supervisor has scheduled   2._____
    your lunch hour from 1 P.M. to 2 P.M. and your co-worker's lunch hour from 12 P.M. to 1
    P.M. Lately, your co-worker has been returning late from lunch each day. As a result, you
    don't get a full hour since you must return to the office by 2 P.M.
    Of the following, the BEST action for you to take FIRST is to

    A.   explain to your co-worker in a courteous manner that his lateness is interfering with
         your right to a full hour for lunch
    B.   tell your co-worker that his lateness must stop or you will report him to your super-
         visor
    C.   report your co-worker's lateness to your supervisor
    D.   leave at 1 P.M. for lunch, whether your co-worker has returned or not

3. Assume that, as an office worker, one of your jobs is to open mail sent to your unit, read   3._____
    the mail for content, and send the mail to the appropriate person to handle. You acciden-
    tally open and begin to read a letter marked *personal* addressed to a co-worker.
    Of the following, the BEST action for you to take is to

    A.   report to your supervisor that your co-worker is receiving personal mail at the office
    B.   destroy the letter so that your co-worker does not know you saw it
    C.   reseal the letter and place it on the co-worker's desk without saying anything
    D.   bring the letter to your co-worker and explain that you opened it by accident

4. Suppose that in evaluating your work, your supervisor gives you an overall good rating,   4._____
    but states that you sometimes turn in work with careless errors.
    The BEST action for you to take would be to

    A.   ask a co-worker who is good at details to proofread your work
    B.   take time to do a careful job, paying more attention to detail
    C.   continue working as usual since occasional errors are to be expected
    D.   ask your supervisor if she would mind correcting your errors

5. Assume that you are taking a telephone message for a co-worker who is not in the office   5._____
    at the time.
    Of the following, the LEAST important item to write on the message is the

    A.   length of the call   B.   name of the caller
    C.   time of the call   D.   telephone number of the caller

Questions 6-13.

DIRECTIONS: Questions 6 through 13 each consist of a sentence which may or may not be an example of good English. The underlined parts of each sentence may be correct or incorrect. Examine each sentence, considering grammar, punctuation, spelling, and capitalization. If the English usage in the underlined parts of the sentence given is better than any of the changes in the underlined words suggested in Options B, C, or D, choose Option A. If the changes in the underlined words suggested in Options B, C, or D would make the sentence correct, choose the correct option. Do not choose an option that will change the meaning of the sentence.

6. This Fall, the office will be closed on Columbus Day, October 9th.   6._____

    A. Correct as is
    B. fall...Columbus Day, October
    C. Fall...columbus day, October
    D. fall...Columbus Day, october

7. This manual discribes the duties performed by an Office Aide.   7._____

    A. Correct as is
    B. describe the duties performed
    C. discribe the duties performed
    D. describes the duties performed

8. There weren't no paper in the supply closet.   8._____

    A. Correct as is   B. weren't any
    C. wasn't any   D. wasn't no

9. The new employees left there office to attend a meeting.   9._____

    A. Correct as is   B. they're
    C. their   D. thier

10. The office worker started working at 8;30 a.m.   10._____

    A. Correct as is   B. 8:30 a.m.
    C. 8;30 a,m.   D. 8:30 am.

11. The alphabet, or A to Z sequence are the basis of most filing systems.   11._____

    A. Correct as is
    B. alphabet, or A to Z sequence, is
    C. alphabet, or A to Z sequence are
    D. alphabet, or A too Z sequence, is

12. Those file cabinets are five feet tall.   12._____

    A. Correct as is   B. Them...feet
    C. Those...foot   D. Them...foot

11

13. The Office Aide checked the <u>register and finding</u> the date of the meeting.   13.____

    A. Correct as is   B. regaster and finding
    C. register and found   D. regaster and found

Questions 14-21.

DIRECTIONS: Each of Questions 14 through 21 has two lists of numbers. Each list contains three sets of numbers. Check each of the three sets in the list on the right to see if they are the same as the corresponding set in the list on the left. Mark your answers:

    A. If none of the sets in the right list are the same as those in the left list
    B. if only one of the sets in the right list are the same as those in the left list
    C. if only two of the sets in the right list are the same as those in the left list
    D. if all three sets in the right list are the same as those in the left list

14. 7354183476   7354983476   14.____
       4474747744   4474747774
       57914302311   57914302311

15. 7143592185   7143892185   15.____
       8344517699   8344518699
       9178531263   9178531263

16. 2572114731   257214731   16.____
       8806835476   8806835476
       8255831246   8255831246

17. 331476853821   331476858621   17.____
       6976658532996   6976655832996
       3766042113715   3766042113745

18. 8806663315   8806663315   18.____
       74477138449   74477138449
       211756663666   211756663666

19. 990006966996   99000696996   19.____
       53022219743   53022219843
       4171171117717   4171171177717

20. 24400222433004   24400222433004   20.____
       5300030055000355   5300030055500355
       20000075532002022   20000075532002022

21. 611166640660001116   611166664066001116   21.____
       7111300117001100733   7111300117001100733
       26666446664476518   26666446664476518

Questions 22-25.

DIRECTIONS: Each of Questions 22 through 25 has two lists of names and addresses. Each
list contains three sets of names and addresses. Check each of the three sets
in the list on the right to see if they are the same as the corresponding set in
the list on the left. Mark your answers:
    A.   if none of the sets in the right list are the same as those in the left
         list
    B.   if only one of the sets in the right list is the same as those in the left
         list
    C.   if only two of the sets in the right list are the same as those in the
         left list
    D.   if all three sets in the right list are the same as those in the left list

22.   Mary T. Berlinger   Mary T. Berlinger   22.____
       2351 Hampton St.   2351 Hampton St.
       Monsey, N.Y. 20117   Monsey, N.Y. 20117

       Eduardo Benes   Eduardo Benes
       473 Kingston Avenue   473 Kingston Avenue
       Central Islip, N.Y. 11734   Central Islip, N.Y. 11734

       Alan Carrington Fuchs   Alan Carrington Fuchs
       17 Gnarled Hollow Road   17 Gnarled Hollow Road
       Los Angeles, CA 91635   Los Angeles, CA 91685

23.   David John Jacobson   David John Jacobson   23.____
       178 35 St. Apt. 4C   178 53 St. Apt. 4C
       New York, N.Y. 00927   New York, N.Y. 00927

       Ann-Marie Calonella   Ann-Marie Calonella
       7243 South Ridge Blvd.   7243 South Ridge Blvd.
       Bakersfield, CA 96714   Bakersfield, CA 96714

       Pauline M. Thompson   Pauline M. Thomson
       872 Linden Ave.   872 Linden Ave.
       Houston, Texas 70321   Houston, Texas 70321

24.   Chester LeRoy Masterton   Chester LeRoy Masterson   24.____
       152 Lacy Rd.   152 Lacy Rd.
       Kankakee, Ill. 54532   Kankakee, Ill. 54532

       William Maloney   William Maloney
       S. LaCrosse Pla.   S. LaCross Pla.
       Wausau, Wisconsin 52146   Wausau, Wisconsin 52146

       Cynthia V. Barnes   Cynthia V. Barnes
       16 Pines Rd.   16 Pines Rd.
       Greenpoint, Miss. 20376   Greenpoint, Miss. 20376

25. Marcel Jean Frontenac
6 Burton On The Water
Calender, Me. 01471

J. Scott Marsden
174 S. Tipton St.
Cleveland, Ohio

Lawrence T. Haney
171 McDonough St.
Decatur, Ga. 31304

Marcel Jean Frontenac
6 Burton On The Water
Calender, Me. 01471

J. Scott Marsden
174 Tipton St.
Cleveland, Ohio

Lawrence T. Haney
171 McDonough St.
Decatur, Ga. 31304

25.____

KEY (CORRECT ANSWERS)

1.	C	11.	B
2.	A	12.	A
3.	D	13.	C
4.	B	14.	B
5.	A	15.	B
6.	A	16.	C
7.	D	17.	A
8.	C	18.	D
9.	C	19.	A
10.	B	20.	C

21. C
22. C
23. B
24. B
25. C

TEST 2

DIRECTIONS: Each question or incomplete statement is followed by several suggested answers or completions. Select the one that BEST answers the question or completes the statement. *PRINT THE LETTER OF THE CORRECT ANSWER IN THE SPACE AT THE RIGHT.*

Questions 1-6.

DIRECTIONS: Questions 1 through 6 are to be answered SOLELY on the basis of the information contained in the following passage.

Duplicating is the process of making a number of identical copies of letters, documents, etc. from an original. Some duplicating processes make copies directly from the original document. Other duplicating processes require the preparation of a special master, and copies are then made from the master. Four of the most common duplicating processes are stencil, fluid, offset, and xerox.

In the stencil process, the typewriter is used to cut the words into a master called a stencil. Drawings, charts, or graphs can be cut into the stencil using a stylus. As many as 3,500 good-quality copies can be reproduced from one stencil. Various grades of finished paper from inexpensive mimeograph to expensive bond can be used.

The fluid process is a good method of copying from 50 to 125 good-quality copies from a master, which is prepared with a special dye. The master is placed on the duplicator, and special paper with a hard finish is moistened and then passed through the duplicator. Some of the dye on the master is dissolved, creating an impression on the paper. The impression becomes lighter as more copies are made; and once the dye on the master is used up, a new master must be made.

The offset process is the most adaptable office duplicating process because this process can be used for making a few copies or many copies. Masters can be made on paper or plastic for a few hundred copies, or on metal plates for as many as 75,000 copies. By using a special technique called photo-offset, charts, photographs, illustrations, or graphs can be reproduced on the master plate. The offset process is capable of producing large quantities of fine, top-quality copies on all types of finished paper.

The xerox process reproduces an exact duplicate from an original. It is the fastest duplicating method because the original material is placed directly on the duplicator, eliminating the need to make a special master. Any kind of paper can be used. The xerox process is the most expensive duplicating process; however, it is the best method of reproducing small quantities of good-quality copies of reports, letters, official documents, memos, or contracts.

1. Of the following, the MOST efficient method of reproducing 5,000 copies of a graph is   1.____

    A. stencil   B. fluid   C. offset   D. xerox

2. The offset process is the MOST adaptable office duplicating process because   2.____

    A. it is the quickest duplicating method
    B. it is the least expensive duplicating method
    C. it can produce a small number or large number of copies
    D. a softer master can be used over and over again

3. Which one of the following duplicating processes uses moistened paper?   3.____

   A. Stencil   B. Fluid   C. Offset   D. Xerox

4. The fluid process would be the BEST process to use for reproducing   4.____

   A. five copies of a school transcript
   B. fifty copies of a memo
   C. five hundred copies of a form letter
   D. five thousand copies of a chart

5. Which one of the following duplicating processes does NOT require a special master?   5.____

   A. Fluid   B. Xerox   C. Offset   D. Stencil

6. Xerox is NOT used for all duplicating jobs because   6.____

   A. it produces poor-quality copies
   B. the process is too expensive
   C. preparing the master is too time-consuming
   D. it cannot produce written reports

7. Assume a city agency has 775 office workers.   7.____
If 2 out of 25 office workers were absent on a particular day, how many office workers reported to work on that day?

   A. 713   B. 744   C. 750   D. 773

Questions 8-11.

DIRECTIONS: In Questions 8 through 11, select the choice that is CLOSEST in meaning to the underlined word.

SAMPLE: This division reviews the fiscal reports of the agency.
         In this sentence, the word fiscal means MOST NEARLY
           A. financial   B. critical   C. basic   D. personnel

        The correct answer is A, financial, because financial is closest to fiscal.

8. A central file eliminates the need to retain duplicate material.   8.____
The word retain means MOST NEARLY

   A. keep   B. change   C. locate   D. process

9. Filing is a routine office task.   9.____
Routine means MOST NEARLY

   A. proper   B. regular   C. simple   D. difficult

10. Sometimes a word, phrase, or sentence must be deleted to correct an error.   10.____
Deleted means MOST NEARLY

   A. removed   B. added   C. expanded   D. improved

11. Your supervisor will <u>evaluate</u> your work.
    <u>Evaluate</u> means MOST NEARLY

    A. judge   B. list   C. assign   D. explain

11._____

Questions 12-19.

DIRECTIONS: The code table below shows 10 letters with matching numbers. For each Question 12 through 19, there are three sets of letters. Each set of letters is followed by a set of numbers which may or may not match their correct letter according to the code table. For each question, check all three sets of letters and numbers and mark your answer:
    A. if no pairs are correctly matched
    B. if only one pair is correctly matched
    C. if only two pairs are correctly matched
    D. if all three pairs are correctly matched

<u>CODE TABLE</u>

T	M	V	D	S	P	R	G	B	H
1	2	3	4	5	6	7	8	9	0

<u>Sample Question:</u>   TMVDSP - 123456
                       RGBHTM - 789011
                       DSPRGB - 256789

In the sample question above, the first set of numbers correctly matches its set of letters. But the second and third pairs contain mistakes. In the second pair, M is incorrectly matched with number 1. According to the code table, letter M should be correctly matched with number 2. In the third pair, the letter D is incorrectly matched with number 2. According to the code table, letter D should be correctly matched with number 4. Since only one of the pairs is correctly matched, the answer to this sample question is B.

12. RSBMRM - 759262
    GDSRVH - 845730
    VDBRTM - 349713

12._____

13. TGVSDR - 183247
    SMHRDP - 520647
    TRMHSR - 172057

13._____

14. DSPRGM - 456782
    MVDBHT - 234902
    HPMDBT - 062491

14._____

15. BVPTRD - 936184
    GDPHMB - 807029
    GMRHMV - 827032

15._____

16. MGVRSH - 283750
    TRDMBS - 174295
    SPRMGV - 567283

16._____

17. SGBSDM - 489542   17.____
    MGHPTM - 290612
    MPBMHT - 269301

18. TDPBHM - 146902   18.____
    VPBMRS - 369275
    GDMBHM - 842902

19. MVPTBV - 236194   19.____
    PDRTMB - 647128
    BGTMSM - 981232

Questions 20-25.

DIRECTIONS: In each of Questions 20 through 25, the names of four people are given. For each question, choose as your answer the one of the four names given which should be filed FIRST according to the usual system of alphabetical filing of names, as described in the following paragraph.

In filing names, you must start with the last name. Names are filed in order of the first letter of the last name, then the second letter, etc. Therefore, BAILY would be filed before BROWN, which would be filed before COLT. A name with fewer letters of the same type comes first; i.e., Smith before Smithe. If the last names are the same, the names are filed alphabetically by the first name. If the first name is an initial, a name with an initial would come before a first name that starts with the same letter as the initial. Therefore, I. BROWN would come before IRA BROWN. Finally, if both last name and first name are the same, the name would be filed alphabetically by the middle name, one again an initial coming before a middle name which starts with the same letter as the initial. If there is no middle name at all, the name would come before those with middle initials or names.

Sample Question: A.   Lester Daniels
                   B.   William Dancer
                   C.   Nathan Danzig
                   D.   Dan Lester

The last names beginning with D are filed before the last name beginning with L. Since DANIELS, DANCER, and DANZIG all begin with the same three letters, you must look at the fourth letter of the last name to determine which name should be filed first. C comes before I or Z in the alphabet, so DANCER is filed before DANIELS or DANZIG. Therefore, the answer to the above sample question is B.

20. A. Scott Biala   B. Mary Byala   20.____
     C. Martin Baylor   D. Francis Bauer

21. A. Howard J. Black   B. Howard Black   21.____
     C. J. Howard Black   D. John H. Black

22. A. Theodora Garth Kingston B. Theadore Barth Kingston   22.____
     C. Thomas Kingston   D. Thomas T. Kingston

23. A. Paulette Mary Huerta   B. Paul M. Huerta   23.____
     C. Paulette L. Huerta   D. Peter A. Huerta

24. A. Martha Hunt Morgan   B. Martin Hunt Morgan   24.____
     C. Mary H. Morgan   D. Martine H. Morgan

25. A. James T. Meerschaum   B. James M. Mershum   25.____
     C. James F. Mearshaum   D. James N. Meshum

————

KEY (CORRECT ANSWERS)

1.	C		11.	A
2.	C		12.	B
3.	B		13.	B
4.	B		14.	C
5.	B		15.	A
6.	B		16.	D
7.	A		17.	A
8.	A		18.	D
9.	B		19.	A
10.	A		20.	D

21.	B
22.	B
23.	B
24.	A
25.	C

————

TEST 3

1. Which one of the following statements about proper telephone usage is NOT always correct?
   When answering the telephone, you should

   A. know whom you are speaking to
   B. give the caller your undivided attention
   C. identify yourself to the caller
   D. obtain the information the caller wishes before you do your other work

   1.____

2. Assume that, as a member of a worker's safety committee in your agency, you are responsible for encouraging other employees to follow correct safety practices. While you are working on your regular assignment, you observe an employee violating a safety rule.
   Of the following, the BEST action for you to take FIRST is to

   A. speak to the employee about safety practices and order him to stop violating the safety rule
   B. speak to the employee about safety practices and point out the safety rule he is violating
   C. bring the matter up in the next committee meeting
   D. report this violation of the safety rule to the employee's supervisor

   2.____

3. Assume that you have been temporarily assigned by your supervisor to do a job which you do not want to do. The BEST action for you to take is to

   A. discuss the job with your supervisor, explaining why you do not want to do it
   B. discuss the job with your supervisor and tell her that you will not do it
   C. ask a co-worker to take your place on this job
   D. do some other job that you like; your supervisor may give the job you do not like to someone else

   3.____

4. Assume that you keep the confidential personnel files of employees in your unit. A friend asks you to obtain some information from the file of one of your co-workers.
   The BEST action to take is to _____ to your friend.

   A. ask the co-worker if you can give the information
   B. ask your supervisor if you can give the information
   C. give the information
   D. refuse to give the information

   4.____

Questions 5-8.

DIRECTIONS: Questions 5 through 8 are to be answered SOLELY on the basis of the information contained in the following passage.

City government is committed to providing a safe and healthy work environment for all city employees. An effective agency safety program reduces accidents by educating employees about the types of careless acts which can cause accidents. Even in an office, accidents can happen. If each employee is aware of possible safety hazards, the number of accidents on the job can be reduced.

Careless use of office equipment can cause accidents and injuries. For example, file cabinet drawers which are filled with papers can be so heavy that the entire cabinet could tip over from the weight of one open drawer.

The bottom drawers of desks and file cabinets should never be left open since employees could easily trip over open drawers and injure themselves.

When reaching for objects on a high shelf, an employee should use a strong, sturdy object such as a step stool to stand on. Makeshift platforms made out of books, papers, or boxes can easily collapse. Even chairs can slide out from under foot, causing serious injury.

Even at an employee's desk, safety hazards can occur. Frayed or cut wires should be repaired or replaced immediately. Computers which are not firmly anchored to the desk or table could fall, causing injury.

Smoking is one of the major causes of fires in the office. A lighted match or improperly extinguished cigarette thrown into a wastebasket filled with paper could cause a major fire with possible loss of life. Where smoking is permitted, ashtrays should be used. Smoking is particularly dangerous in offices where flammable chemicals are used.

5. The goal of an effective safety program is to   5._____

    A.   reduce office accidents
    B.   stop employees from smoking on the job
    C.   encourage employees to continue their education
    D.   eliminate high shelves in offices

6. Desks and file cabinets can become safety hazards when   6._____

    A.   their drawers are left open
    B.   they are used as wastebaskets
    C.   they are makeshift
    D.   they are not anchored securely to the floor

7. Smoking is especially hazardous when it occurs   7._____

    A.   near exposed wires
    B.   in a crowded office
    C.   in an area where flammable chemicals are used
    D.   where books and papers are stored

8. Accidents are likely to occur when   8._____

    A.   employees' desks are cluttered with books and papers
    B.   employees are not aware of safety hazards
    C.   employees close desk drawers
    D.   step stools are used to reach high objects

9. Assume that part of your job as a worker in the accounting division of a city agency is to   9.____
    answer the telephone. When you first answer the telephone, it is LEAST important to tell
    the caller

      A. your title   B. your name
      C. the name of your unit   D. the name of your agency

10. Assume that you are assigned to work as a receptionist, and your duties are to answer   10.____
    phones, greet visitors, and do other general office work. You are busy with a routine job
    when several visitors approach your desk.
    The BEST action to take is to

      A. ask the visitors to have a seat and assist them after your work is completed
      B. tell the visitors that you are busy and they should return at a more convenient time
      C. stop working long enough to assist the visitors
      D. continue working and wait for the visitors to ask you for assistance

11. Assume that your supervisor has chosen you to take a special course during working   11.____
    hours to learn a new payroll procedure. Although you know that you were chosen
    because of your good work record, a co-worker, who feels that he should have been cho-
    sen, has been telling everyone in your unit that the choice was unfair.
    Of the following, the BEST way to handle this situation FIRST is to

      A. suggest to the co-worker that everything in life is unfair
      B. contact your union representative in case your co-worker presents a formal griev-
          ance
      C. tell your supervisor about your co-worker's complaints and let her handle the situa-
          tion
      D. tell the co-worker that you were chosen because of your superior work record

12. Assume that while you are working on an assignment which must be completed quickly,   12.____
    a supervisor from another unit asks you to obtain information for her.
    Of the following, the BEST way to respond to her request is to

      A. tell her to return in an hour since you are busy
      B. give her the names of some people in her own unit who could help her
      C. tell her you are busy and refer her to a co-worker
      D. tell her that you are busy and ask her if she could wait until you finish your assign-
          ment

13. A co-worker in your unit is often off from work because of illness. Your supervisor assigns   13.____
    the co-worker's work to you when she is not there. Lately, doing her work has interfered
    with your own job.
    The BEST action for you to take FIRST is to

      A. discuss the problem with your supervisor
      B. complete your own work before starting your co-worker's work
      C. ask other workers in your unit to assist you
      D. work late in order to get the jobs done

14. During the month of June, 40,587 people attended a city-owned swimming pool. In July, 13,014 more people attended the swimming pool than the number that had attended in June. In August, 39,655 people attended the swimming pool.
The TOTAL number of people who attended the swimming pool during the months of June, July, and August was

    A. 80,242   B. 93,256   C. 133,843   D. 210,382

14.____

Questions 15-22.

DIRECTIONS: Questions 15 through 22 test how well you understand what you read. It will be necessary for you to read carefully because your answers to these questions must be based ONLY on the information in the following paragraphs.

The telephone directory is made up of two books. The first book consists of the introductory section and the alphabetical listing of names section. The second book is the classified directory (also known as the yellow pages). Many people who are familiar with one book do not realize how useful the other can be. The efficient office worker should become familiar with both books in order to make the best use of this important source of information.

The introductory section gives general instructions for finding numbers in the alphabetical listing and classified directory. This section also explains how to use the telephone company's many services, including the operator and information services, gives examples of charges for local and long-distance calls, and lists area codes for the entire country. In addition, this section provides a useful postal zip code map.

The alphabetical listing of names section lists the names, addresses, and telephone numbers of subscribers in an area. Guide names, or *telltales*, are on the top corner of each page. These guide names indicate the first and last name to be found on that page. *Telltales* help locate any particular name quickly. A cross-reference spelling is also given to help locate names which are spelled several different ways. City, state, and federal government agencies are listed under the major government heading. For example, an agency of the federal government would be listed under *United States Government*.

The classified directory, or yellow pages, is a separate book. In this section are advertising services, public transportation line maps, shopping guides, and listings of businesses arranged by the type of product or services they offer. This book is most useful when looking for the name or phone number of a business when all that is known is the type of product offered and the address, or when trying to locate a particular type of business in an area. Businesses listed in the classified directory can usually be found in the alphabetical listing of names section. When the name of the business is known, you will find the address or phone number more quickly in the alphabetical listing of names section.

15. The introductory section provides

    A. shopping guides   B. government listings
    C. business listings   D. information services

15.____

16. Advertising services would be found in the

    A. introductory section   B. alphabetical listing of names section
    C. classified directory   D. information services

16.____

17. According to the information in the above passage for locating government agencies, the   17._____
    Information Office of the Department of Consumer Affairs of New York City government
    would be alphabetically listed FIRST under

    A. *I* for Information Offices
    B. *D* for Department of Consumer Affairs
    C. *N* for New York City
    D. *G* for government

18. When the name of a business is known, the QUICKEST way to find the phone number is   18.__ _
    to look in the

    A. classified directory
    B. introductory section
    C. alphabetical listing of names section
    D. advertising service section

19. The QUICKEST way to find the phone number of a business when the type of service a   19._____
    business offers and its address is known is to look in the

    A. classified directory
    B. alphabetical listing of names section
    C. introductory section
    D. information service

20. What is a *telltale?*   20._____

    A. An alphabetical listing
    B. A guide name
    C. A map
    D. A cross-reference listing

21. The BEST way to find a postal zip code is to look in the   21._____

    A. classified directory
    B. introductory section
    C. alphabetical listing of names section
    D. government heading

22. To help find names which have several different spellings, the telephone directory pro-   22._____
    vides

    A. cross-reference spelling   B. *telltales*
    C. spelling guides   D. advertising services

23. Assume that your agency has been given $2025 to purchase file cabinets.   23._____
    If each file cabinet costs $135, how many file cabinets can your agency purchase?

    A. 8   B. 10   C. 15   D. 16

24. Assume that your unit ordered 14 staplers at a total cost of $30.20, and each stapler cost the same.
The cost of one stapler was MOST NEARLY

    A. $1.02   B. $1.61   C. $2.16   D. $2.26

24.____

25. Assume that you are responsible for counting and recording licensing fees collected by your department. On a particular day, your department collected in fees 40 checks in the amount of $6 each, 80 checks in the amount of $4 each, 45 twenty dollar bills, 30 ten dollar bills, 42 five dollar bills, and 186 one dollar bills.
The TOTAL amount in fees collected on that day was

    A. $1,406   B. $1,706   C. $2,156   D. $2,356

25.____

26. Assume that you are responsible for your agency's petty cash fund. During the month of February, you pay out 7 $2.00 subway fares and one taxi fare for $10.85. You pay out nothing else from the fund. At the end of February, you count the money left in the fund and find 3 one dollar bills, 4 quarters, 5 dimes, and 4 nickels. The amount of money you had available in the petty cash fund at the BEGINNING of February was

    A. $4.70   B. $16.35   C. $24.85   D. $29.55

26.____

27. You overhear your supervisor criticize a co-worker for handling equipment in an unsafe way. You feel that the criticism may be unfair.
Of the following, it would be BEST for you to

    A. take your co-worker aside and tell her how you feel about your supervisor's comments
    B. interrupt the discussion and defend your co-worker to your supervisor
    C. continue working as if you had not overheard the discussion
    D. make a list of other workers who have violated safety rules and give it to your supervisor

27.____

28. Assume that you have been assigned to work on a long-term project with an employee who is known for being uncooperative.
In beginning to work with this employee, it would be LEAST desirable for you to

    A. understand why the person is uncooperative
    B. act in a calm manner rather than an emotional manner
    C. be appreciative of the co-worker's work
    D. report the co-worker's lack of cooperation to your supervisor

28.____

29. Assume that you are assigned to sell tickets at a city-owned ice skating rink. An adult ticket costs $4.50, and a children's ticket costs $2.25. At the end of a day, you find that you have sold 36 adult tickets and 80 children's tickets.
The TOTAL amount of money you collected for that day was

    A. $244.80   B. $318.00   C. $342.00   D. $348.00

29.____

30. If each office worker files 487 index cards in one hour, how many cards can 26 office workers file in one hour?

    A. 10,662   B. 12,175   C. 12,662   D. 14,266

30.____

KEY (CORRECT ANSWERS)

1.	D	16.	C
2.	B	17.	C
3.	A	18.	C
4.	D	19.	A
5.	A	20.	B
6.	A	21.	B
7.	C	22.	A
8.	B	23.	C
9.	A	24.	C
10.	C	25.	C
11.	C	26.	D
12.	D	27.	C
13.	A	28.	D
14.	C	29.	C
15.	D	30.	C

EXAMINATION SECTION
TEST 1

DIRECTIONS: Each question or incomplete statement is followed by several suggested answers or completions. Select the one that BEST answers the question or completes the statement. *PRINT THE LETTER OF THE CORRECT ANSWER IN THE SPACE AT THE RIGHT.*

1. Assume that a few co-workers meet near your desk and talk about personal matters during working hours. Lately, this practice has interfered with your work.
   In order to stop this practice, the BEST action for you to take FIRST is to

   A. ask your supervisor to put a stop to the co-workers' meeting near your desk
   B. discontinue any friendship with this group
   C. ask your co-workers not to meet near your desk
   D. request that your desk be moved to another location

   1.____

2. In order to maintain office coverage during working hours, your supervisor has scheduled your lunch hour from 1 P.M. to 2 P.M. and your co-worker's lunch hour from 12 P.M. to 1 P.M. Lately, your co-worker has been returning late from lunch each day. As a result, you don't get a full hour since you must return to the office by 2 P.M.
   Of the following, the BEST action for you to take FIRST is to

   A. explain to your co-worker in a courteous manner that his lateness is interfering with your right to a full hour for lunch
   B. tell your co-worker that his lateness must stop or you will report him to your supervisor
   C. report your co-worker's lateness to your supervisor
   D. leave at 1 P.M. for lunch, whether your co-worker has returned or not

   2.____

3. Assume that, as an office worker, one of your jobs is to open mail sent to your unit, read the mail for content, and send the mail to the appropriate person to handle. You accidentally open and begin to read a letter marked *personal* addressed to a co-worker.
   Of the following, the BEST action for you to take is to

   A. report to your supervisor that your co-worker is receiving personal mail at the office
   B. destroy the letter so that your co-worker does not know you saw it
   C. reseal the letter and place it on the co-worker's desk without saying anything
   D. bring the letter to your co-worker and explain that you opened it by accident

   3.____

4. Suppose that in evaluating your work, your supervisor gives you an overall good rating, but states that you sometimes turn in work with careless errors.
   The BEST action for you to take would be to

   A. ask a co-worker who is good at details to proofread your work
   B. take time to do a careful job, paying more attention to detail
   C. continue working as usual since occasional errors are to be expected
   D. ask your supervisor if she would mind correcting your errors

   4.____

5. Assume that you are taking a telephone message for a co-worker who is not in the office at the time.
   Of the following, the LEAST important item to write on the message is the

   A. length of the call   B. name of the caller
   C. time of the call   D. telephone number of the caller

   5.____

Questions 6-13.

DIRECTIONS: Questions 6 through 13 each consist of a sentence which may or may not be an example of good English. The underlined parts of each sentence may be correct or incorrect. Examine each sentence, considering grammar, punctuation, spelling, and capitalization. If the English usage in the underlined parts of the sentence given is better than any of the changes in the underlined words suggested in Options B, C, or D, choose Option A. If the changes in the underlined words suggested in Options B, C, or D would make the sentence correct, choose the correct option. Do not choose an option that will change the meaning of the sentence.

6. This <u>Fall</u>, the office will be closed on <u>Columbus Day, October</u> 9th.   6.____

    A. Correct as is
    B. fall...Columbus Day, October
    C. Fall...columbus day, October
    D. fall...Columbus Day, october

7. This manual <u>discribes the duties performed</u> by an Office Aide.   7.____

    A. Correct as is
    B. describe the duties performed
    C. discribe the duties performed
    D. describes the duties performed

8. There <u>weren't no</u> paper in the supply closet.   8.____

    A. Correct as is   B. weren't any
    C. wasn't any   D. wasn't no

9. The new employees left <u>there</u> office to attend a meeting.   9.____

    A. Correct as is   B. they're
    C. their   D. thier

10. The office worker started working at <u>8;30 a.m.</u>   10.____

    A. Correct as is   B. 8:30 a.m.
    C. 8;30 a,m.   D. 8:30 am.

11. The <u>alphabet, or A to Z sequence</u> are the basis of most filing systems.   11.____

    A. Correct as is
    B. alphabet, or A to Z sequence, is
    C. alphabet, or A to Z sequence are
    D. alphabet, or A too Z sequence, is

12. <u>Those</u> file cabinets are five <u>feet</u> tall.   12.____

    A. Correct as is   B. Them...feet
    C. Those...foot   D. Them...foot

13. The Office Aide checked the <u>register and finding</u> the date of the meeting.   13.____

    A. Correct as is   B. regaster and finding
    C. register and found   D. regaster and found

Questions 14-21.

DIRECTIONS: Each of Questions 14 through 21 has two lists of numbers. Each list contains
              three sets of numbers. Check each of the three sets in the list on the right to
              see if they are the same as the corresponding set in the list on the left. Mark
              your answers:
              A. If none of the sets in the right list are the same as those in the left
                  list
              B. if only one of the sets in the right list are the same as those in the
                  left list
              C. if only two of the sets in the right list are the same as those in the
                  left list
              D. if all three sets in the right list are the same as those in the left list

14. 7354183476   7354983476   14.____
     4474747744   4474747774
     57914302311   57914302311

15. 7143592185   7143892185   15.____
     8344517699   8344518699
     9178531263   9178531263

16. 2572114731   257214731   16.____
     8806835476   8806835476
     8255831246   8255831246

17. 331476853821   331476858621   17.____
     6976658532996   6976655832996
     3766042113715   3766042113745

18. 8806663315   8806663315   18.____
     74477138449   74477138449
     211756663666   211756663666

19. 990006966996   99000696996   19.____
     53022219743   53022219843
     4171171117717   4171171177717

20. 24400222433004   24400222433004   20.____
     5300030055000355   5300030055500355
     20000075532002022   20000075532002022

21. 611166640660001116   61116664066001116   21.____
     7111300117001100733   7111300117001100733
     26666446664476518   26666446664476518

29

Questions 22-25.

DIRECTIONS: Each of Questions 22 through 25 has two lists of names and addresses. Each list contains three sets of names and addresses. Check each of the three sets in the list on the right to see if they are the same as the corresponding set in the list on the left. Mark your answers:

- A. if none of the sets in the right list are the same as those in the left list
- B. if only one of the sets in the right list is the same as those in the left list
- C. if only two of the sets in the right list are the same as those in the left list
- D. if all three sets in the right list are the same as those in the left list

22. Mary T. Berlinger   Mary T. Berlinger   22.____
     2351 Hampton St.   2351 Hampton St.
     Monsey, N.Y. 20117   Monsey, N.Y. 20117

     Eduardo Benes   Eduardo Benes
     473 Kingston Avenue   473 Kingston Avenue
     Central Islip, N.Y. 11734 Central Islip, N.Y. 11734

     Alan Carrington Fuchs   Alan Carrington Fuchs
     17 Gnarled Hollow Road   17 Gnarled Hollow Road
     Los Angeles, CA 91635   Los Angeles, CA 91685

23. David John Jacobson   David John Jacobson   23.____
     178 35 St. Apt. 4C   178 53 St. Apt. 4C
     New York, N.Y. 00927   New York, N.Y. 00927

     Ann-Marie Calonella   Ann-Marie Calonella
     7243 South Ridge Blvd.   7243 South Ridge Blvd.
     Bakersfield, CA 96714   Bakersfield, CA 96714

     Pauline M. Thompson   Pauline M. Thomson
     872 Linden Ave.   872 Linden Ave.
     Houston, Texas 70321   Houston, Texas 70321

24. Chester LeRoy Masterton   Chester LeRoy Masterson   24.____
     152 Lacy Rd.   152 Lacy Rd.
     Kankakee, Ill. 54532   Kankakee, Ill. 54532

     William Maloney   William Maloney
     S. LaCrosse Pla.   S. LaCross Pla.
     Wausau, Wisconsin 52146   Wausau, Wisconsin 52146

     Cynthia V. Barnes   Cynthia V. Barnes
     16 Pines Rd.   16 Pines Rd.
     Greenpoint, Miss. 20376   Greenpoint, Miss. 20376

25. Marcel Jean Frontenac
6 Burton On The Water
Calender, Me. 01471

J. Scott Marsden
174 S. Tipton St.
Cleveland, Ohio

Lawrence T. Haney
171 McDonough St.
Decatur, Ga. 31304

Marcel Jean Frontenac
6 Burton On The Water
Calender, Me. 01471

J. Scott Marsden
174 Tipton St.
Cleveland, Ohio

Lawrence T. Haney
171 McDonough St.
Decatur, Ga. 31304

25.____

———

KEY (CORRECT ANSWERS)

1.	C		11.	B
2.	A		12.	A
3.	D		13.	C
4.	B		14.	B
5.	A		15.	B
6.	A		16.	C
7.	D		17.	A
8.	C		18.	D
9.	C		19.	A
10.	B		20.	C

21.	C
22.	C
23.	B
24.	B
25.	C

———

TEST 2

DIRECTIONS: Each question or incomplete statement is followed by several suggested answers or completions. Select the one that BEST answers the question or completes the statement. *PRINT THE LETTER OF THE CORRECT ANSWER IN THE SPACE AT THE RIGHT.*

Questions 1-6.

DIRECTIONS: Questions 1 through 6 are to be answered SOLELY on the basis of the information contained in the following passage.

Duplicating is the process of making a number of identical copies of letters, documents, etc. from an original. Some duplicating processes make copies directly from the original document. Other duplicating processes require the preparation of a special master, and copies are then made from the master. Four of the most common duplicating processes are stencil, fluid, offset, and xerox.

In the stencil process, the typewriter is used to cut the words into a master called a stencil. Drawings, charts, or graphs can be cut into the stencil using a stylus. As many as 3,500 good-quality copies can be reproduced from one stencil. Various grades of finished paper from inexpensive mimeograph to expensive bond can be used.

The fluid process is a good method of copying from 50 to 125 good-quality copies from a master, which is prepared with a special dye. The master is placed on the duplicator, and special paper with a hard finish is moistened and then passed through the duplicator. Some of the dye on the master is dissolved, creating an impression on the paper. The impression becomes lighter as more copies are made; and once the dye on the master is used up, a new master must be made.

The offset process is the most adaptable office duplicating process because this process can be used for making a few copies or many copies. Masters can be made on paper or plastic for a few hundred copies, or on metal plates for as many as 75,000 copies. By using a special technique called photo-offset, charts, photographs, illustrations, or graphs can be reproduced on the master plate. The offset process is capable of producing large quantities of fine, top-quality copies on all types of finished paper.

The xerox process reproduces an exact duplicate from an original. It is the fastest duplicating method because the original material is placed directly on the duplicator, eliminating the need to make a special master. Any kind of paper can be used. The xerox process is the most expensive duplicating process; however, it is the best method of reproducing small quantities of good-quality copies of reports, letters, official documents, memos, or contracts.

1. Of the following, the MOST efficient method of reproducing 5,000 copies of a graph is   1._____

    A. stencil   B. fluid   C. offset   D. xerox

2. The offset process is the MOST adaptable office duplicating process because   2._____

    A. it is the quickest duplicating method
    B. it is the least expensive duplicating method
    C. it can produce a small number or large number of copies
    D. a softer master can be used over and over again

3. Which one of the following duplicating processes uses moistened paper?   3._____

     A. Stencil   B. Fluid   C. Offset   D. Xerox

4. The fluid process would be the BEST process to use for reproducing   4._____

     A. five copies of a school transcript
     B. fifty copies of a memo
     C. five hundred copies of a form letter
     D. five thousand copies of a chart

5. Which one of the following duplicating processes does NOT require a special master?   5._____

     A. Fluid   B. Xerox   C. Offset   D. Stencil

6. Xerox is NOT used for all duplicating jobs because   6._____

     A. it produces poor-quality copies
     B. the process is too expensive
     C. preparing the master is too time-consuming
     D. it cannot produce written reports

7. Assume a city agency has 775 office workers.   7._____
If 2 out of 25 office workers were absent on a particular day, how many office workers reported to work on that day?

     A. 713   B. 744   C. 750   D. 773

Questions 8-11.

DIRECTIONS: In Questions 8 through 11, select the choice that is CLOSEST in meaning to the underlined word.

SAMPLE: This division reviews the <u>fiscal</u> reports of the agency.
In this sentence, the word <u>fiscal</u> means MOST NEARLY
     A. financial   B. critical   C. basic   D. personnel

     The correct answer is A, financial, because financial is closest to <u>fiscal</u>.

8. A central file eliminates the need to <u>retain</u> duplicate material.   8._____
The word <u>retain</u> means MOST NEARLY

     A. keep   B. change   C. locate   D. process

9. Filing is a <u>routine</u> office task.   9._____
<u>Routine</u> means MOST NEARLY

     A. proper   B. regular   C. simple   D. difficult

10. Sometimes a word, phrase, or sentence must be <u>deleted</u> to correct an error.   10._____
<u>Deleted</u> means MOST NEARLY

     A. removed   B. added   C. expanded   D. improved

11. Your supervisor will <u>evaluate</u> your work.
    <u>Evaluate</u> means MOST NEARLY

    A. judge   B. list   C. assign   D. explain

11._____

Questions 12-19.

DIRECTIONS: The code table below shows 10 letters with matching numbers. For each Question 12 through 19, there are three sets of letters. Each set of letters is followed by a set of numbers which may or may not match their correct letter according to the code table. For each question, check all three sets of letters and numbers and mark your answer:
- A. if no pairs are correctly matched
- B. if only one pair is correctly matched
- C. if only two pairs are correctly matched
- D. if all three pairs are correctly matched

<u>CODE TABLE</u>

T	M	V	D	S	P	R	G	B	H
1	2	3	4	5	6	7	8	9	0

<u>Sample Question:</u>   TMVDSP - 123456
                           RGBHTM - 789011
                           DSPRGB - 256789

In the sample question above, the first set of numbers correctly matches its set of letters. But the second and third pairs contain mistakes. In the second pair, M is incorrectly matched with number 1. According to the code table, letter M should be correctly matched with number 2. In the third pair, the letter D is incorrectly matched with number 2. According to the code table, letter D should be correctly matched with number 4. Since only one of the pairs is correctly matched, the answer to this sample question is B.

12.   RSBMRM - 759262
      GDSRVH - 845730
      VDBRTM - 349713

12._____

13.   TGVSDR - 183247
      SMHRDP - 520647
      TRMHSR - 172057

13._____

14.   DSPRGM - 456782
      MVDBHT - 234902
      HPMDBT - 062491

14._____

15.   BVPTRD - 936184
      GDPHMB - 807029
      GMRHMV - 827032

15._____

16.   MGVRSH - 283750
      TRDMBS - 174295
      SPRMGV - 567283

16._____

17.	SGBSDM	-	489542
	MGHPTM	-	290612
	MPBMHT	-	269301

17.____

18.	TDPBHM	-	146902
	VPBMRS	-	369275
	GDMBHM	-	842902

18.____

19.	MVPTBV	-	236194
	PDRTMB	-	647128
	BGTMSM	-	981232

19.____

Questions 20-25.

DIRECTIONS: In each of Questions 20 through 25, the names of four people are given. For each question, choose as your answer the one of the four names given which should be filed FIRST according to the usual system of alphabetical filing of names, as described in the following paragraph.

In filing names, you must start with the last name. Names are filed in order of the first letter of the last name, then the second letter, etc. Therefore, BAILY would be filed before BROWN, which would be filed before COLT. A name with fewer letters of the same type comes first; i.e., Smith before Smithe. If the last names are the same, the names are filed alphabetically by the first name. If the first name is an initial, a name with an initial would come before a first name that starts with the same letter as the initial. Therefore, I. BROWN would come before IRA BROWN. Finally, if both last name and first name are the same, the name would be filed alphabetically by the middle name, one again an initial coming before a middle name which starts with the same letter as the initial. If there is no middle name at all, the name would come before those with middle initials or names.

Sample Question: A. Lester Daniels
B. William Dancer
C. Nathan Danzig
D. Dan Lester

The last names beginning with D are filed before the last name beginning with L. Since DANIELS, DANCER, and DANZIG all begin with the same three letters, you must look at the fourth letter of the last name to determine which name should be filed first. C comes before I or Z in the alphabet, so DANCER is filed before DANIELS or DANZIG. Therefore, the answer to the above sample question is B.

20.	A.	Scott Biala	B.	Mary Byala	20.____
	C.	Martin Baylor	D.	Francis Bauer	
21.	A.	Howard J. Black	B.	Howard Black	21.____
	C.	J. Howard Black	D.	John H. Black	
22.	A.	Theodora Garth Kingston	B.	Theadore Barth Kingston	22.____
	C.	Thomas Kingston	D.	Thomas T. Kingston	
23.	A.	Paulette Mary Huerta	B.	Paul M. Huerta	23.____
	C.	Paulette L. Huerta	D.	Peter A. Huerta	

24. A. Martha Hunt Morgan   B. Martin Hunt Morgan   24.____
     C. Mary H. Morgan   D. Martine H. Morgan

25. A. James T. Meerschaum   B. James M. Mershum   25.____
     C. James F. Mearshaum   D. James N. Meshum

KEY (CORRECT ANSWERS)

1.	C	11.	A
2.	C	12.	B
3.	B	13.	B
4.	B	14.	C
5.	B	15.	A
6.	B	16.	D
7.	A	17.	A
8.	A	18.	D
9.	B	19.	A
10.	A	20.	D

21.	B
22.	B
23.	B
24.	A
25.	C

TEST 3

DIRECTIONS: Each question or incomplete statement is followed by several suggested answers or completions. Select the one that BEST answers the question or completes the statement. *PRINT THE LETTER OF THE CORRECT ANSWER IN THE SPACE AT THE RIGHT.*

1. Which one of the following statements about proper telephone usage is NOT always cor-   1.____
   rect?
   When answering the telephone, you should

   A. know whom you are speaking to
   B. give the caller your undivided attention
   C. identify yourself to the caller
   D. obtain the information the caller wishes before you do your other work

2. Assume that, as a member of a worker's safety committee in your agency, you are   2.____
   responsible for encouraging other employees to follow correct safety practices. While you
   are working on your regular assignment, you observe an employee violating a safety
   rule.
   Of the following, the BEST action for you to take FIRST is to

   A. speak to the employee about safety practices and order him to stop violating the
      safety rule
   B. speak to the employee about safety practices and point out the safety rule he is
      violating
   C. bring the matter up in the next committee meeting
   D. report this violation of the safety rule to the employee's supervisor

3. Assume that you have been temporarily assigned by your supervisor to do a job which   3.____
   you do not want to do. The BEST action for you to take is to

   A. discuss the job with your supervisor, explaining why you do not want to do it
   B. discuss the job with your supervisor and tell her that you will not do it
   C. ask a co-worker to take your place on this job
   D. do some other job that you like; your supervisor may give the job you do not like to
      someone else

4. Assume that you keep the confidential personnel files of employees in your unit. A friend   4.____
   asks you to obtain some information from the file of one of your co-workers.
   The BEST action to take is to _____ to your friend.

   A. ask the co-worker if you can give the information
   B. ask your supervisor if you can give the information
   C. give the information
   D. refuse to give the information

Questions 5-8.

DIRECTIONS: Questions 5 through 8 are to be answered SOLELY on the basis of the information contained in the following passage.

City government is committed to providing a safe and healthy work environment for all city employees. An effective agency safety program reduces accidents by educating employees about the types of careless acts which can cause accidents. Even in an office, accidents can happen. If each employee is aware of possible safety hazards, the number of accidents on the job can be reduced.

Careless use of office equipment can cause accidents and injuries. For example, file cabinet drawers which are filled with papers can be so heavy that the entire cabinet could tip over from the weight of one open drawer.

The bottom drawers of desks and file cabinets should never be left open since employees could easily trip over open drawers and injure themselves.

When reaching for objects on a high shelf, an employee should use a strong, sturdy object such as a step stool to stand on. Makeshift platforms made out of books, papers, or boxes can easily collapse. Even chairs can slide out from under foot, causing serious injury.

Even at an employee's desk, safety hazards can occur. Frayed or cut wires should be repaired or replaced immediately. Computers which are not firmly anchored to the desk or table could fall, causing injury.

Smoking is one of the major causes of fires in the office. A lighted match or improperly extinguished cigarette thrown into a wastebasket filled with paper could cause a major fire with possible loss of life. Where smoking is permitted, ashtrays should be used. Smoking is particularly dangerous in offices where flammable chemicals are used.

5. The goal of an effective safety program is to   5.____

    A. reduce office accidents
    B. stop employees from smoking on the job
    C. encourage employees to continue their education
    D. eliminate high shelves in offices

6. Desks and file cabinets can become safety hazards when   6.____

    A. their drawers are left open
    B. they are used as wastebaskets
    C. they are makeshift
    D. they are not anchored securely to the floor

7. Smoking is especially hazardous when it occurs   7.____

    A. near exposed wires
    B. in a crowded office
    C. in an area where flammable chemicals are used
    D. where books and papers are stored

8. Accidents are likely to occur when   8.____

    A. employees' desks are cluttered with books and papers
    B. employees are not aware of safety hazards
    C. employees close desk drawers
    D. step stools are used to reach high objects

9. Assume that part of your job as a worker in the accounting division of a city agency is to answer the telephone. When you first answer the telephone, it is LEAST important to tell the caller

    A. your title   B. your name
    C. the name of your unit   D. the name of your agency

9.____

10. Assume that you are assigned to work as a receptionist, and your duties are to answer phones, greet visitors, and do other general office work. You are busy with a routine job when several visitors approach your desk.
The BEST action to take is to

    A. ask the visitors to have a seat and assist them after your work is completed
    B. tell the visitors that you are busy and they should return at a more convenient time
    C. stop working long enough to assist the visitors
    D. continue working and wait for the visitors to ask you for assistance

10.____

11. Assume that your supervisor has chosen you to take a special course during working hours to learn a new payroll procedure. Although you know that you were chosen because of your good work record, a co-worker, who feels that he should have been chosen, has been telling everyone in your unit that the choice was unfair.
Of the following, the BEST way to handle this situation FIRST is to

    A. suggest to the co-worker that everything in life is unfair
    B. contact your union representative in case your co-worker presents a formal grievance
    C. tell your supervisor about your co-worker's complaints and let her handle the situation
    D. tell the co-worker that you were chosen because of your superior work record

11.____

12. Assume that while you are working on an assignment which must be completed quickly, a supervisor from another unit asks you to obtain information for her.
Of the following, the BEST way to respond to her request is to

    A. tell her to return in an hour since you are busy
    B. give her the names of some people in her own unit who could help her
    C. tell her you are busy and refer her to a co-worker
    D. tell her that you are busy and ask her if she could wait until you finish your assignment

12.____

13. A co-worker in your unit is often off from work because of illness. Your supervisor assigns the co-worker's work to you when she is not there. Lately, doing her work has interfered with your own job.
The BEST action for you to take FIRST is to

    A. discuss the problem with your supervisor
    B. complete your own work before starting your co-worker's work
    C. ask other workers in your unit to assist you
    D. work late in order to get the jobs done

13.____

14. During the month of June, 40,587 people attended a city-owned swimming pool. In July, 13,014 more people attended the swimming pool than the number that had attended in June. In August, 39,655 people attended the swimming pool.
The TOTAL number of people who attended the swimming pool during the months of June, July, and August was

    A. 80,242   B. 93,256   C. 133,843   D. 210,382

14._____

Questions 15-22.

DIRECTIONS: Questions 15 through 22 test how well you understand what you read. It will be necessary for you to read carefully because your answers to these questions must be based ONLY on the information in the following paragraphs.

The telephone directory is made up of two books. The first book consists of the introductory section and the alphabetical listing of names section. The second book is the classified directory (also known as the yellow pages). Many people who are familiar with one book do not realize how useful the other can be. The efficient office worker should become familiar with both books in order to make the best use of this important source of information.

The introductory section gives general instructions for finding numbers in the alphabetical listing and classified directory. This section also explains how to use the telephone company's many services, including the operator and information services, gives examples of charges for local and long-distance calls, and lists area codes for the entire country. In addition, this section provides a useful postal zip code map.

The alphabetical listing of names section lists the names, addresses, and telephone numbers of subscribers in an area. Guide names, or *telltales,* are on the top corner of each page. These guide names indicate the first and last name to be found on that page. *Telltales* help locate any particular name quickly. A cross-reference spelling is also given to help locate names which are spelled several different ways. City, state, and federal government agencies are listed under the major government heading. For example, an agency of the federal government would be listed under *United States Government.*

The classified directory, or yellow pages, is a separate book. In this section are advertising services, public transportation line maps, shopping guides, and listings of businesses arranged by the type of product or services they offer. This book is most useful when looking for the name or phone number of a business when all that is known is the type of product offered and the address, or when trying to locate a particular type of business in an area. Businesses listed in the classified directory can usually be found in the alphabetical listing of names section. When the name of the business is known, you will find the address or phone number more quickly in the alphabetical listing of names section.

15. The introductory section provides

    A. shopping guides   B. government listings
    C. business listings   D. information services

15._____

16. Advertising services would be found in the

    A. introductory section   B. alphabetical listing of names section
    C. classified directory   D. information services

16._____

17. According to the information in the above passage for locating government agencies, the Information Office of the Department of Consumer Affairs of New York City government would be alphabetically listed FIRST under

17._____

    A. *I* for Information Offices
    B. *D* for Department of Consumer Affairs
    C. *N* for New York City
    D. *G* for government

18. When the name of a business is known, the QUICKEST way to find the phone number is to look in the

18.___ _

    A. classified directory
    B. introductory section
    C. alphabetical listing of names section
    D. advertising service section

19. The QUICKEST way to find the phone number of a business when the type of service a business offers and its address is known is to look in the

19._____

    A. classified directory
    B. alphabetical listing of names section
    C. introductory section
    D. information service

20. What is a *telltale?*

20._____

    A. An alphabetical listing
    B. A guide name
    C. A map
    D. A cross-reference listing

21. The BEST way to find a postal zip code is to look in the

21._____

    A. classified directory
    B. introductory section
    C. alphabetical listing of names section
    D. government heading

22. To help find names which have several different spellings, the telephone directory provides

22._____

    A. cross-reference spelling   B. *telltales*
    C. spelling guides   D. advertising services

23. Assume that your agency has been given $2025 to purchase file cabinets. If each file cabinet costs $135, how many file cabinets can your agency purchase?

23._____

    A. 8   B. 10   C. 15   D. 16

24. Assume that your unit ordered 14 staplers at a total cost of $30.20, and each stapler cost the same.
The cost of one stapler was MOST NEARLY

    A. $1.02   B. $1.61   C. $2.16   D. $2.26

24.____

25. Assume that you are responsible for counting and recording licensing fees collected by your department. On a particular day, your department collected in fees 40 checks in the amount of $6 each, 80 checks in the amount of $4 each, 45 twenty dollar bills, 30 ten dollar bills, 42 five dollar bills, and 186 one dollar bills.
The TOTAL amount in fees collected on that day was

    A. $1,406   B. $1,706   C. $2,156   D. $2,356

25.____

26. Assume that you are responsible for your agency's petty cash fund. During the month of February, you pay out 7 $2.00 subway fares and one taxi fare for $10.85. You pay out nothing else from the fund. At the end of February, you count the money left in the fund and find 3 one dollar bills, 4 quarters, 5 dimes, and 4 nickels. The amount of money you had available in the petty cash fund at the BEGINNING of February was

    A. $4.70   B. $16.35   C. $24.85   D. $29.55

26.____

27. You overhear your supervisor criticize a co-worker for handling equipment in an unsafe way. You feel that the criticism may be unfair.
Of the following, it would be BEST for you to

    A. take your co-worker aside and tell her how you feel about your supervisor's comments
    B. interrupt the discussion and defend your co-worker to your supervisor
    C. continue working as if you had not overheard the discussion
    D. make a list of other workers who have violated safety rules and give it to your supervisor

27.____

28. Assume that you have been assigned to work on a long-term project with an employee who is known for being uncooperative.
In beginning to work with this employee, it would be LEAST desirable for you to

    A. understand why the person is uncooperative
    B. act in a calm manner rather than an emotional manner
    C. be appreciative of the co-worker's work
    D. report the co-worker's lack of cooperation to your supervisor

28.____

29. Assume that you are assigned to sell tickets at a city-owned ice skating rink. An adult ticket costs $4.50, and a children's ticket costs $2.25. At the end of a day, you find that you have sold 36 adult tickets and 80 children's tickets.
The TOTAL amount of money you collected for that day was

    A. $244.80   B. $318.00   C. $342.00   D. $348.00

29.____

30. If each office worker files 487 index cards in one hour, how many cards can 26 office workers file in one hour?

    A. 10,662   B. 12,175   C. 12,662   D. 14,266

30.____

KEY (CORRECT ANSWERS)

1.	D		16.	C
2.	B		17.	C
3.	A		18.	C
4.	D		19.	A
5.	A		20.	B
6.	A		21.	B
7.	C		22.	A
8.	B		23.	C
9.	A		24.	C
10.	C		25.	C
11.	C		26.	D
12.	D		27.	C
13.	A		28.	D
14.	C		29.	C
15.	D		30.	C

———

EXAMINATION SECTION
TEST 1

DIRECTIONS: Each question or incomplete statement is followed by several suggested answers or completions. Select the one that BEST answers the question or completes the statement. *PRINT THE LETTER OF THE CORRECT ANSWER IN THE SPACE AT THE RIGHT.*

1. As a clerk in an office in a city agency, you have just been given a new assignment by your supervisor. The assignment was previously done by another clerk.
   Before beginning work on this assignment, it is MOST important that you

   A. find out who did the assignment previously
   B. understand your supervisor's instructions for doing the assignment
   C. notify the other clerks in the office that you have just received a new assignment
   D. understand how the assignment is related to the work of other clerks in the office

   1.____

2. Assume that you are a clerk in a city department. Your supervisor has given you an important job that he wants completed as quickly as possible. You will be unable to complete the job by the end of the day, and you will be unable to work on the job in the next several days because you will be away from the office.
   Of the following, the MOST appropriate action for you to take before leaving the office at the end of the day is to

   A. lock your work in your desk so that the work will not be disturbed
   B. ask another clerk in the office to finish the job while you are away
   C. tell your supervisor how much of the job has been done and how much remains to be done
   D. leave a note on your supervisor's desk, advising him that you will continue to work on the job as soon as you return to the office

   2.____

3. Assume that, as a newly appointed clerk in a city department, you are doing an assignment according to a method that your supervisor has told you to use. You believe that you would be less likely to make errors if you were to do the assignment by a different method, although the method your supervisor has told you to use is faster.
   For you to discuss your method with your supervisor would be

   A. *desirable* because he may not know the value of your method
   B. *undesirable* because he may know of your method and may prefer the faster one
   C. *desirable* because your method may show your supervisor that you are able to do accurate work
   D. *undesirable* because your method may not be as helpful to you as you believe it to be

   3.____

4. Assume that you are responsible for receiving members of the public who visit your department for information. At a time when there are several persons seeking information, a man asks you for information in a rude and arrogant manner. Of the following, the BEST action for you to take in handling this man is to

   A. give him the information in the same manner in which he spoke to you
   B. ignore his request until he asks for the information in a more polite manner

   4.____

C. give him the information politely, without commenting to him on his manner
D. ask him to request the information in a polite manner so as not to annoy other people seeking information

5. As a clerk in a city agency, you are assigned to issue publications to members of the public who request the applications in person. Your supervisor has told you that under no circumstances are you to issue more than one application to each person. A person enters the office and asks for two applications, explaining that he wants the second one for use in the event that he makes an error in filling out the application.
Of the following, the MOST appropriate action for you to take in this situation is to

    5.____

A. give the person two applications since he may not know how to fill out the application
B. ask your supervisor for permission to give the person two applications
C. give one application to the person and advise him to come back later for another one
D. issue one application to the person and inform him that only one application may be issued to an individual

6. Suppose that as a clerk in an office of a city department, you have been assigned by your supervisor to assist Mr. Jones, another clerk in the office, and to do his work in his absence. Part of Mr. Jones' duties are to give routine information to visitors who request the information. Several months later, shortly after Mr. Jones has begun a three-week vacation, a visitor enters the office and asks for some routine information which is available to the public. He explains that he previously had gotten similar information from Mr. Jones.
Of the following, the MOST advisable action for you to take is to

    6.____

A. inform the visitor that Mr. Jones is on vacation but that you will attempt to obtain the information
B. advise the visitor to return to the office when Mr. Jones will have returned from vacation
C. tell the visitor that you will have Mr. Jones mail him the information as soon as he returns from vacation
D. attempt to contact Mr. Jones to ask him whether the information should be given to the visitor

7. Miss Smith is a clerk in the information section of a city department.
Of the following, the MOST desirable way for Miss Smith to answer a telephone call to the section is to say,

    7.____

A. "Hello. Miss Smith speaking."
B. "Miss Smith speaking. May I ask who is calling?"
C. "Hello. May I be of service to you?"
D. "Information Section, Miss Smith."

8. When preparing papers for filing, it is NOT desirable to

    8.____

A. smooth papers that are wrinkled
B. use paper clips to keep related papers together in the files
C. arrange the papers in the order in which they will be filed
D. mend torn papers with cellophane tape

9. Assume that you are a clerk in the mail room of a city department. One of your duties is 9.____
to open the letters addressed to the department and to route them to the appropriate
offices. One of the letters you open evidently requires the attention of two different offices
in the department.
In this situation, the one of the following which is the BEST action for you to take is to

   A. make two duplicate copies of the letter, send one to each office, and keep the original on file in the mail room
   B. send the letter to one of the offices with a request that the letter be forwarded to the
   second office
   C. return the letter to the writer with a request that he write separate letters to each of
   the two offices
   D. request the head of each office to send one of his employees to the mail room to
   decide what should be done with the letter

10. As a mail clerk in a city department, you are responsible for opening incoming mail and 10.____
routing the letters to the appropriate offices in the department.
The one of the following situations in which it would be MOST appropriate for you to
attach a letter to the envelope in which the letter arrives is when the

   A. name and address of the sender, which are on the envelope, are missing from the
   letter
   B. letter contains important or confidential information
   C. enclosures the envelope is supposed to contain are missing from the envelope
   D. envelope is not addressed to a specific office in the department

11. In writing a letter, it is important that the letter be paragraphed properly. 11.____
Of the following, the CHIEF value of proper paragraphing is to

   A. shorten the contents of the letter
   B. assist the writer by shortening the time required to write the letter
   C. aid the reader to understand the contents of the letter more readily
   D. reduce the time required to type the letter

12. A mailing list is a list containing the names and addresses of the individuals and organi- 12.____
zations with which a public agency corresponds frequently. Such a list is sometimes kept
on 3"x5" cards.
Of the following, the MOST important reason for an agency to keep its mailing list on
cards is that

   A. the mailing list changes frequently
   B. more than one office in the agency uses the mailing list
   C. the mailing list is used frequently
   D. only part of the mailing list is used at any one time

13. Under a subject filing system, letters are filed in folders labeled according to subject mat- 13.____
ter. Assume that you have been asked to file a large number of letters under such a filing
system.
Of the following, the FIRST step that you should take in filing these letters is to

   A. arrange the letters alphabetically under each subject
   B. determine under which subject each letter is to be filed

C. arrange the letters by date under each subject
D. prepare cross-references for each letter that should be filed under more than one subject

14. Your supervisor assigns you to file a number of letters in an alphabetical file drawer. In the course of your work, you notice that several letters in the file have been unintentionally misfiled.
Of the following, the MOST appropriate action for you to take in this situation is to

14._____

A. complete your filing assignment and then go through the file again to pick out any misfiled letters for refiling
B. leave the misfiled letters where they are in order to avoid disturbing the order of the file
C. put the misfiled letters in their proper places as you discover these letters
D. insert a note in the misfiled letters' proper places indicating where the misfiled letters may be found

15. Suppose that your supervisor gives you a folder containing a large number of letters arranged in the order of the dates they were received and a list of names of persons in alphabetical order. He asks you to determine, without disturbing the order of the letters, if there is a letter in the folder from each person on the list.
Of the following, the BEST method to use in doing this assignment is to

15._____

A. determine whether the number of letters in the folder is the same as the number of names on the list
B. look at each letter to see who wrote it, and then place a light check mark on each letter that has been written by a person on the list
C. prepare a list of the names of the writers of the letters that are in the folder, and then place a light check mark next to each of the names on this list if the name appears on the list of persons your supervisor gave you
D. look at each letter to see who wrote it, and then place a light check mark next to the name of the person on the list who wrote the letter

16. Whenever material is requested from a file under which the material is filed according to subject, the person requesting the material should be required to make out a requisition slip.
Of the following, the information that ordinarily would be LEAST useful to include on such a requisition slip is the

16._____

A. subject of the material requested
B. date the material is requested
C. reason why the material is being requested
D. name of the person requesting the material

17. A tickler file is GENERALLY used

17._____

A. as a reminder of work to be done
B. to store inactive records
C. as an index of the records contained in a filing system
D. to store miscellaneous important records

18. A listing adding machine prints, on a roll or strip of paper, the numbers added and their sum.
Of the following, the CHIEF advantage of printing the numbers and their sum on the strip of paper is to

    A. provide a check on the accuracy of the machine
    B. show that the addition was done by machine
    C. permit the machine operator to make hand-written corrections in the numbers and their sum
    D. provide a record of the numbers and their sum

18._____

Questions 19-21.

DIRECTIONS: Questions 19 to 21 are to be answered SOLELY on the basis of the information contained in the following paragraph.

In order to organize records properly, it is necessary to start from their very beginning and to trace each copy of the record to find out how it is used, how long it is used, and what may finally be done with it. Although several copies of the record are made, one copy should be marked as the copy of record. This is the formal legal copy, held to meet the requirements of the law. The other copies may be retained for brief periods for reference purposes, but these copies should not be kept after their usefulness as reference ends. There is another reason for tracing records through the office and that is to determine how long it takes the copy of record to reach the central file. The copy of record must not be kept longer than necessary by the section of the office which has prepared it, but should be sent to the central file as soon as possible so that it can be available to the various sections of the office. The central file can make the copy of record available to the various sections of the office at an early date only if it arrives at the central file as quickly as possible. Just as soon as its immediate or active service period is ended, the copy of record should be removed from the central file and put into the inactive file in the office to be stored for whatever length of time may be necessary to meet legal requirements, and then destroyed.

19. According to the above paragraph, a reason for tracing records through an office is to

    A. determine how long the central file must keep the records
    B. organize records properly
    C. find out how many copies of each record are required
    D. identify the copy of record

19._____

20. According to the above paragraph, in order for the central file to have the copy of record available as soon as possible for the various sections of the office, it is MOST important that the

    A. copy of record to be sent to the central file meets the requirements of the law
    B. copy of record is not kept in the inactive file too long
    C. section preparing the copy of record does not unduly delay in sending it to the central file
    D. central file does not keep the copy of record beyond its active service period

20._____

21. According to the above paragraph, the length of time a copy of a record is kept in the   21.____
inactive file of an office depends CHIEFLY on the

    A.   requirements of the law
    B.   length of time that is required to trace the copy of record through the office
    C.   use that is made of the copy of record
    D.   length of the period that the copy of record is used for reference purposes

22. As a clerk, you may be assigned the duty of opening and sorting the mail coming to your   22.____
department.
The one of the following which is the BEST reason for not discarding the envelopes in
which letters come from members of the public until you have glanced at the letters is
that

    A.   it is rarely necessary to return a letter to the writer in the original envelope
    B.   the subject of a letter can, of course, be determined only from the letter itself
    C.   the envelopes should usually be filed together with the letters
    D.   members of the public frequently neglect to include a return address in their letters

23. Suppose that your supervisor has asked you and another clerk to proofread a letter. The   23.____
other clerk is reading rapidly to you from the original copy while you are checking the letter.
For you to interrupt his reading and make an immediate notation of each error you find
is

    A.   *wise;* you might otherwise overlook an error
    B.   *foolish;* such action slows down the reading
    C.   *foolish;* such action demonstrates that the copy is not accurate
    D.   *wise;* such action demonstrates that the rate of reading may be increased

24. Suppose that the name files in your office contain filing guides on which appear the let-   24.____
ters of the alphabet. The letters X, Y, and Z, unlike the other letters of the alphabet, are
grouped together and appear on a single guide.
Of the following, the BEST reason for combining these three letters into a single filing
unit is probably that

    A.   provision must be made for expanding the file if that should become necessary
    B.   there is usually insufficient room for filing guides towards the end of a long file
    C.   the letters X, Y, and Z are at the end of the alphabet
    D.   relatively few names begin with these letters of the alphabet

25. You are requested by your supervisor to replace each card you take out of the files with   25.____
an *out-of-file* slip. The *out-of-file* slip indicates which card has been removed from the file
and where the card may be found. Of the following, the CHIEF value of the *out-of-file* slip
is that a clerk looking for a card which happens to have been removed by another clerk

    A.   will know that the card has been returned to the file
    B.   can substitute the *out-of-file* slip for the original card
    C.   will not waste time searching for the card under the impression that it has been
misfiled
    D.   is not likely to misfile a card he has been using for some other purpose

26. The sum of 284.5, 3016.24, 8.9736, and 94.15 is MOST NEARLY 　　26._____

    A. 3402.9   B. 3403.0   C. 3403.9   D. 4036.1

27. If 8394.6 is divided by 29.17, the result is MOST NEARLY 　　27._____

    A. 288   B. 347   C. 2880   D. 3470

28. If two numbers are multiplied together, the result is 3752. If one of the two numbers is 56, 　　28._____
the other number is

    A. 41   B. 15   C. 109   D. 67

29. The sum of the fractions 1/4, 2/3, 3/8, 5/6, and 3/4 is 　　29._____

    A. 20/33   B. 1 19/24   C. 2 1/4   D. 2 7/8

30. The fraction 7/16 expressed as a decimal is 　　30._____

    A. .1120   B. .2286   C. .4375   D. .4850

31. If .10 is divided by 50, the result is 　　31._____

    A. .002   B. .02   C. .2   D. 2

32. The number 60 is 40% of 　　32._____

    A. 24   B. 84   C. 96   D. 150

33. If 3/8 of a number is 96, the number is 　　33._____

    A. 132   B. 36   C. 256   D. 156

34. A city department uses an average of 25 10-cent, 35 15-cent, and 350 20-cent postage 　　34._____
stamps each day. The total cost of stamps used by the department in a five-day period is

    A. $14.75   B. $77.75   C. $145.25   D. $388.75

35. A city department issued 12,000 applications in 2007. The number of applications that 　　35._____
the department issued in 2005 was 25% greater than the number it issued in 2007.
If the department issued 10% fewer applications in 2003 than it did in 2005, the number it issued in 2003 was

    A. 16,500   B. 13,500   C. 9,900   D. 8,100

36. A clerk can add 40 columns of figures an hour by using an adding machine and 20 col- 　　36._____
umns of figures an hour without using an adding machine.
The total number of hours it would take him to add 200 columns if he does 3/5 of the
work by machine and the rest without the machine is

    A. 6   B. 7   C. 8   D. 9

37. In 2004, a city department bought 500 dozen pencils at 40 cents per dozen. In 2007, only 　　37._____
75% as many pencils were bought as were bought in 2004, but the price was 20% higher
than the 2004 price.
The total cost of the pencils bought in 2007 was

    A. $180   B. $187.50   C. $240   D. $250

38. A clerk is assigned to check the accuracy of the entries on 490 forms. He checks 40 forms an hour. After working one hour on this task, he is joined by another clerk, who checks these forms at the rate of 35 an hour.
The total number of hours required to do the entire assignment is

38.____

    A. 5   B. 6   C. 7   D. 8

39. Assume that there are a total of 420 employees in a city agency. Thirty percent of the employees are clerks, and 1/7 are typists.
The difference between the number of clerks and the number of typists is

39.____

    A. 126   B. 66   C. 186   D. 80

40. Assume that a duplicating machine produces copies of a bulletin at a cost of 2 cents per copy. The machine produces 120 copies of the bulletin per minute.
If the cost of producing a certain number of copies was $12, how many minutes of operation did it take the machine to produce this number of copies?

40.____

    A. 5   B. 2   C. 10   D. 6

KEY (CORRECT ANSWERS)

1.	B	11.	C	21.	A	31.	A
2.	C	12.	A	22.	D	32.	D
3.	A	13.	B	23.	A	33.	C
4.	C	14.	C	24.	D	34.	D
5.	D	15.	D	25.	C	35.	B
6.	A	16.	C	26.	C	36.	B
7.	D	17.	A	27.	A	37.	A
8.	B	18.	D	28.	D	38.	C
9.	B	19.	B	29.	D	39.	B
10.	A	20.	C	30.	C	40.	A

TEST 2

DIRECTIONS: Each question or incomplete statement is followed by several suggested answers or completions. Select the one that BEST answers the question or completes the statement. *PRINT THE LETTER OF THE CORRECT ANSWER IN THE SPACE AT THE RIGHT.*

Questions 1-13.

DIRECTIONS: Each of Questions 1 to 13 consists of a word in capitals followed by four suggested meanings of the word. For each question, indicate in the correspondingly numbered space at the right the letter preceding the word which means MOST NEARLY the same as the word in capitals.

1. AUTHORIZE   1.____

   A. write   B. permit   C. request   D. recommend

2. ASSESS   2.____

   A. set a value on   B. belong
   C. think highly of   D. increase

3. CONVENTIONAL   3.____

   A. democratic   B. convenient   C. modern   D. customary

4. DEPLETE   4.____

   A. replace   B. exhaust   C. review   D. withhold

5. INTERVENE   5.____

   A. sympathize with   B. differ
   C. ask for an opinion   D. interfere

6. HAZARDOUS   6.____

   A. dangerous   B. unusual   C. slow   D. difficult

7. SUBSTANTIATE   7.____

   A. replace   B. suggest   C. verify   D. suffer

8. DISCORD   8.____

   A. remainder   B. disagreement   C. pressure   D. dishonest

9. TENACIOUS   9.____

   A. vicious   B. irritable   C. truthful   D. unyielding

10. ALLEVIATE   10.____

   A. relieve   B. appreciate   C. succeed   D. admit

11. FALLACY   11.____

   A. basis   B. false idea
   C. guilt   D. lack of respect

12. SCRUTINIZE   12.____

    A. reject   B. bring about   C. examine   D. insist upon

13. IMMINENT   13.____

    A. anxious   B. well-known   C. important   D. about to happen

Questions 14-25.

DIRECTIONS: Each of Questions 14 to 25 consists of a sentence which may be classified appropriately under one of the following four categories:
    A. incorrect because of faulty grammar or sentence structure
    B. incorrect because of faulty punctuation
    C. incorrect because of faulty capitalization
    D. correct

        Examine each sentence carefully. Then, in the correspondingly numbered space at the right, indicate the letter preceding the category which is the BEST of the four suggested above. Each incorrect sentence contains only one type of error. Consider a sentence correct if it contains no errors, although there may be other correct ways of expressing the same thought.

14. All the clerks, including those who have been appointed recently are required to work on the new assignment.   14.____

15. The office manager asked each employee to work one Saturday a month.   15.____

16. Neither Mr. Smith nor Mr. Jones was able to finish his assignment on time.   16.____

17. The task of filing these cards is to be divided equally between you and he.   17.____

18. He is an employee whom we consider to be efficient.   18.____

19. I believe that the new employees are not as punctual as us.   19.____

20. The employees, working in this office, are to be congratulated for their work.   20.____

21. The supervisor entered the room and said, "The work must be completed today."   21.____

22. The employees were given their assignments and, they were asked to begin work immediately.   22.____

23. The letter will be sent to the United States senate this week.   23.____

24. When the supervisor entered the room, he noticed that the book was laying on the desk.   24.____

25. The price of the pens were higher than the price of the pencils.   25.____

Questions 26-35.

DIRECTIONS: Each of Questions 26 to 35 consists of a group of four words. One word in each group is INCORRECTLY spelled. For each question, indicate in the correspondingly numbered space at the right, the letter preceding the word which is INCORRECTLY spelled.

26. A. grateful   B. fundimental   C. census   D. analysis   26.____

27. A. installment   B. retrieve   C. concede   D. dissapear   27.____

28. A. accidentaly   B. dismissal   C. conscientious   D. indelible   28.____

29. A. perceive   B. carreer   C. anticipate   D. acquire   29.____

30. A. facillity   B. reimburse   C. assortment   D. guidance   30.____

31. A. plentiful   B. across   C. advantagous   D. similar   31.____

32. A. omission   B. pamphlet   C. guarrantee   D. repel   32.____

33. A. maintenance   B. always   C. liable   D. anouncement   33.____

34. A. exaggerate   B. sieze   C. condemn   D. commit   34.____

35. A. pospone   B. altogether   C. grievance   D. excessive   35.____

Questions 36-41.

DIRECTIONS: Questions 36 to 41 are to be answered SOLELY on the basis of the information and directions given below.

Assume that you are a clerk assigned to the personnel bureau of a department. Your
supervisor has asked you to classify the employees in your agency into the following four
groups:

A.   Female employees who are college graduates, who are less than 35
years of age, and who earn at least $36,000 a year;

B.   Male employees who are not college graduates, who are less than 35
years of age, and who earn at least $38,000 a year but not more than
$44,000 a year;

C.   Female employees who are 35 years of age or older, who are not college graduates, and who earn at least $30,000 a year but less than
$36,000 a year;

D.   Male employees who are college graduates, who are 35 years of age
or older, and who earn more than $44,000 a year.

NOTE: In each question, consider only the information which will assist you in classifying
each employee. Any information which is of no assistance in classifying an employee
should not be considered.

SAMPLE: Mr. Smith, a city resident, is 60 years of age, and is a college graduate. His salary
is $45,600 a year.

The correct answer to this sample is D, since the employee is a male college
graduate, is more than 35 years of age, and earns more than $44,000 a year.
Questions 36 to 41 contain information from the personnel records in the department. For
each question, indicate in the correspondingly numbered space at the right the letter preceding the appropriate group into which you would place each employee.

36.   Mrs. Brown is a 33-year-old accountant who was graduated from college with honors.   36.____
Her present annual salary is $43,480.

37. Mr. Queen has had two promotions since beginning work for the department eight years ago at the age of 29. A college graduate, he receives $50,800 a year as supervisor in charge of a bureau.

37.____

38. Miss Arthur earns $35,400 a year and has worked in the department for five years. Now 36 years of age, she attends high school in the evenings and hopes to obtain a high school diploma.

38.____

39. At 34 years of age, Mr. Smith earns $43,960 per annum. After he was graduated from high school, he attended college for two years, but he did not complete his college course.

39.____

40. Mr. Rose is a 28-year-old high school graduate earning $38,200 a year. He intends to attend college in the evenings to study public administration.

40.____

41. Mr. Johnson, a veteran, attended college in the evenings for six years before he obtained a degree in engineering. At 37 years of age, he earns an annual salary of $53,200.

41.____

Questions 42-50.

DIRECTIONS: Each of Questions 42 to 50 consists of four names. For each question, select the one of the four names that should be THIRD if the four names were arranged in alphabetical order in accordance with the Rules of Alphabetical Filing given below. Read these rules carefully. Then, for each question indicate in the correspondingly numbered space at the right the letter preceding the name that should be THIRD in alphabetical order.

RULES FOR ALPHABETICAL FILING

NAMES OF INDIVIDUALS
(1) The names of individuals are filed in strict alphabetical order: first according to the last name, then according to first name or initial, and finally according to middle name or initial. For example: William Jones precedes George Kirk, and Arthur S. Blake precedes Charles M. Blake.

(2) When the last names are identical, the one with an initial instead of a first name precedes the one with a first name beginning with the same initial. For example: J. Green precedes Joseph Green.

(3) When identical last names also have identical first names, the one without a middle name or initial precedes the one with a middle name or initial. For example: Robert Jackson precedes both Robert C. Jackson and Robert Chester Jackson.

(4) When last names are identical and the first names are also identical, the one with a middle initial precedes the one with a middle name beginning with the same initial. For example: Peter A. Brown precedes Peter Alvin Brown.

(5) Prefixes such as De, El, La, and Van are considered parts of the names they precede. For example: Wilfred De Wald precedes Alexander Duval.

(6) Last names beginning with "Mac" or "Mc" are filed as spelled.

(7) Abbreviated names are treated as if they were spelled out. For example: Jos. is filed as Joseph, and Robt. is filed as Robert.

(8) Titles and designations such as Dr., Mrs., Prof. are disregarded in filing.

NAMES OF BUSINESS ORGANIZATIONS

(1) The names of business organisations are filed exactly as written, except that an organization bearing the name of an individual is filed alphabetically according to the name of the individual in accordance with the rules for filing names of individuals given above. For example: Thomas Allison Machine Company precedes Northern Baking Company.

(2) When numerals occur in a name, they are treated as if they were spelled out. For example: 6 stands for six, and 4th stands for fourth.

(3) When the following words occur in names, they are disregarded: the, of, and.

SAMPLE:

A.	Fred Town	(2)
B.	Jack Towne	(3)
C.	D. Town	(1)
D.	Jack S. Towne	(4)

The numbers in parentheses indicate the proper alphabetical order in which these names should be filed. Since the name that should be filed THIRD is Jack Towne, the answer is B.

42. A. Herbert Restman
    B. H. Restman
    C. Harry Restmore
    D. H. Restmore   42.____

43. A. Martha Eastwood
    B. Martha E. Eastwood
    C. Martha Edna Eastwood
    D. M. Eastwood   43.____

44. A. Timothy Macalan
    B. Fred McAlden
    C. Thomas MacAllister
    D. Mrs. Frank McAllen   44.____

45. A. Elm Trading Co.
    B. El Dorado Trucking Corp.
    C. James Eldred Jewelry Store
    D. Eldridge Printing, Inc.   45.____

46. A. Edward La Gabriel
    B. Marie Doris Gabriel
    C. Marjorie N. Gabriel
    D. Marjorie N. Gabriel   46.____

47. A. Peter La Vance
    B. George Van Meer
    C. Wallace De Vance
    D. Leonard Vance

48. A. Fifth Avenue Book Shop
    B. Mr. Wm. A. Fifner
    C. 52nd Street Association
    D. Robert B. Fiffner

49. A. Dr. Chas. D. Peterson
    B. Miss Irene F. Petersen
    C. Lawrence E. Peterson
    D. Prof. N.A. Petersen

50. A. 71st Street Theater
    B. The Seven Seas Corp.
    C. 7th Ave. Service Co.
    D. Walter R. Sevan and Co.

47.____

48.____

49.____

50.____

KEY (CORRECT ANSWERS)

1. B	11. B	21. D	31. C	41. D
2. A	12. C	22. B	32. C	42. D
3. D	13. D	23. C	33. D	43. B
4. B	14. B	24. A	34. B	44. B
5. D	15. C	25. A	35. A	45. D
6. A	16. D	26. B	36. A	46. C
7. C	17. A	27. D	37. D	47. D
8. B	18. D	28. A	38. C	48. A
9. D	19. A	29. B	39. B	49. A
10. A	20. B	30. A	40. B	50. C

EXAMINATION SECTION
TEST 1

DIRECTIONS: Each question or incomplete statement is followed by several suggested answers or completions. Select the one that BEST answers the question or completes the statement. *PRINT THE LETTER OF THE CORRECT ANSWER IN THE SPACE AT THE RIGHT.*

1. A push-button telephone with six buttons, one of which is a *hold* button, is often used when more than one outside line is needed.
    If you are talking on one line of this type of telephone when another call comes in, what is the procedure to follow if you want to answer the second call but keep the first call on the line? Push the

    A. *hold* button at the same time as you push the *pickup* button of the ringing line
    B. *hold* button and then push the *pickup* button of the ringing line
    C. *pickup* button of the ringing line and then push the *hold* button
    D. *pickup* button of the ringing line and push the *hold* button when you return to the original line

    1.____

2. Suppose that you are asked to prepare a petty cash statement for March. The original and one copy are to go to the personnel office. One copy is to go to the fiscal office, and another copy is to go to your supervisor. The last copy is for your files.
    In preparing the statement and the copies, how many sheets of copy paper should you use?

    A. 3   B. 4   C. 5   D. 8

    2.____

3. Which one of the following is the LEAST important advantage of putting the subject of a letter in the heading to the right of the address?
    It

    A. makes filing of the copy easier
    B. makes more space available in the body of the letter
    C. simplifies distribution of letters
    D. simplifies determination of the subject of the letter

    3.____

4. Of the following, the MOST efficient way to put 100 copies of a one-page letter into 9 1/2" x 4 1/8" envelopes for mailing is to fold _____ into an envelope.

    A. each letter and insert it immediately after folding
    B. each letter separately until all 100 are folded; then insert each one
    C. the 100 letters two at a time, then separate them and insert each one
    D. two letters together, slip them apart, and insert each one

    4.____

5. When preparing papers for filing, it is NOT desirable to

    A. smooth papers that are wrinkled
    B. use paper clips to keep related papers together in the files
    C. arrange the papers in the order in which they will be filed
    D. mend torn papers with cellophane tape

    5.____

6. Of the following, the BEST reason for a clerical unit to have its own duplicating machine is that the unit 6._____

    A. uses many forms which it must reproduce internally
    B. must make two copies of each piece of incoming mail for a special file
    C. must make seven copies of each piece of outgoing mail
    D. must type 200 envelopes each month for distribution to the same offices

7. Several offices use the same photocopying machine. 7._____
If each office must pay its share of the cost of running this machine, the BEST way of determining how much of this cost should be charged to each of these offices is to

    A. determine the monthly number of photocopies made by each office
    B. determine the monthly number of originals submitted for photocopying by each office
    C. determine the number of times per day each office uses the photocopy machine
    D. divide the total cost of running the photocopy machine by the total number of offices using the machine

8. Which one of the following would it be BEST to use to indicate that a file folder has been removed from the files for temporary use in another office? 8._____
A(n)

    A. cross-reference card   B. tickler file marker
    C. aperture card   D. out guide

9. Which one of the following is the MOST important objective of filing? 9._____

    A. Giving a secretary something to do in her spare time
    B. Making it possible to locate information quickly
    C. Providing a place to store unneeded documents
    D. Keeping extra papers from accumulating on workers' desks

10. If a check has been made out for an incorrect amount, the BEST action for the writer of the check to take is to 10._____

    A. erase the original amount and enter the correct amount
    B. cross out the original amount with a single line and enter the correct amount above it
    C. black out the original amount so that it cannot be read and enter the correct amount above it
    D. write a new check

11. Which one of the following BEST describes the usual arrangement of a tickler file? 11._____

    A. Alphabetical   B. Chronological
    C. Numerical   D. Geographical

12. Which one of the following is the LEAST desirable filing practice? 12._____

    A. Using staples to keep papers together
    B. Filing all material without regard to date
    C. Keeping a record of all materials removed from the files
    D. Writing filing instructions on each paper prior to filing

13. Assume that one of your duties is to keep records of the office supplies used by your unit   13._____
for the purpose of ordering new supplies when the old supplies run out. The information
that will be of MOST help in letting you know when to reorder supplies is the

    A. quantity issued   B. quantity received
    C. quantity on hand   D. stock number

Questions 14-19.

DIRECTIONS: Questions 14 through 19 consist of sets of names and addresses. In each
question, the name and address in Column II should be an exact copy of the
name and address in Column I. If there is:
    a mistake *only* in the name, mark your answer A;
    a mistake *only* in the address, mark your answer B;
    a mistake in *both* name and address, mark your answer C;
    no mistake in *either* name or address, mark your answer D.

SAMPLE QUESTION

Column I	Column II
Michael Filbert	Michael Filbert
456 Reade Street	645 Reade Street
New York, N.Y. 10013	New York, N.Y. 10013

Since there is a mistake only in the address (the street number should be 456 instead of 645), the answer to the sample question is B.

COLUMN I	COLUMN II	
14. Esta Wong 141 West 68 St. New York, N.Y. 10023	Esta Wang 141 West 68 St. New York, N.Y. 10023	14._____
15. Dr. Alberto Grosso 3475 12th Avenue Brooklyn, N.Y. 11218	Dr. Alberto Grosso 3475 12th Avenue Brooklyn, N.Y. 11218	15._____
16. Mrs. Ruth Bortlas 482 Theresa Ct. Far Rockaway, N.Y. 11691	Ms. Ruth Bortlas 482 Theresa Ct. Far Rockaway, N.Y. 11169	16._____
17. Mr. and Mrs. Howard Fox 2301 Sedgwick Ave. Bronx, N.Y. 10468	Mr. and Mrs. Howard Fox 231 Sedgwick Ave. Bronx, N.Y. 10468	17._____
18. Miss Marjorie Black 223 East 23 Street New York, N.Y. 10010	Miss Margorie Black 223 East 23 Street New York, N.Y. 10010	18._____
19. Michelle Herman 806 Valley Rd. Old Tappan, N.J. 07675	Michelle Hermann 806 Valley Dr. Old Tappan, N.J. 07675	19._____

Questions 20-25.

DIRECTIONS: Questions 20 through 25 are to be answered SOLELY on the basis of the information in the following passage.

Basic to every office is the need for proper lighting. Inadequate lighting is a familiar cause of fatigue and serves to create a somewhat dismal atmosphere in the office. One requirement of proper lighting is that it be of an appropriate intensity. Intensity is measured in foot-candles. According to the Illuminating Engineering Society of New York, for casual seeing tasks such as in reception rooms, inactive file rooms, and other service areas, it is recommended that the amount of light be 30 foot-candles. For ordinary seeing tasks such as reading and work in active file rooms and in mail rooms, the recommended lighting is 100 foot-candles. For very difficult seeing tasks such as accounting, transcribing, and business machine use, the recommended lighting is 150 foot-candles.

Lighting intensity is only one requirement. Shadows and glare are to be avoided. For example, the larger the proportion of a ceiling filled with lighting units, the more glare-free and comfortable the lighting will be. Natural lighting from windows is not too dependable because on dark wintry days, windows yield little usable light, and on sunny, summer afternoons, the glare from windows may be very distracting. Desks should not face the windows. Finally, the main lighting source ought to be overhead and to the left of the user.

20. According to the above passage, insufficient light in the office may cause   20.____

    A. glare
    B. shadows
    C. tiredness
    D. distraction

21. Based on the above passage, which of the following must be considered when planning   21.____
lighting arrangements?
The

    A. amount of natural light present
    B. amount of work to be done
    C. level of difficulty of work to be done
    D. type of activity to be carried out

22. It can be inferred from the above passage that a well-coordinated lighting scheme is   22.____
LIKELY to result in

    A. greater employee productivity
    B. elimination of light reflection
    C. lower lighting cost
    D. more use of natural light

23. Of the following, the BEST title for the above passage is   23.____

    A. Characteristics of Light
    B. Light Measurement Devices
    C. Factors to Consider When Planning Lighting Systems
    D. Comfort vs. Cost When Devising Lighting Arrangements

24. According to the above passage, a foot-candle is a measurement of the 24.____

    A. number of bulbs used
    B. strength of the light
    C. contrast between glare and shadow
    D. proportion of the ceiling filled with lighting units

25. According to the above passage, the number of foot-candles of light that would be 25.____
needed to copy figures onto a payroll is _____ foot-candles.

    A. less than 30   B. 30
    C. 100   D. 150

KEY (CORRECT ANSWERS)

1.	B		11.	B
2.	B		12.	B
3.	B		13.	C
4.	A		14.	A
5.	B		15.	D
6.	A		16.	C
7.	A		17.	B
8.	D		18.	A
9.	B		19.	C
10.	D		20.	C

21.	D
22.	A
23.	C
24.	B
25.	D

TEST 2

DIRECTIONS: Each question or incomplete statement is followed by several suggested answers or completions. Select the one that BEST answers the question or completes the statement. *PRINT THE LETTER OF THE CORRECT ANSWER IN THE SPACE AT THE RIGHT.*

1. Assume that a supervisor has three subordinates who perform clerical tasks. One of the employees retires and is replaced by someone who is transferred from another unit in the agency. The transferred employee tells the supervisor that she has worked as a clerical employee for two years and understands clerical operations quite well. The supervisor then assigns the transferred employee to a desk, tells the employee to begin working, and returns to his own desk.
   The supervisor's action in this situation is

   A. *proper;* experienced clerical employees do not require training when they are transferred to new assignments
   B. *improper;* before the supervisor returns to his desk, he should tell the other two subordinates to watch the transferred employee perform the work
   C. *proper;* if the transferred employee makes any mistakes, she will bring them to the supervisor's attention
   D. *improper;* the supervisor should find out what clerical tasks the transferred employee has performed and give her instruction in those which are new or different

1.____

2. Assume that you are falling behind in completing your work assignments and you believe that your workload is too heavy.
   Of the following, the BEST course of action for you to take FIRST is to

   A. discuss the problem with your supervisor
   B. decide which of your assignments can be postponed
   C. try to get some of your co-workers to help you out
   D. plan to take some of the work home with you in order to catch up

2.____

3. Suppose that one of the clerks under your supervision is filling in monthly personnel forms. She asks you to explain a particular personnel regulation which is related to various items on the forms. You are not thoroughly familiar with the regulation.
   Of the following responses you may make, the one which will gain the MOST respect from the clerk and which is generally the MOST advisable is to

   A. tell the clerk to do the best she can and that you will check her work later
   B. inform the clerk that you are not sure of a correct explanation but suggest a procedure for her to follow
   C. give the clerk a suitable interpretation so that she will think you are familiar with all regulations
   D. tell the clerk that you will have to read the regulation more thoroughly before you can give her an explanation

3.____

4. Charging out records until a specified due date, with prompt follow-up if they are not returned, is a

4.____

A. *good* idea; it may prevent the records from being kept needlessly on someone's desk for long periods of time
B. *good* idea; it will indicate the extent of your authority to other departments
C. *poor* idea; the person borrowing the material may make an error because of the pressure put upon him to return the records
D. *poor* idea; other departments will feel that you do not trust them with the records and they will be resentful

Questions 5-9.

DIRECTIONS: Questions 5 through 9 consist of three lines of code letters and numbers. The numbers on each line should correspond with the code letters on the same line in accordance with the table below.

Code Letter	P	L	I	J	B	O	H	U	C	G
Corresponding Number	0	1	2	3	4	5	6	7	8	9

On some of the lines, an error exists in the coding. Compare the letters and numbers in each question carefully. If you find an error or errors on
only *one* of the lines in the question, mark your answer A;
any *two* lines in the question, mark your answer B;
all *three* lines in the question, mark your answer C;
none of the lines in the question, mark your answer D.

SAMPLE QUESTION

JHOILCP   3652180
BICLGUP   4286970
UCIBHLJ   5824613

In the above sample, the first line is correct since each code letter listed has the correct corresponding number. On the second line, an error exists because code letter L should have the number 1 instead of the number 6. On the third line, an error exists because the code letter U should have the number 7 instead of the number 5. Since there are errors on two of the three lines, the correct answer is B.

5.   BULJCIP   4713920   5._____
     HIGPOUL   6290571
     OCUHJBI   5876342

6.   CUBLOIJ   8741023   6._____
     LCLGCLB   1818914
     JPUHIOC   3076158

7.   OIJGCBPO   52398405   7._____
     UHPBLIOP   76041250
     CLUIPGPC   81720908

8.	BPCOUOJI	40875732	8._____
	UOHCIPLB	75682014	
	GLHUUCBJ	92677843	
9.	HOIOHJLH	65256361	9._____
	IOJJHHBP	25536640	
	OJHBJOPI	53642502	

Questions 10-13.

DIRECTIONS: Questions 10 through 13 are to be answered SOLELY on the basis of the information given in the following passage.

The mental attitude of the employee toward safety is exceedingly important in preventing
accidents. All efforts designed to keep safety on the employee's mind and to keep accident
prevention a live subject in the office will help substantially in a safety program. Although it
may seem strange, it is common for people to be careless. Therefore, safety education is a
continuous process.

Safety rules should be explained, and the reasons for their rigid enforcement should be
given to employees. Telling employees to be careful or giving similar general safety warnings
and slogans is probably of little value. Employees should be informed of basic safety funda-
mentals. This can be done through staff meetings, informal suggestions to employees, mov-
ies, and safety instruction cards. Safety instruction cards provide the employees with specific
suggestions about safety and serve as a series of timely reminders helping to keep safety on
the minds of employees. Pictures, posters, and cartoon sketches on bulletin boards that are
located in areas continually used by employees arouse the employees' interest in safety. It is
usually good to supplement this type of safety promotion with intensive individual follow-up.

10.   The above passage implies that the LEAST effective of the following safety measures is   10._____

    A.   rigid enforcement of safety rules
    B.   getting employees to think in terms of safety
    C.   elimination of unsafe conditions in the office
    D.   telling employees to stay alert at all times

11.   The reason given by the passage for maintaining ongoing safety education is that   11._____

    A.   people are often careless
    B.   office tasks are often dangerous
    C.   the value of safety slogans increases with repetition
    D.   safety rules change frequently

12.   Which one of the following safety aids is MOST likely to be preferred by the passage?   12._____
    A

    A.   cartoon of a man tripping over a carton and yelling, *Keep aisles clear!*
    B.   poster with a large number one and a caption saying, *Safety First*
    C.   photograph of a very neatly arranged office
    D.   large sign with the word *THINK* in capital letters

13. Of the following, the BEST title for the above passage is

    A. Basic Safety Fundamentals
    B. Enforcing Safety Among Careless Employees
    C. Attitudes Toward Safety
    D. Making Employees Aware of Safety

13.____

Questions 14-21.

DIRECTIONS: Questions 14 through 21 are to be answered SOLELY on the basis of the information and the chart given below.

    The following chart shows expenses in five selected categories for a one-year period, expressed as percentages of these same expenses during the previous year. The chart compares two different offices. In Office T (represented by ▨▨▨▨▨), a cost reduction program has been tested for the past year. The other office, Office Q (represented by ▨▨▨), served as a control, in that no special effort was made' to reduce costs during the past year.

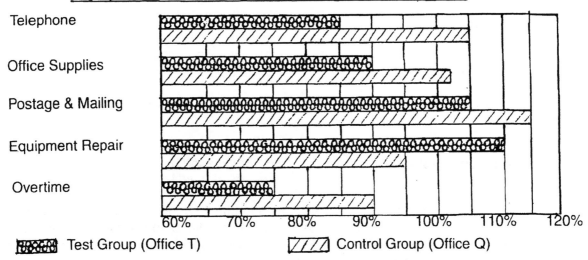

RESULTS OF OFFICE COST REDUCTION PROGRAM

Expenses of Test and Control Groups for 2016
Expressed as Percentages of Same Expenses for 2015

▨▨▨ Test Group (Office T)   ▨▨▨ Control Group (Office Q)

14. In Office T, which category of expense showed the greatest percentage REDUCTION from 2015 to 2016?

    A. Telephone   B. Office Supplies
    C. Postage & Mailing   D. Overtime

14.____

15. In which expense category did Office T show the BEST results in percentage terms when compared to Office Q?

    A. Telephone   B. Office Supplies
    C. Postage & Mailing   D. Overtime

15.____

16. According to the above chart, the cost reduction program was LEAST effective for the 16.____
    expense category of

    A. Office Supplies   B. Postage & Mailing
    C. Equipment Repair   D. Overtime

17. Office T's telephone costs went down during 2016 by approximately how many percent- 17.____
    age points?

    A. 15   B. 20   C. 85   D. 105

18. Which of the following changes occurred in expenses for Office Supplies in Office Q in 18.____
    the year 2016 as compared with the year 2015?
    They

    A. increased by more than 100%
    B. remained the same
    C. decreased by a few percentage points
    D. increased by a few percentage points

19. For which of the following expense categories do the results in Office T and the results in 19.____
    Office Q differ MOST NEARLY by 10 percentage points?

    A. Telephone   B. Postage & Mailing
    C. Equipment Repair   D. Overtime

20. In which expense category did Office Q's costs show the GREATEST percentage 20.____
    increase in 2016?

    A. Telephone   B. Office Supplies
    C. Postage & Mailing   D. Equipment Repair

21. In Office T, by approximately what percentage did overtime expense change during the 21.____
    past year?
    It

    A. *increased* by 15%   B. *increased* by 75%
    C. *decreased* by 10%   D. *decreased* by 25%

22. In a particular agency, there were 160 accidents in 2007. Of these accidents, 75% were 22.____
    due to unsafe acts and the rest were due to unsafe conditions. In the following year, a
    special safety program was established. The number of accidents in 2009 due to unsafe
    acts was reduced to 35% of what it had been in 2007.
    How many accidents due to unsafe acts were there in 2009?

    A. 20   B. 36   C. 42   D. 56

23. At the end of every month, the petty cash fund of Agency A is reimbursed for payments 23.____
    made from the fund during the month. During the month of February, the amounts paid
    from the fund were entered on receipts as follows: 10 bus fares of 35¢ each and one taxi
    fare of $3.50.
    At the end of the month, the money left in the fund was in the following denominations:
    15 one dollar bills, 4 quarters, 10 dimes, and 20 nickels.
    If the petty cash fund is reduced by 20% for the following month, how much money will
    there be available in the petty cash fund for March?

    A. $11.00   B. $20.00   C. $21.50   D. $25.00

24. The one of the following records which it would be MOST advisable to keep in alphabeti- 24.____
cal order is a

    A. continuous listing of phone messages, including time and caller, for your supervi-
sor
    B. listing of individuals currently employed by your agency in a particular title
    C. record of purchases paid for by the petty cash fund
    D. dated record of employees who have borrowed material from the files in your office

25. Assume that you have been asked to copy by hand a column of numbers with two deci- 25.____
mal places from one record to another. Each number consists of three, four, and five digits.
In order to copy them quickly and accurately, you should copy

    A. each number exactly, making sure that the column of digits farthest to the right is in
a straight line and all other columns are lined up
    B. the column of digits farthest to the right and then copy the next column of digits
moving from right to left
    C. the column of digits farthest to the left and then copy the next column of digits mov-
ing from left to right
    D. the digits to the right of each decimal point and then copy the digits to the left of
each decimal point

———

KEY (CORRECT ANSWERS)

1.	D	11.	A
2.	A	12.	A
3.	D	13.	D
4.	A	14.	D
5.	A	15.	A
6.	C	16.	C
7.	D	17.	A
8.	B	18.	D
9.	C	19.	B
10.	D	20.	C

21.	D
22.	C
23.	B
24.	B
25.	A

———

WRITTEN ENGLISH EXPRESSION

EXAMINATION SECTION
TEST 1

DIRECTIONS: In each of the sentences below, four portions are underlined and lettered. Read each sentence and decide whether any of the underlined parts contains an error in spelling, punctuation, or capitalization, or employs grammatical usage which would be inappropriate for carefully written English. If so, note the letter printed under the unacceptable form and print it in the space at the right. If all four of the underlined portions are acceptable as they stand, print the letter E. No sentence contains more than one unacceptable form.

1. A low ceiling is when the atmospheric conditions make flying inadvisable.
             A   B   C   D

1.____

2. They couldn't tell who the card was from.
   A   B   C   D

2.____

3. No one but you and I are to help him.
       A   B C   D

3.____

4. To him fall the duties of foster parent.
    A   B   C   D

4.____

5. If the world should somehow find peace within itself, so that all her people would
          A   B   C   D
stop fighting everlastingly...that would be the day!

5.____

6. Every one of the teachers prepared his lessons in a consumate manner.
    A   B   C   D

6.____

7. Didn't they used to pay promptly?
   A   B   C   D

7.____

8. The services rendered by these people and their share in making the work a
           A   B   C

success is to be commended.
       D

8.____

9. They couldn't tell whom the cable was recieved from.
   A B   C   D

9.____

10. We like these better than those kind.
       A B   C D

10.____

11. It is a test of you more than I.
    A B   C   D

11.____

12. The person in charge being him there can be no change in policy.
      A   B C   D

12.____

13. A large amount of information and news are to be found there.
     A B   C   D

13.____

14. I should have liked to have seen it again.
        A   B   C D

14.____

15. The desire to travel made him restless
        A   B C D

15.____

16. Should that effect their decision?
    A   B   C D

16.____

17. Do as we do for the celebration of the childrens' event.
    A B C   D

17.____

18. Do either of you care to join us?
    A B C D

18.____

19. A child's food requirements differ from the adult
      A   B   C   D

19.____

20. A large family, including two uncles and four grandparents, live at the
       A   B   C D
    hotel.

20.____

21. <u>If they would have done</u>   <u>that,</u>   <u>they</u>   <u>might have</u>   succeeded.
           A   B   C   D

21.____

22. <u>Neither</u>   the hot days   <u>or</u>   the humid nights   <u>annoy</u>   <u>our</u>   Southern visitor.
       A   B   C   D

22.____

23. Some   <u>people do not</u>   <u>gain favor</u>   <u>because</u>   they are   <u>kind of</u>   tactless.
           A   B   C   D

23.____

24. <u>No sooner</u>   had the turning point   <u>come</u>   <u>than</u>   a new   <u>embarassing</u>   issue
         A   B   C   D
   arose.

24.____

25. An usher   <u>seldom</u>   <u>rises</u>   <u>above</u>   a   <u>theatre manager</u>.
              A   B   C   D

25.____

KEY (CORRECT ANSWERS)

1.	B		11.	D
2.	C		12.	C
3.	B		13.	C
4.	E		14.	B
5.	C		15.	E
6.	D		16.	B
7.	C		17.	D
8.	D		18.	A
9.	D		19.	D
10.	C		20.	C

21.	A
22.	B
23.	D
24.	D
25.	C

TEST 2

DIRECTIONS: In each of the sentences below, four portions are underlined and lettered. Read each sentence and decide whether any of the underlined parts contains an error in spelling, punctuation, or capitalization, or employs grammatical usage which would be inappropriate for carefully written English. If so, note the letter printed under the unacceptable form and print it in the space at the right. If all four of the underlined portions are acceptable as they stand, print the letter E. No sentence contains more than one unacceptable form.

1. The <u>epic,</u> "Gone With the <u>Wind,</u>" deals with events that <u>ocurred</u> during the Civil
    A   B   C

    War <u>era.</u>
         D

1.____

2. <u>Shall</u> you <u>be</u> <u>at home,</u> <u>let us say,</u> on Sunday at two o'clock?
   A   B   C   D

2.____

3. We <u>see</u> Mr. <u>Lewis'</u> <u>take</u> his car <u>out of the garage</u> daily.
    A   B   C   D

3.____

4. We <u>have</u> <u>no</u> place <u>to keep</u> our rubbers, <u>only</u> in the hall closet.
       A   B   C   D

4.____

5. <u>Isn't it</u> true <u>what</u> <u>you</u> <u>told</u> me about the best way to prepare for an exami-
   A   B   C   D
    nation?

5.____

6. <u>"Who</u> <u>shall</u> I say called," the butler <u>asked</u> <u>?</u>
    A   B   C   D

6.____

7. The museum <u>is</u> often visited by students who <u>are</u> fond of <u>Primitive</u> paintings,
            A   B   C

    and by <u>patent</u> attorneys.
          D

7.____

8. I <u>rose</u> <u>to nominate</u> the <u>superintendant,</u> the man <u>who</u> most of us felt was
   A   B   C   D
    the best.

8.____

9. ___

9. The child <u>was</u> sent to the store to <u>purchase</u> a bottle of milk and <u>brought</u> home
A   B   C

fresh rolls, <u>too.</u>
D

10. ___

10. The garden tool <u>was sent</u> <u>to be sharpened</u> and a new handle <u>to be</u> <u>put on.</u>
A   B   C   D

11. ___

11. At the end of her vacation, Joan came home with little money <u>,</u> <u>nevertheless</u> <u>,</u>
A   B   C

it was a joyous <u>occasion.</u>
D

12. ___

12. We <u>people</u> have <u>opportunities</u> to show the rest of the world how real democracy
A   B

functions and <u>leads</u> to the <u>perfectability</u> of man.
C   D

13. ___

13. The guide paddled along and then <u>fell into</u> a <u>reverie</u> <u>where</u> he <u>related</u> the
A   B   C   D

history of the region.

14. ___

14. We <u>should have</u> investigated the <u>cause of</u> the noise in the <u>Hotel</u> by <u>bringing</u>
A   B   C   D

the car to a halt.

15. ___

15. The first few strokes of the brush <u>were</u> enough <u>to convince</u> me that Tom could paint
A   B

<u>much better</u> <u>than</u> <u>me.</u>
C   D

16. ___

16. We inquired <u>whether</u> we <u>could see</u> the owner of the store, after we <u>waited</u>
A   B   C

<u>for one hour.</u>
D

17. The irratation of the high-strung parent was aggravated by the slightest noise that
         A   B   C

    the baby made.
            D

17.____

18. There is a large demand for men interested in the field of
        A   B   C

    Information Retrieval.
          D

18.____

19. Snow after the rains delay the coming crops.
     A   B   C   D

19.____

20. They intend to partially do away with ceremonies.
     A   B   C   D

20.____

21. If that be done and turns out badly we shall see horror.
    A   B   C   D

21.____

22. The new plant is to be electrically lighted; increasing brightness by 50%.
              A   B   C   D

22.____

23. The reason the speaker was offended was that the audience was inat-
       A   B   C   D
    tentive.

23.____

24. There appear to be conditions that govern the behavioral Sciences.
         A   B   C   D

24.____

25. Either of the men are influential enough to control the situation.
     A   B   C   D

25.____

KEY (CORRECT ANSWERS)

1.	C		11.	A
2.	E		12.	D
3.	B		13.	C
4.	D		14.	C
5.	B		15.	D
6.	D		16.	C
7.	C		17.	A
8.	C		18.	D
9.	C		19.	C
10.	C		20.	E

21.	C
22.	C
23.	E
24.	D
25.	B

TEST 3

DIRECTIONS: In each of the sentences below, four portions are underlined and lettered. Read each sentence and decide whether any of the underlined parts contains an error in spelling, puncutation, or capitalization, or employs grammatical usage which would be inappropriate for carefully written English. If so, note the letter printed under the unacceptable form and print it in the space at the right. If all four of the underlined portions are acceptable as they stand, print the letter E. No sentence contains more than one unacceptable form.

1. <u>Who</u> <u>did</u> you predict <u>would win</u> the election <u>this</u> year?
    A   B   C   D

1.____

2. <u>It</u> takes a <u>lot</u> <u>more</u> effort <u>to sell</u> houses this year than last year.
   A   B   C   D

2.____

3. <u>Having pranced</u> into the arena <u>with little grace and unsteady hoof</u>
        A   B

   <u>for the jumps ahead,</u>   <u>the driver reined his horse.</u>
            C   D

3.____

4. Once the dog wagged <u>it's</u> tail, <u>you</u> knew <u>it</u> <u>was</u> a friendly animal.
                         A   B   C   D

4.____

5. The record of the winning team was <u>among</u> the <u>most</u> <u>noteworthy</u>
                                    A   B   C

   <u>of the season.</u>
       D

5.____

6. <u>When</u> <u>asked</u> to choose corn, cabbage, <u>or</u> potatoes, the diner selected the
    A   B   C

   <u>latter.</u>
    D

6.____

7. The maid <u>wasn't</u> <u>so</u> small <u>that</u> she <u>couldn't</u> reach the top window for clean-
             A   B   C   D

   ing.

7.____

8. Many people <u>feel</u> that powdered coffee <u>produces</u> a <u>really</u> <u>abhorent</u> flavor.
                A   B   C   D

8._____

9. <u>Would you mind</u> <u>me</u> <u>trying</u> that coat on for <u>size?</u>
      A   B   C   D

9._____

10. This chair <u>looks</u> <u>much</u> <u>different</u> <u>than</u> the chair we selected in the store.
           A   B   C   D

10._____

11. After <u>trying</u> unsuccessfully <u>to land</u> a <u>job</u> in the city, Will <u>settled</u> in the coun-
       A   B   C   D

try on a farm.

11._____

12. On the last attempt, the pole-vaulter <u>came</u> <u>nearly</u> <u>to getting</u> <u>hurt.</u>
                             A   B   C   D

12._____

13. The <u>observance</u> of <u>armistice day</u> <u>throughout the world</u> offers an opportunity
         A   B   C

<u>to reflect</u> on the horrors of war.
    D

13._____

14. <u>Outside of</u> the mistakes in spelling, the child's letter <u>was</u> a <u>very</u> good <u>one.</u>
      A   B   C   D

14._____

15. <u>Scisors</u> <u>are</u> always dangerous <u>for</u> a child to <u>handle.</u>
     A   B   C   D

15._____

16. I assure <u>you</u> <u>that</u> I <u>will not yield</u> to pressure <u>to sell</u> my interest.
         A   B   C   D

16._____

17. Ask <u>him</u> <u>if</u> he <u>recalls</u> the incident which <u>tookplace</u> at our first meeting.
      A   B   C   D

17._____

18. The manager <u>felt</u> <u>like as not to order</u> his <u>usher - captain</u> <u>to surrender</u> his uniform.
            A   B   C   D

18._____

19. The mother of the bride climaxed the occasion by exlaiming, "I want my children
                              A   B   C

    should be happy forever."
    D

19.____

20. We read in the papers where the prospects for peace are improving.
        A   B   C   D

20.____

21. "Can I share the cab with you?" was frequently heard during the period of
     A   B   C   D

     gas rationing.

21.____

22. Had the police suspected the ruse, they would have taken relevent pre-
     A   B   C   D

     cautions.

22.____

23. The teacher admonished the other students neither to speak to John, nor
                               A   B   C

    should they annoy him.
    D

23.____

24. Fortunately, we had been told that there was but one availible service
                  A   B   C   D

    station in that area.

24.____

25. We haven't hardly enough time to make it.
        A   B   C   D

25.____

KEY (CORRECT ANSWERS)

1.	E		11.	B
2.	B		12.	B
3.	D		13.	B
4.	A		14.	A
5.	E		15.	A
6.	D		16.	E
7.	B		17.	B
8.	D		18.	B
9.	B		19.	D
10.	A		20.	C

21.	A
22.	D
23.	D
24.	D
25.	A

TEST 4

In each of the sentences below, four portions are underlined and lettered. Read each sentence and decide whether any of the underlined parts contains an error in spelling, punctuation, or capitalization, or employs grammatical usage which would be inappropriate for carefully written English. If so, note the letter printed under the unacceptable form and print it in the space at the right. If all four of the underlined portions are acceptable as they stand, print the letter E. No sentence contains more than one unacceptable form.

1. He either will fail in his attempt or will seek other Government employ-
           A   B   C   D
    ment.

2. After each side gave their version, the case was closed.
    A   B   C   D

3. Every one of the cars were tagged by the police.
    A   B   C   D

4. They can't seem to see it when I explain the theory.
          A   B   C   D

5. It is difficult to find the genuine signature between all those submitted.
    A   B   C   D

6. She can't understand why they don't remember who to give the letter to .
                             A   B   C   D

7. Every man and woman in America is interested in his tax bill.
    A   B   C   D

8. A guard was called to prevent them carrying away souvenirs.
               A   B   C   D

9. Neither you nor I am to blame for the sudden slump in business.
    A   B   C D

1.____

2.____

3.____

4.____

5.____

6.____

7.____

8.____

9.____

10. _____

10. To <u>you</u> and <u>him</u> <u>belong</u> the <u>credit.</u>
      A   B   C   D

11. _____

11. The auctioneer had <u>less</u> items to <u>sell</u> this year <u>than</u> last <u>year.</u>
            A   B   C   D

12. _____

12. <u>Theirs</u> <u>instead of</u> <u>his</u> instructions <u>will be followed.</u>
    A   B   C   D

13. _____

13. <u>It</u> is the <u>same</u> at his local <u>broker's</u> Frank <u>Smith.</u>
    A   B   C   D

14. _____

14. The teacher <u>politely</u> <u>requested</u> <u>each</u> pupil to <u>step in</u> the room.
           A   B   C   D

15. _____

15. <u>Too</u> many parents <u>leave</u> <u>their</u> children do as <u>they</u> please.
    A   B   C   D

16. _____

16. <u>He</u> arrived <u>safe,</u> his papers <u>untouched,</u> his composure <u>unrufled.</u>
    A   B   C   D

17. _____

17. I <u>do not</u> have <u>any</u> faith in <u>John</u> <u>running</u> for office.
      A   B   C   D

18. _____

18. The musicians began to play <u>tunefully</u> <u>;</u> <u>keeping</u> the proper tempo <u>indicated</u>
                          A   B   C   D

for the selection.

19. _____

19. <u>Mary's</u> maid of honor bought the <u>kind of</u> <u>an</u> <u>outfit</u> suitable for an afternoon
    A   B   C   D

wedding.

20. _____

20. After the debate, <u>every one</u> of the <u>Speakers</u> realized that, <u>given</u> another
                    A   B   C

chance, he <u>could have done</u> better.
              D

21. The reason <u>given</u> by the physician for the patient's trouble <u>was</u> <u>because</u> of his

             A   B   C

    poor eating <u>habits.</u>

                D

21._____

22. The fog was so <u>thick</u> that the driver <u>couldn't</u> <u>hardly</u> see more than ten feet <u>ahead.</u>

                   A   B   C   D

22._____

23. I suggest that you <u>present</u> the medal to <u>who</u> you <u>deem</u> <u>best.</u>

                    A   B   C   D

23._____

24. A decision made by a man <u>without much deliberation</u> is sometimes <u>no</u> different

                                    A   B

    <u>than</u> a <u>slow one.</u>

      C   D

24._____

25. <u>By the time</u> Jones <u>graduates from</u> <u>Dental School,</u> he <u>will be</u> twenty-six years of

        A   B   C   D

    age.

25._____

KEY (CORRECT ANSWERS)

1.	D		11.	A
2.	C		12.	A
3.	C		13.	D
4.	C		14.	D
5.	C		15.	B
6.	C		16.	D
7.	E		17.	C
8.	C		18.	B
9.	E		19.	C
10.	C		20.	B

21.	C
22.	B
23.	B
24.	D
25.	C

TEST 5

Questions 1-18.

DIRECTIONS: Each of the sentences numbered 1 to 18 may be classified most appropriately under one of the following three categories:
- A. faulty because of incorrect grammar
- B. faulty because of incorrect punctuation
- C. correct

Examine each sentence carefully. Then, in the space at the right, print the letter preceding the option which is best of those suggested above. All incorrect sentences contain but one type of error. Consider a sentence correct if it contains none of the types of errors mentioned, even though there may be other correct ways of expressing the same thought.

1. He sent the notice to the clerk who you hired yesterday. 1._____

2. It must be admitted, however that you were not informed of this change. 2._____

3. Only the employees who have served in this grade for at least two years are eligible for promotion. 3._____

4. The work was divided equally between she and Mary. 4._____

5. He thought that you were not available at that time. 5._____

6. When the messenger returns; please give him this package. 6._____

7. The new secretary prepared, typed, addressed, and delivered, the notices. 7._____

8. Walking into the room, his desk can be seen at the rear. 8._____

9. Although John has worked here longer than she, he produces a smaller amount of work. 9._____

10. She said she could of typed this report yesterday. 10._____

11. Neither one of these procedures are adequate for the efficient performance of this task. 11._____

12. The typewriter is the tool of the typist; the cash register, the tool of the cashier. 12._____

13. "The assignment must be completed as soon as possible" said the supervisor. 13._____

14. As you know, office handbooks are issued to all new employees. 14._____

15. Writing a speech is sometimes easier than to deliver it before an audience. 15._____

16. Mr. Brown our accountant, will audit the accounts next week. 16._____

17. Give the assignment to whomever is able to do it most efficiently. 17._____

18. The supervisor expected either your or I to file these reports. 18._____

Questions 19-28.

DIRECTIONS: Each of the following sentences may be classified most appropriately under one of the following four categories:
  A. faulty because of incorrect grammar
  B. faulty because of incorrect punctuation
  C. faulty because of incorrect spelling
  D. correct

Examine each sentence carefully. Then, in the space at the right, print the letter preceding the option which is best of those suggested above. All incorrect sentences contain but one type of error. Consider a sentence correct if it contains none of the types of errors mentioned, even though there may be other correct ways of expressing the same thought.

19. The fire apparently started in the storeroom, which is usually locked.   19._____

20. On approaching the victim two bruises were noticed by this officer.   20._____

21. The officer, who was there examined the report with great care.   21._____

22. Each employee in the office had a separate desk.   22._____

23. All employees including members of the clerical staff, were invited to the lecture.   23._____

24. The suggested procedure is similar to the one now in use.   24._____

25. No one was more pleased with the new procedure than the chauffeur.   25._____

26. He tried to pursuade her to change the procedure.   26._____

27. The total of the expenses charged to petty cash were high.   27._____

28. An understanding between him and I was finally reached.   28._____

KEY (CORRECT ANSWERS)

1.	A	11.	A
2.	B	12.	C
3.	C	13.	B
4.	A	14.	C
5.	C	15.	A
6.	B	16.	B
7.	B	17.	A
8.	A	18.	A
9.	C	19.	D
10.	A	20.	A

21.	B
22.	C
23.	B
24.	D
25.	D
26.	C
27.	A
28.	A

WRITTEN ENGLISH EXPRESSION

EXAMINATION SECTION
TEST 1

Questions 1-5.

DIRECTIONS: Each of the following sentences may be classified under one of the following four categories:
- A. faulty because of incorrect grammar
- B. faulty because of incorrect punctuation
- C. faulty because of incorrect capitalization or incorrect spelling
- D. correct

Examine each sentence carefully. Then, in the space at the right, print the letter preceding the option which is best of those suggested above. All incorrect sentences contain but one type of error. Consider a sentence correct if it contains none of the types of errors mentioned, even though there may be other correct ways of expressing the same thought.

1. They told both he and I that the prisoner had escaped.   1.____

2. Any superior officer, who, disregards the just complaints of his subordinates, is remiss in the performance of his duty.   2.____

3. Only those members of the national organization who resided in the Middle West attended the conference in Chicago.   3.____

4. We told him to give the investigation assignment to whoever was available.   4.____

5. Please do not disappoint and embarass us by not appearing in court.   5.____

Questions 6-10.

DIRECTIONS: Each of the following sentences may be classified under one of the following four categories:
- A. faulty because of incorrect spelling only
- B. faulty because of incorrect grammar or word usage only
- C. faulty because of one error in spelling and one error in grammar or word usage
- D. correct

Examine each sentence carefully. Then, in the space at the right, print the letter preceding the option which is best of those suggested above. All incorrect sentences contain but one type of error. Consider a sentence correct if it contains none of the types of errors mentioned, even though there may be other correct ways of expressing the same thought.

6. Although the officer's speech proved to be entertaining, the topic was not relevant to the main theme of the conference.   6.____

7. In February all new officers attended a training course in which they were learned their   7._____
principal duties and the fundamental operating procedures of the department.

8. I personally seen inmate Jones threaten inmates Smith and Green with bodily harm if   8._____
they refused to participate in the plot.

9. To the layman, who on a chance visit to the prison observes everything functioning   9._____
smoothly, the maintenance of prison discipline may seem to be a relatively easily realiz-
able objective.

10. The prisoners in cell block fourty were forbidden to lay on the cell cots during the recre-   10._____
ation hour.

Questions 11-22.

DIRECTIONS: Each of the following sentences may be classified under one of the following
four categories:
A. faulty because of incorrect grammar
B. faulty because of incorrect punctuation
C. faulty because of incorrect capitalization or incorrect spelling
D. correct
Examine each sentence carefully. Then, in the space at the right, print the letter preceding the option which is best of those suggested above. All incorrect
sentences contain but one type of error. Consider a sentence correct if it contains none of the types of errors mentioned, even though there may be other
correct ways of expressing the same thought.

11. I cannot encourage you any.   11._____

12. You always look well in those sort of clothes.   12._____

13. Shall we go to the park?   13._____

14. The man whome he introduced was Mr. Carey.   14._____

15. She saw the letter laying here this morning.   15._____

16. It should rain before the Afternoon is over.   16._____

17. They have already went home.   17._____

18. That Jackson will be elected is evident.   18._____

19. He does not hardly approve of us.   19._____

20. It was he, who won the prize.   20._____

21. Shall we go to the park.   21._____

22. They are, alike, in this particular.   22._____

KEY (CORRECT ANSWERS)

1.	A		11.	A
2.	B		12.	A
3.	C		13.	D
4.	D		14.	C
5.	C		15.	A
6.	A		16.	C
7.	C		17.	A
8.	B		18.	D
9.	D		19.	A
10.	C		20.	B

21. B
22. B

TEST 2

DIRECTIONS: Among the sentences in this test are some which cannot be accepted in formal, written English for one or another of the following reasons:

POOR DICTION: The use of a word which is improper either because its meaning does not fit the sentence or because it is not acceptable in formal writing.
Example;   The audience was strongly <u>effected</u> by the senator's speech.

VERBOSITY: Repetitious elements adding nothing to the meaning of the sentence and not justified by any need for special emphasis.
Example: At that time there was <u>then</u> no right of petition.

FAULTY GRAMMAR: Word forms and expressions which do not conform to the grammatical and structural usages required by formal written English (errors in case, number, parallelism, and the like).
Example;   Everyone in the delegation had <u>their</u> reasons for opposing the measure.

No sentence has more than one kind of error. Some sentences have no errors. Read each sentence carefully; then, in the space at the right, print the letter:
    D if the sentence contains an error in <u>diction</u>
    V if the sentence is <u>verbose</u>
    G if the sentence contains <u>faulty grammar</u>
    O if the sentence contains <u>none</u> of these errors.

1. I will not go unless I receive a special invitation.   1.____

2. The pilot shouted decisive orders to his assistant as the plane burst into flames.   2.____

3. She acts like her feelings were hurt.   3.____

4. Please come here and try and help me finish this piece of work.   4.____

5. As long as you are ready, you may as well start promptly and on time.   5.____

6. My younger brother insists that he is as tall as me.   6.____

7. A spiritual person is usually deeply concerned with mundane affairs.   7.____

8. Speaking from practical experience, I advise you to give up those unquestionably quixotic schemes.   8.____

9. We walked as long as there was any light to guide us.   9.____

10. Realizing I had forgotten my gloves, I returned to the theatre, using a flashlight and turned down every seat.   10.____

11. The winters were hard and dreary, nothing could live without shelter.   11.____

12. Not one in a thousand readers take the matter seriously.   12.____

13. This tire has so many defections that it is worthless.   13.____

14. The jury were divided in their views.   14.____

15. He was so credulous that his friends found it hard to deceive him.   15.____

16. The emperor's latest ukase is sure to stir up such resentment that the people will revolt. 16.____

17. When you go to the library tomorrow, please bring this book to the librarian in the reference room.   17.____

18. His speech is so precise as to seem infected.   18.____

19. I had sooner serve overseas before I remain inactive at home.   19.____

20. We read each other's letters together.   20.____

KEY (CORRECT ANSWERS)

1. O
2. V   Eliminate decisive
3. G   Use as though instead of like
4. V   Eliminate and try
5. V   Eliminate and on time

6. G   I instead of me
7. D   Mundane means worldly; what is needed here is religious or ethereal
8. O
9. O
10. G   To achieve parallelism and balance, rewrite as follows: "...and, using a flashlight, turned down every seat."
11. G   Semicolon (;) after dreary instead of comma (,)
12. G   Takes, not take
13. D   Defects, not defections
14. O
15. D   Easy, not hard
16. O
17. D   Take, not bring
18. D   Affected, not infected
19. G   Replace before I by than
20. V   Eliminate together

TEST 3

DIRECTIONS: Among the sentences in this test are some which cannot be accepted in formal, written English for one or another of the following reasons:

POOR DICTION: The use of a word which is improper either because its meaning does not fit the sentence or because it is not acceptable in formal writing.
Example: The audience was strongly <u>effected</u> by the senator's speech.

VERBOSITY: Repetitious elements adding nothing to the meaning of the sentence and not justified by any need for special emphasis.
Example; At that time there was <u>then</u> no right of petition.

FAULTY GRAMMAR: Word forms and expressions which do not conform to the grammatical and structural usages required by formal written English (errors in case, number, parallelism, and the like).
Example; Everyone in the delegation had <u>their</u> reasons for opposing the measure.

No sentence has more than one kind of error. Some sentences have no errors. Read each sentence carefully; then, in the space at the right, print the letter:
    D if the sentence contains an error in <u>diction</u>
    V if the sentence is <u>verbose</u>
    G if the sentence contains <u>faulty grammar</u>
    O if the sentence contains <u>none</u> of these errors.

1. Choose an author as you choose a friend.   1._____

2. Home is home, be it ever so humble and so plain.   2._____

3. Invidious smokers usually find it difficult to break the habit.   3._____

4. You always look devastating in that sort of clothes.   4._____

5. We had no sooner entered the room when the bell rang.   5._____

6. A box of choice figs was sent him for Christmas.   6._____

7. Neither Charles or his brother finished his assignment.   7._____

8. There goes the last piece of cake and the last spoonful of ice cream.   8._____

9. Diamonds are more desired than any precious stones.   9._____

10. The administrator's unconscionable demands elated the workers.   10._____

11. Never before, to the best of my recollection, has there been such promising students.   11._____

12. It is only because your manners are so objectionable that you are not invited to the party.   12._____

13. An altruistic proverb is: "God helps those who help themselves."   13._____

14. I fully expected that the children would be at their desks and to find them ready to begin work. 14.____

15. A complete system of railroads covers and crisscrosses the entire country. 15.____

16. Our vacation being over, I am sorry to say. 16.____

17. It is so dark that I can't hardly see. 17.____

18. Either you or I am right; we cannot both be right. 18.____

19. After it had laid in the rain all night, it was not fit for use again. 19.____

20. Although the meaning was implicit, the statement required further explanation. 20.____

KEY (CORRECT ANSWERS)

1. O
2. V   Eliminate <u>and so plain</u>
3. D   *Inveterate*, not <u>invidious</u>
4. D   *Well*, not <u>devastating</u>
5. G   *Than*, for <u>well</u>
6. O
7. G   *Nor*, for <u>or</u>
8. G   *Go*, for <u>goes</u>
9. G   Insert *other* after <u>any</u>
10. D   *Embittered*, not <u>elated</u>
11. G   *Have*, not <u>has</u>
12. O
13. D   Not <u>altruistic</u>, *selfish*
14. G   To assure parallelism and balance, place comma (,) after desks, and eliminate <u>and to find them</u>
15. V   Eliminate <u>and crisscrosses</u>
16. G   Replace <u>being</u> by *is*
17. G   *Can hardly see*, not <u>can't hardly see</u>
18. O
19. D, G   *Lain*, not <u>laid</u>
20. O

TEST 4

DIRECTIONS: Among the sentences in this test are some which cannot be accepted in formal, written English for one or another of the following reasons:

POOR DICTION: The use of a word which is improper either because its meaning does not fit the sentence or because it is not acceptable in formal writing.
<u>Example:</u>   The audience was strongly <u>effected</u> by the senator's speech.

VERBOSITY: Repetitious elements adding nothing to the meaning of the sentence and not justified by any need for special emphasis.
<u>Example:</u>   At that time there was <u>then</u> no right of petition.

FAULTY GRAMMAR: Word forms and expressions which do not conform to the grammatical and structural usages required by formal written English (errors in case, number, parallelism, and the like).
<u>Example:</u>   Everyone in the delegation had <u>their</u> reasons for opposing the measure.

No sentence has more than one kind of error. Some sentences have no errors. Read each sentence carefully; then, in the space at the right, print the letter:
    D if the sentence contains an error in <u>diction</u>
    V if the sentence is <u>verbose</u>
    G if the sentence contains <u>faulty grammar</u>
    O if the sentence contains <u>none</u> of these errors

1.   Neither Tom nor John were present for the rehearsal.   1._____

2.   She admired the cavalier manner with which her husband treated her.   2._____

3.   The happiness or misery of men's lives depend on their early training.   3._____

4.   Honor as well as profit are to be gained by those studies.   4._____

5.   The egg business is only incidental to the regular business of the general store.   5._____

6.   It was superior in every way to the book previously read.   6._____

7.   We found his captious suggestions to be friendly and constructive.   7._____

8.   His testimony today is completely and radically different from that of yesterday.   8._____

9.   If you would have studied the problem carefully you would have found the solution more quickly.   9._____

10.   The large tips he received made the job a highly lucid one despite its long hours.   10._____

11.   The flowers smelled so sweet that the whole house was perfumed.   11._____

12.   When either or both habits becomes fixed, the student improves.   12._____

13.   Neither his words nor his action were justifiable.   13._____

14. A calm almost always comes before a storm.   14.____

15. The gallery with all its pictures were destroyed.   15.____

16. Those trees which are not deciduous remain green and attractive all winter.   16.____

17. Whom did they say won?   17.____

18. The man whom I thought was my friend deceived me.   18.____

19. Send whoever will do the work.   19.____

20. The question of who should be leader arose and the power he should have.   20.____

KEY (CORRECT ANSWERS)

  1. G   *Was*, not <u>were</u>
  2. D   *Resented* for <u>admired</u>
  3. G   *Depends* for <u>depend</u>
  4. G   *Is* for <u>are</u>
  5. O
  6. O
  7. D   *Careful*, not <u>captious</u>
  8. V   Eliminate <u>completely and radically</u>
  9. G   *Had you studied...* is to be substituted for <u>If you would have studied</u>
10. D   *Lucrative*, not <u>lucid</u>
11. O
12. G   *Become*, not <u>becomes</u>
13. G   Use *was* instead of <u>were</u>
14. O
15. G   *Was destroyed*, not <u>were destroyed</u>
16. O
17. G   *Who*, not <u>whom</u>
18. G   *Who*, not <u>whom</u>
19. O
20. G   Attain parallelism by placing <u>arose</u> at the end of this sentence

---

TEST 5

DIRECTIONS: Among the sentences in this test are some which cannot be accepted in formal, written English for one or another of the following reasons:

POOR DICTION: The use of a word which is improper either because its meaning does not fit the sentence or because it is not acceptable in formal writing.
Example; The audience was strongly effected by the senator's speech.

VERBOSITY: Repetitious elements adding nothing to the meaning of the sentence and not justified by any need for special emphasis.
Example: At that time there was then no right of petition.

FAULTY GRAMMAR: Word forms and expressions which do not conform to the grammatical and structural usages required by formal written English (errors in case, number, parallelism, and the like).
Example: Everyone in the delegation had their reasons for opposing the measure.

No sentence has more than one kind of error. Some sentences have no errors. Read each sentence carefully; then, in the space at the right, print the letter:
   D if the sentence contains an error in diction
   V if the sentence is verbose
   G if the sentence contains faulty grammar
   O if the sentence contains none of these errors

1.   The town consists of three distinct sections, of which the western one is by far the larger.   1._____

2.   Of London and Paris, the former is the wealthiest.   2._____

3.   The omniscient clap of thunder was not followed by a storm.   3._____

4.   Chicago is larger than any city in Illinois.   4._____

5.   America is the greatest nation, and of all other nations England is the greater.   5._____

6.   Amalgamating their forces helped the two generals to defeat the enemy.   6._____

7.   There are very good and sufficient grounds for such a decision.   7._____

8.   Due to bad weather, the game was postponed.   8._____

9.   The door opens, and in walks John and Mary.   9._____

10.   Where but America is there greater prosperity?   10._____

11.   The coffee grounds left a sedentary deposit in the cup.   11._____

12.   I can but do my best.   12._____

13.   I cannot help but comparing him with his predecessor.   13._____

14.   Many of Aesop's Fables are parodies from which we can profit.   14._____

15. I wish that I was in Florida now.   15._____

16. I like this kind of grapes better than any other.   16._____

17. The remainder of the time was spent in prayer.   17._____

18. Immigration is when people come into a foreign country to live.   18._____

19. He coughed continuously last winter.   19._____

20. The method is different than the one that was formerly used.   20._____

———————

KEY (CORRECT ANSWERS)

1. G   *Largest* for <u>larger</u>
2. G   Wealthier for <u>wealthiest</u>
3. D   *Ominous,* not <u>omniscient</u>
4. G   Insert *other* before <u>city</u>
5. G   *Greatest* should replace <u>greater</u> at the end of this sentence
6. O
7. V   Eliminate <u>and sufficient</u>
8. G   *Because of,* not <u>due to</u>
9. G   *Walk,* not <u>walks</u>
10. G   Insert *in* before <u>America</u>
11. D   *Sedimentary,* not <u>sedentary</u>
12. O
13. G   Eliminate <u>but</u>
14. D   *Parables,* not <u>parodies</u>
15. G   *Were,* not <u>was</u>
16. O
17. O
18. G   Rewrite: *Immigration denotes people coming into...*
19. D   *Continually,* not <u>continuously</u>
20. G   *From,* not <u>than</u>

———————

READING COMPREHENSION
UNDERSTANDING AND INTERPRETING WRITTEN MATERIAL
EXAMINATION SECTION
TEST 1

DIRECTIONS: Each question or incomplete statement is followed by several suggested answers or completions. Select the one that BEST answers the question or completes the statement. *PRINT THE LETTER OF THE CORRECT ANSWER IN THE SPACE AT THE RIGHT.*

Questions 1-2.

DIRECTIONS: Questions 1 and 2 are to be answered SOLELY on the basis of the following passage.

The employees in a unit or division of a government agency may be referred to as a work group. Within a government agency which has existed for some time, the work groups will have evolved traditions of their own. The persons in these work groups acquire these traditions as part of the process of work adjustment within their groups. Usually, a work group in a large organization will contain *oldtimers*, *newcomers*, and *in-betweeners*. Like the supervisor of a group, who is not necessarily an oldtimer or the oldest member, oldtimers usually have great influence. They can recall events unknown to others and are a storehouse of information and advice about current problems in the light of past experience. They pass along the traditions of the group to the others who, in turn, become oldtimers themselves. Thus, the traditions of the group which have been honored and revered by long acceptance are continued.

1. According to the above passage, the traditions of a work group within a government   1._____
    agency are developed

    A. at the time the group is established
    B. over a considerable period of time
    C. in order to give recognition to oldtimers
    D. for the group before it is established

2. According to the above passage, the oldtimers within a work group   2._____

    A. are the means by which long accepted practices and customs are perpetuated
    B. would best be able to settle current problems that arise
    C. are honored because of the changes they have made in the traditions
    D. have demonstrated that they have learned to do their work well

Questions 3-4.

DIRECTIONS: Questions 3 and 4 are to be answered SOLELY on the basis of the following passage.

In public agencies, the success of a person assigned to perform first-line supervisory duties depends in large part upon the personal relations between him and his subordinate employees. The goal of supervising effort is something more than to obtain compliance with procedures established by some central office. The major objective is work accomplishment. In order for this goal to be attained, employees must want to attain it and must exercise initiative in their work. Only if employees are generally satisfied with the type of supervision which exists in an organization will they put forth their best efforts.

3. According to the above passage, in order for employees to try to do their work as well as they can, it is essential that   3.___

    A.   they participate in determining their working conditions and rates of pay
    B.   their supervisors support the employees' viewpoints in meetings with higher management
    C.   they are content with the supervisory practices which are being used
    D.   their supervisors make the changes in working procedures that the employees request

4. It can be inferred from the above passage that the goals of a unit in a public agency will not be reached unless the employees in the unit   4.___

    A.   wish to reach them and are given the opportunity to make individual contributions to the work
    B.   understand the relationship between the goals of the unit and goals of the agency
    C.   have satisfactory personal relationships with employees of other units in the agency
    D.   carefully follow the directions issued by higher authorities

Questions 5-9.

DIRECTIONS: Questions 5 through 9 are to be answered SOLELY on the basis of the following passage.

If an employee thinks he can save money, time, or material for the city or has an idea about how to do something better than it is being done, he shouldn't keep it to himself. He should send his ideas to the Employees' Suggestion Program, using the special form which is kept on hand in all departments. An employee may send in as many ideas as he wishes. To make sure that each idea is judged fairly, the name of the suggester is not made known until an award is made. The awards are certificates of merit or cash prizes ranging from $10 to $500.

5. According to the above passage, an employee who knows how to do a job in a better way should   5.___

    A.   be sure it saves enough time to be worthwhile
    B.   get paid the money he saves for the city
    C.   keep it to himself to avoid being accused of causing a speed-up
    D.   send his idea to the Employees' Suggestion Program

6. In order to send his idea to the Employees' Suggestion Program, an employee should   6._____

    A. ask the Department of Personnel for a special form
    B. get the special form in his own department
    C. mail the idea using Special Delivery
    D. send it on plain, white letter-size paper

7. An employee may send to the Employees' Suggestion Program   7._____

    A. as many ideas as he can think of
    B. no more than one idea each week
    C. no more than ten ideas in a month
    D. only one idea on each part of the job

8. The reason the name of an employee who makes a suggestion is not made known at first is to   8._____

    A. give the employee a larger award
    B. help the judges give more awards
    C. insure fairness in judging
    D. only one idea on each part of the job

9. An employee whose suggestion receives an award may be given a   9._____

    A. bonus once a year   B. certificate for $10
    C. cash prize of up to $500   D. salary increase of $500

Questions 10-12.

DIRECTIONS: Questions 10 through 12 are to be answered SOLELY on the basis of the following passage.

According to the rules of the Department of Personnel, the work of every permanent city employee is reviewed and rated by his supervisor at least once a year. The civil service rating system gives the employee and his supervisor a chance to talk about the progress made during the past year as well as about those parts of the job in which the employee needs to do better. In order to receive a pay increase each year, the employee must have a satisfactory service rating. Service ratings also count toward an employee's final mark on a promotion examination.

10. According to the above passage, a permanent city employee is rated AT LEAST once   10._____

    A. before his work is reviewed
    B. every six months
    C. yearly by his supervisor
    D. yearly by the Department of Personnel

11. According to the above passage, under the rating system the supervisor and the employee can discuss how   11._____

    A. much more work needs to be done next year
    B. the employee did his work last year

C.   the work can be made easier next year
D.   the work of the Department can be increased

12.   According to the above passage, a permanent city employee will NOT receive a yearly   12.___
      pay increase

      A.   if he received a pay increase the year before
      B.   if he used his service rating for his mark on a promotion examination
      C.   if his service rating is unsatisfactory
      D.   unless he got some kind of a service rating

Questions 13-16.

DIRECTIONS: Questions 13 through 16 are to be answered SOLELY on the basis of the
            following passage.

It is an accepted fact that the rank and file employee can frequently advance worthwhile
suggestions toward increasing efficiency. For this reason, an Employees' Suggestion System
has been developed and put into operation. Suitable means have been provided at each
departmental location for the confidential submission of suggestions. Numerous suggestions
have been received thus far and, after study, about five percent of the ideas submitted are
being translated into action. It is planned to set up, eventually, monetary awards for all worthwhile suggestions.

13.   According to the above passage, a MAJOR reason why an Employees' Suggestion Sys-   13.___
      tem was established is that

      A.   an organized program of improvement is better than a haphazard one
      B.   employees can often give good suggestions to increase efficiency
      C.   once a fact is accepted, it is better to act on it than to do nothing
      D.   the suggestions of rank and file employees were being neglected

14.   According to the above passage, under the Employees' Suggestion System,   14.___

      A.   a file of worthwhile suggestions will eventually be set up at each departmental
           location
      B.   it is possible for employees to turn in suggestions without fellow employees know-
           ing of it
      C.   means have been provided for the regular and frequent collection of suggestions
           submitted
      D.   provision has been made for the judging of worthwhile suggestions by an Employ-
           ees' Suggestion Committee

15.   According to the above passage, it is reasonable to assume that   15.___

      A.   all suggestions must be turned in at a central office
      B.   employees who make worthwhile suggestions will be promoted
      C.   not all the prizes offered will be monetary ones
      D.   prizes of money will be given for the best suggestions

16. According to the above passage, of the many suggestions made,　　　　　16.____

    A. all are first tested
    B. a small part are put into use
    C. most are very worthwhile
    D. samples are studied

Questions 17-20.

DIRECTIONS: Questions 17 through 20 are to be answered SOLELY on the basis of the following passage.

Employees may be granted leaves of absence without pay at the discretion of the Personnel Officer. Such a leave without pay shall begin on the first working day on which the employee does not report for duty and shall continue to the first day on which the employee returns to duty. The Personnel Division may vary the dates of the leave for the record so as to conform with payroll periods, but in no case shall an employee be off the payroll for a different number of calendar days than would have been the case if the actual dates mentioned above had been used. An employee who has vacation or overtime to his credit, which is available for normal use, may take time off immediately prior to beginning a leave of absence without pay, chargeable against all or part of such vacation or overtime.

17. According to the above passage, the Personnel Officer must　　　　　17.____

    A. decide if a leave of absence without pay should be granted
    B. require that a leave end on the last working day of a payroll period
    C. see to it that a leave of absence begins on the first working day of a pay period
    D. vary the dates of a leave of absence to conform with a payroll period

18. According to the above passage, the exact dates of a leave of absence without pay may　　18.____
be varied provided that the

    A. calendar days an employee is off the payroll equal the actual leave granted
    B. leave conforms to an even number of payroll periods
    C. leave when granted made provision for variance to simplify payroll records
    D. Personnel Officer approves the variation

19. According to the above passage, a leave of absence without pay must extend from the　　19.____

    A. first day of a calendar period to the first day the employee resumes work
    B. first day of a payroll period to the last calendar day of the leave
    C. first working day missed to the first day on which the employee resumes work
    D. last day on which an employee works through the first day he returns to work

20. According to the above passage, an employee may take extra time off just before the　　20.____
start of a leave of absence without pay if

    A. he charges this extra time against his leave
    B. he has a favorable balance of vacation or overtime which has been frozen
    C. the vacation or overtime that he would normally use for a leave without pay has not been charged in this way before
    D. there is time to his credit which he may use

Question 21.

DIRECTIONS: Question 21 is to be answered SOLELY on the basis of the following passage.

In considering those things which are motivators and incentives to work, it might be just as erroneous not to give sufficient weight to money as an incentive as it is to give too much weight. It is not a problem of establishing a rank-order of importance, but one of knowing that motivation is a blend or mixture rather than a pure element. It is simple to say that cultural factors count more than financial considerations, but this leads only to the conclusion that our society is financial-oriented.

21.   Based on the above passage, in our society, cultural and social motivations to work are   21.____

    A.   things which cannot be avoided
    B.   melded to financial incentives
    C.   of less consideration than high pay
    D.   not balanced equally with economic or financial considerations

Question 22.

DIRECTIONS: Question 22 is to be answered SOLELY on the basis of the following passage.

A general principle of training and learning with respect to people is that they learn more readily if they receive *feedback*. Essential to maintaining proper motivational levels is knowledge of results which indicate level of progress. Feedback also assists the learning process by identifying mistakes. If this kind of information were not given to the learner, then improper or inappropriate job performance may be instilled.

22.   Based on the above passage, which of the following is MOST accurate?   22.____

    A.   Learning will not take place without feedback.
    B.   In the absence of feedback, improper or inappropriate job performance will be learned.
    C.   To properly motivate a learner, the learner must have his progress made known to him.
    D.   Trainees should be told exactly what to do if they are to learn properly.

Question 23.

DIRECTIONS: Question 23 is to be answered SOLELY on the basis of the following passage.

In a democracy, the obligation of public officials is twofold. They must not only do an efficient and satisfactory job of administration, but also they must persuade the public that it is an efficient and satisfactory job. It is a burden which, if properly assumed, will make democracy work and perpetuate reform government.

23.   The above passage means that   23.____

    A.   public officials should try to please everybody
    B.   public opinion is instrumental in determining the policy of public officials

C. satisfactory performance of the job of administration will eliminate opposition to its work
D. frank and open procedure in a public agency will aid in maintaining progressive government

Question 24.

DIRECTIONS: Question 24 is to be answered SOLELY on the basis of the following passage.

Upon retirement for service, a member shall receive a retirement allowance which shall consist of an annuity which shall be the actuarial equivalent of his accumulated deductions at the time of his retirement and a pension, in addition to his annuity, which shall be equal to one service-fraction of his final compensation, multiplied by the number of years of service since he last became a member credited to him, and a pension which is the actuarial equivalent of the reserve-for-increased-take-home-pay to which he may then be entitled, if any.

24. According to the above passage, a retirement allowance shall consist of a(n)   24._____

A. annuity, plus a pension, plus an actuarial equivalent
B. annuity, plus a pension, plus reserve-for-increased-take-home-pay, if any
C. annuity, plus reserve-for-increased-take-home-pay, if any, plus final compensation
D. pension, plus reserve-for-increased-take-home-pay, if any, plus accumulated deductions

Question 25.

DIRECTIONS: Question 25 is to be answered SOLELY on the basis of the following passage.

Membership in the retirement system shall cease upon the occurrence of any one of the following conditions: when the time out of service of any member who has total service of less than 25 years, shall aggregate more than 5 years; when the time out of service of any member who has total service of 25 years or more, shall aggregate more than 10 years; when any member shall have withdrawn more than 50% of his accumulated deductions; or when any member shall have withdrawn the cash benefit provided by Section B3-35.0 of the Administrative Code.

25. According to the information in the above passage, membership in the retirement system   25._____
shall cease when an employee

A. with 17 years of service has been on a leave of absence for 3 years
B. withdraws 50% of his accumulated deductions
C. with 28 years of service has been out of service for 10 years
D. withdraws his cash benefits

KEY (CORRECT ANSWERS)

1.	B		11.	B
2.	A		12.	C
3.	C		13.	B
4.	A		14.	B
5.	D		15.	D
6.	B		16.	B
7.	A		17.	A
8.	C		18.	A
9.	B		19.	C
10.	C		20.	D

21.	B
22.	C
23.	D
24.	B
25.	D

TEST 2

DIRECTIONS: Each question or incomplete statement is followed by several suggested answers or completions. Select the one that BEST answers the question or completes the statement. *PRINT THE LETTER OF THE CORRECT ANSWER IN THE SPACE AT THE RIGHT.*

Questions 1-6.

DIRECTIONS: Questions 1 through 6 are to be answered SOLELY on the basis of the following passage from an old office manual.

Since almost every office has some contact with data-processed records, a stenographer should have some understanding of the basic operations of data processing. Data processing systems now handle about one-third of all office paperwork. On punched cards, magnetic tape, or on other mediums, data are recorded before being fed into the computer for processing. A machine such as the keypunch is used to convert the data written on the source document into the coded symbols on punched cards or tapes. After data has been converted, it must be verified to guarantee absolute accuracy of conversion. In this manner, data becomes a permanent record which can be read by electronic computers that compare, store, compute, and otherwise process data at high speeds.

One key person in a computer installation is a programmer, the man or woman who puts business and scientific problems into special symbolic languages that can be read by the computer. Jobs done by the computer range all the way from payroll operations to chemical process control, but most computer applications are directed toward management data. About half of the programmers employed by business come to their positions with college degrees; the remaining half are promoted to their positions from within the organization on the basis of demonstrated ability without regard to education.

1. Of the following, the BEST title for the above passage is   1._____

    A. THE STENOGRAPHER AS DATA PROCESSOR
    B. THE RELATION OF KEYPUNCHING TO STENOGRAPHY
    C. UNDERSTANDING DATA PROCESSING
    D. PERMANENT OFFICE RECORDS

2. According to the above passage, a stenographer should understand the basic operations   2._____
of data processing because

    A. almost every office today has contact with data processed by computer
    B. any office worker may be asked to verify the accuracy of data
    C. most offices are involved in the production of permanent records
    D. data may be converted into computer language by typing on a keypunch

3. According to the above passage, the data which the computer understands is MOST   3._____
often expressed as

    A. a scientific programming language
    B. records or symbols punched on tape, cards, or other mediums
    C. records on cards
    D. records on tape

4. According to the above passage, computers are used MOST often to handle   4.____

    A. management data
    B. problems of higher education
    C. the control of chemical processes
    D. payroll operations

5. Computer programming is taught in many colleges and business schools.   5.____
The above passage implies that programmers in industry

    A. must have professional training
    B. need professional training to advance
    C. must have at least a college education to do adequate programming tasks
    D. do not need college education to do programming work

6. According to the above passage, data to be processed by computer should be   6.____

    A. recent   B. basic
    C. complete   D. verified

Questions 7-10.

DIRECTIONS: Questions 7 through 10 are to be answered SOLELY on the basis of the following passage.

There is nothing that will take the place of good sense on the part of the stenographer. You may be perfect in transcribing exactly what the dictator says and your speed may be adequate, but without an understanding of the dictator's intent as well as his words, you are likely to be a mediocre secretary.

A serious error that is made when taking dictation is putting down something that does not make sense. Most people who dictate material would rather be asked to repeat and explain than to receive transcribed material which has errors due to inattention or doubt. Many dictators request that their grammar be corrected by their secretaries, but unless specifically asked to do so, secretaries should not do it without first checking with the dictator. Secretaries should be aware that, in some cases, dictators may use incorrect grammar or slang expressions to create a particular effect.

Some people dictate commas, periods, and paragraphs, while others expect the stenographer to know when, where, and how to punctuate. A well-trained secretary should be able to indicate the proper punctuation by listening to the pauses and tones of the dictator's voice.

A stenographer who has taken dictation from the same person for a period of time should be able to understand him under most conditions, By increasing her tact, alertness, and efficiency, a secretary can become more competent.

7. According to the above passage, which of the following statements concerning the dicta-   7.____
tion of punctuation is CORRECT?

    A. Dictator may use incorrect punctuation to create a desired style
    B. Dictator should indicate all punctuation
    C. Stenographer should know how to punctuate based on the pauses and tones of the dictator
    D. Stenographer should not type any punctuation if it has not been dictated to her

8. According to the above passage, how should secretaries handle grammatical errors in a   8.____
dictation? Secretaries should

    A. *not correct* grammatical errors unless the dictator is aware that this is being done
    B. *correct* grammatical errors by having the dictator repeat the line with proper pauses
    C. *correct* grammatical errors if they have checked the correctness in a grammar book
    D. *correct* grammatical errors based on their own good sense

9. If a stenographer is confused about the method of spacing and indenting of a report   9.____
which has just been dictated to her, she GENERALLY should

    A. do the best she can
    B. ask the dictator to explain what she should do
    C. try to improve her ability to understand dictated material
    D. accept the fact that her stenographic ability is not adequate

10. In the last line of the first paragraph, the word *mediocre* means MOST NEARLY   10.____

    A. superior   B. respected
    C. disregarded   D. second-rate

Questions 11-12.

DIRECTIONS: Questions 11 and 12 are to be answered SOLELY on the basis of the following passage.

    The number of legible carbon copies required to be produced determines the weight of the carbon paper to be used. When only one copy is made, heavy carbon paper is satisfactory. Most typists, however, use medium-weight carbon paper and find it serviceable for up to three or four copies. If five or more copies are to be made, it is wise to use light carbon paper. On the other hand, the finish of carbon paper to be used depends largely on the stroke of the typist and, in lesser degree, on the number of copies to be made and on whether the typewriter has pica or elite type. A soft-finish carbon paper should be used if the typist's touch is light or if a noiseless machine is used. It is desirable for the average typist to use medium-finish carbon paper for ordinary work, when only a few carbon copies are required. Elite type requires a harder carbon finish than pica type for the same number of copies.

11. According to the above passage, the lighter the carbon paper used,   11.____

    A. the softer the finish of the carbon paper will be
    B. the greater the number of legible carbon copies that can be made
    C. the greater the number of times the carbon paper can be used
    D. the lighter the typist's touch should be

12. According to the above passage, the MOST important factor which determines whether   12.____
the finish of carbon paper to be used in typing should be hard, medium, or soft is

    A. the touch of the typist
    B. the number of carbon copies required
    C. whether the type in the typewriter is pica or elite
    D. whether a machine with pica type will produce the same number of carbon copies as a machine with elite type

Questions 13-16.

DIRECTIONS: Questions 13 through 16 are to be answered SOLELY on the basis of the fol-
              lowing passage.

Modern office methods, geared to ever higher speeds and aimed at ever greater efficiency, are largely the result of the typewriter. The typewriter is a substitute for handwriting
and, in the hands of a skilled typist, not only turns out letters and other documents at least
three times faster than a penman can do the work, but turns out the greater volume more uni-
formly and legibly. With the use of carbon paper and onionskin paper, identical copies can be
made at the same time.

The typewriter, besides its effect on the conduct of business and government, has had a
very important effect on the position of women. The typewriter has done much to bring
women into business and government, and today there are vastly more women than men typists. Many women have used the keys of the typewriter to climb the ladder to responsible
managerial positions.

The typewriter, as its name implies, employs type to make an ink impression on paper.
For many years, the manual typewriter was the standard machine used. Today, the electric
typewriter is dominant, and completely automatic electronic typewriters are coming into wider
use.

The mechanism of the office manual typewriter includes a set of keys arranged systematically in rows; a semicircular frame of type, connected to the keys by levers; the carriage, or
paper carrier; a rubber roller, called a platen, against which the type strikes; and an inked rib-
bon which make the impression of the type character when the key strikes it.

13. The above passage mentions a number of good features of the combination of a skilled   13.____
    typist and a typewriter. Of the following, the feature which is NOT mentioned in the pas-
    sage is

    A. speed   B. reliability
    C. uniformity   D. legibility

14. According to the above passage, a skilled typist can   14.____

    A. turn out at least five carbon copies of typed matter
    B. type at least three times faster than a penman can write
    C. type more than 80 words a minute
    D. readily move into a managerial position

15. According to the above passage, which of the following is NOT part of the mechanism of   15.____
    a manual typewriter?

    A. Carbon paper   B. Platen
    C. Paper carrier   D. Inked ribbon

16. According to the above passage, the typewriter has helped   16.____

    A. men more than women in business
    B. women in career advancement into management
    C. men and women equally, but women have taken better advantage of it
    D. more women than men, because men generally dislike routine typing work

Questions 17-21.

DIRECTIONS: Questions 17 through 21 are to be answered SOLELY on the basis of the following passage.

The recipient gains an impression of a typewritten letter before he begins to read the
message. Factors which provide for a good first impression include margins and spacing that
are visually pleasing, formal parts of the letter which are correctly placed according to the
style of the letter, copy which is free of obvious erasures and over-strikes, and transcript that
is even and clear. The problem for the typist is that of how to produce that first, positive
impression of her work.

There are several general rules which a typist can follow when she wishes to prepare a
properly spaced letter on a sheet of letterhead. Ordinarily, the width of a letter should not be
less than four inches nor more than six inches. The side margins should also have a desirable
relation to the bottom margin and the space between the letterhead and the body of the letter.
Usually the most appealing arrangement is when the side margins are even and the bottom
margin is slightly wider than the side margins. In some offices, however, standard line length
is used for all business letters, and the secretary then varies the spacing between the date
line and the inside address according to the length of the letter.

17.   The BEST title for the above passage would be   17._____

A.   WRITING OFFICE LETTERS
B.   MAKING GOOD FIRST IMPRESSIONS
C.   JUDGING WELL-TYPED LETTERS
D.   GOOD PLACING AND SPACING FOR OFFICE LETTERS

18.   According to the above passage, which of the following might be considered the way in   18._____
which people very quickly judge the quality of work which has been typed? By

A.   measuring the margins to see if they are correct
B.   looking at the spacing and cleanliness of the typescript
C.   scanning the body of the letter for meaning
D.   reading the date line and address for errors

19.   What, according to the above passage, would be definitely UNDESIRABLE as the aver-   19._____
age line length of a typed letter?

A.   4"   B.   6"
C.   5"   D.   7"

20.   According to the above passage, when the line length is kept standard, the secretary   20._____

A.   does not have to vary the spacing at all since this also is standard
B.   adjusts the spacing between the date line and inside address for different lengths
of letters
C.   uses the longest line as a guideline for spacing between the date line and inside
address
D.   varies-the number of spaces between the lines

21. According to the above passage, side margins are MOST pleasing when they   21.____

    A. are even and somewhat smaller than the bottom margin
    B. are slightly wider than the bottom margin
    C. vary with the length of the letter
    D. are figured independently from the letterhead and the body of the letter

Questions 22-25.

DIRECTIONS: Questions 22 through 25 are to be answered SOLELY on the basis of the following passage.

Typed pages can reflect the simplicity of modern art in a machine age. Lightness and evenness can be achieved by proper layout and balance of typed lines and white space. Instead of solid, cramped masses of uneven, crowded typing, there should be a pleasing balance up and down as well as horizontal.

To have real balance, your page must have a center. The eyes see the center of the sheet slightly above the real center. This is the way both you and the reader see it. Try imagining a line down the center of the page that divides the paper in equal halves. On either side of your paper, white space and blocks of typing need to be similar in size and shape. Although left and right margins should be equal, top and bottom margins need not be as exact. It looks better to hold a bottom border wider than a top margin, so that your typing rests upon a cushion of white space. To add interest to the appearance of the page, try making one paragraph between one-half and two-thirds the size of an adjacent paragraph.

Thus, by taking full advantage of your typewriter, the pages that you type will not only be accurate but will also be attractive.

22. It can be inferred from the above passage that the basic importance of proper balancing   22.____
on a typed page is that proper balancing

    A. makes a typed page a work of modern art
    B. provides exercise in proper positioning of a typewriter
    C. increases the amount of typed copy on the paper
    D. draws greater attention and interest to the page

23. A reader will tend to see the center of a typed page   23.____

    A. somewhat higher than the true center
    B. somewhat lower than the true center
    C. on either side of the true center
    D. about two-thirds of an inch above the true center

24. Which of the following suggestions is NOT given by the above passage?   24.____

    A. Bottom margins may be wider than top borders.
    B. Keep all paragraphs approximately the same size.
    C. Divide your page with an imaginary line down the middle.
    D. Side margins should be equalized.

25. Of the following, the BEST title for the above passage is

25.____

    A. INCREASING THE ACCURACY OF THE TYPED PAGE
    B. DETERMINATION OF MARGINS FOR TYPED COPY
    C. LAYOUT AND BALANCE OF THE TYPED PAGE
    D. HOW TO TAKE FULL ADVANTAGE OF THE TYPEWRITER

KEY (CORRECT ANSWERS)

1.	C		11.	B
2.	A		12.	A
3.	B		13.	C
4.	A		14.	B
5.	D		15.	A
6.	D		16.	B
7.	C		17.	D
8.	A		18.	B
9.	B		19.	D
10.	D		20.	B

21.	A
22.	D
23.	A
24.	B
25.	C

TEST 3

DIRECTIONS: Each question or incomplete statement is followed by several suggested answers or completions. Select the one that BEST answers the question or completes the statement. *PRINT THE LETTER OF THE CORRECT ANSWER IN THE SPACE AT THE RIGHT.*

Questions 1-5.

DIRECTIONS: Questions 1 through 5 are to be answered SOLELY on the basis of the following passage.

A written report is a communication of information from one person to another. It is an account of some matter especially investigated, however routine that matter may be. The ultimate basis of any good written report is facts, which become known through observation and verification. Good written reports may seem to be no more than general ideas and opinions. However, in such cases, the facts leading to these opinions were gathered, verified, and reported earlier, and the opinions are dependent upon these facts. Good style, proper form, and emphasis cannot make a good written report out of unreliable information and bad judgment; but on the other hand, solid investigation and brilliant thinking are not likely to become very useful until they are effectively communicated to others. If a person's work calls for written reports, then his work is often no better than his written reports.

1. Based on the information in the above passage, it can be concluded that opinions expressed in a report should be

   A. based on facts which are gathered and reported
   B. emphasized repeatedly when they result from a special investigation
   C. kept to a minimum
   D. separated from the body of the report

1.__

2. In the above passage, the one of the following which is mentioned as a way of establishing facts is

   A. authority   B. reporting
   C. communication   D. verification

2.__

3. According to the above passage, the characteristic shared by ALL written reports is that they are

   A. accounts of routine matters   B. transmissions of information
   C. reliable and logical   D. written in proper form

3.__

4. Which of the following conclusions can logically be drawn from the information given in the above passage?

   A. Brilliant thinking can make up for unreliable information in a report.
   B. One method of judging an individual's work is the quality of the written reports he is required to submit.
   C. Proper form and emphasis can make a good report out of unreliable information.
   D. Good written reports that seem to be no more than general ideas should be rewritten.

4.__

5. Which of the following suggested titles would be MOST appropriate for the above pas-   5.___
   sage?

    A. GATHERING AND ORGANIZING FACTS
    B. TECHNIQUES OF OBSERVATION
    C. NATURE AND PURPOSE OF REPORTS
    D. REPORTS AND OPINIONS: DIFFERENCES AND SIMILARITIES

Questions 6-8.

DIRECTIONS: Questions 6 through 8 are to be answered SOLELY on the basis of the follow-
               ing passage.

The most important unit of the mimeograph machine is a perforated metal drum over
which is stretched a cloth ink pad. A reservoir inside the drum contains the ink which flows
through the perforations and saturates the ink pad. To operate the machine, the operator first
removes from the machine the protective sheet, which keeps the ink from drying while the
machine is not in use. He then hooks the stencil face down on the drum, draws the stencil
smoothly over the drum, and fastens the stencil at the bottom. The speed with which the
drum turns determines the blackness of the copies printed. Slow turning gives heavy, black
copies; fast turning gives light, clear-cut reproductions. If reproductions are run on other than
porous paper, slip-sheeting is necessary to prevent smearing. Often, the printed copy fails to
drop readily as it comes from the machine. This may be due to static electricity. To remedy
this difficulty, the operator fastens a strip of tinsel from side to side near the impression roller
so that the printed copy just touches the soft stems of the tinsel as it is ejected from the
machine, thus grounding the static electricity to the frame of the machine.

6. According to the above passage,   6.___

    A. turning the drum fast produces light copies
    B. stencils should be placed face up on the drum
    C. ink pads should be changed daily
    D. slip-sheeting is necessary when porous paper is being used

7. According to the above passage, when a mimeograph machine is not in use,   7.___

    A. the ink should be drained from the drum
    B. the ink pad should be removed
    C. the machine should be covered with a protective sheet
    D. the counter should be set at zero

8. According to the above passage, static electricity is grounded to the frame of the mimeo-   8.___
   graph machine by means of

    A. a slip-sheeting device
    B. a strip of tinsel
    C. an impression roller
    D. hooks located at the top of the drum

Questions 9-10.

DIRECTIONS: Questions 9 and 10 are to be answered SOLELY on the basis of the following passage.

The proofreading of material typed from copy is performed more accurately and more speedily when two persons perform this work as a team. The person who did not do the typing should read aloud the original copy while the person who did the typing should check the reading against the typed copy. The reader should speak very slowly and repeat the figures, using a different grouping of numbers when repeating the figures. For example, in reading 1967, the reader may say *one-nine-six-seven* on first reading the figure and *nineteen-sixty-seven* on repeating the figure. The reader should read all punctuation marks, taking nothing for granted. Since mistakes can occur anywhere, everything typed should be proofread. To avoid confusion, the proofreading team should use the standard proofreading marks, which are given in most dictionaries.

9.   According to the above passage, the   9.____

   A.   person who holds the typed copy is called the reader
   B.   two members of a proofreading team should take turns in reading the typed copy aloud
   C.   typed copy should be checked by the person who did the typing
   D.   person who did not do the typing should read aloud from the typed copy

10.   According to the above passage,   10.____

   A.   it is unnecessary to read the period at the end of a sentence
   B.   typographical errors should be noted on the original copy
   C.   each person should develop his own set of proofreading marks
   D.   figures should be read twice

Questions 11-16.

DIRECTIONS: Questions 11 through 16 are to be answered SOLELY on the basis of the above passage.

Basic to every office is the need for proper lighting. Inadequate lighting is a familiar cause of fatigue and serves to create a somewhat dismal atmosphere in the office. One requirement of proper lighting is that it be of an appropriate intensity. Intensity is measured in foot candles. According to the Illuminating Engineering Society of New York, for casual seeing tasks such as in reception rooms, inactive file rooms, and other service areas, it is recommended that the amount of light be 30 foot-candles. For ordinary seeing tasks such as reading, work in active file rooms, and in mailrooms, the recommended lighting is 100 foot-candles. For very difficult seeing tasks such as accounting, transcribing, and business machine use, the recommended lighting is 150 foot-candles.

Lighting intensity is only one requirement. Shadows and glare are to be avoided. For example, the larger the proportion of a ceiling filled with lighting units, the more glare-free and comfortable the lighting will be. Natural lighting from windows is not too dependable because on dark wintry days, windows yield little usable light, and on sunny summer afternoons, the glare from windows may be very distracting. Desks should not face the windows. Finally, the main lighting source ought to be overhead and to the left of the user,

11. According to the above passage, insufficient light in the office may cause

    A. glare   B. tiredness
    C. shadows   D. distraction

11._____

12. Based on the above passage, which of the following must be considered when planning lighting arrangements? The

    A. amount of natural light present
    B. amount of work to be done
    C. level of difficulty of work to be done
    D. type of activity to be carried out

12._____

13. It can be inferred from the above passage that a well-coordinated lighting scheme is LIKELY to result in

    A. greater employee productivity
    B. elimination of light reflection
    C. lower lighting cost
    D. more use of natural light

13._____

14. Of the following, the BEST title for the above passage is

    A. CHARACTERISTICS OF LIGHT
    B. LIGHT MEASUREMENT DEVICES
    C. FACTORS TO CONSIDER WHEN PLANNING LIGHTING SYSTEMS
    D. COMFORT VS. COST WHEN DEVISING LIGHTING ARRANGEMENTS

14._____

15. According to the above passage, a foot-candle is a measurement of the

    A. number of bulbs used
    B. strength of the light
    C. contrast between glare and shadow
    D. proportion of the ceiling filled with lighting units

15._____

16. According to the above passage, the number of foot-candles of light that would be needed to copy figures onto a payroll is _____ foot-candles.

    A. less than 30   B. 100
    C. 30   D. 150

16._____

Questions 17-23.

DIRECTIONS: Questions 17 through 23 are to be answered SOLELY on the basis of the following passage, which is the Fee Schedule of a hypothetical college.

FEE SCHEDULE

A. A candidate for any baccalaureate degree is not required to pay tuition fees for undergraduate courses until he exceeds 128 credits, Candidates exceeding 128 credits in undergraduate courses are charged at the rate of $100 a credit for each credit of undergraduate course work in excess of 128. Candidates for a baccalaureate degree who are taking graduate courses must pay the same fee as any other student taking graduate courses

B. Non-degree students and college graduates are charged tuition fees for courses, whether undergraduate or graduate, at the rate of $180 a credit. For such students, there is an additional charge of $150 for each class hour per week in excess of the number of course credits. For example, if a three-credit course meets five hours a week, there is an additional charge for the extra two hours. Graduate courses are shown with a (G) before the course number.

C. All students are required to pay the laboratory fees indicated after the number of credits given for that course.

D. All students must pay a $250 general fee each semester.

E. Candidates for a baccalaureate degree are charged a $150 medical insurance fee for each semester. All other students are charged a $100 medical insurance fee each semester.

17. Miss Burton is not a candidate for a degree. She registers for the following courses in the spring semester: Economics 12, 4 hours a week, 3 credits; History (G) 23, 4 hours a week, 3 credits; English 1, 2 hours a week, 2 credits. The TOTAL amount in fees that Miss Burton must pay is   17.____

    A. less than $2000
    B. at least $2000 but less than $2100
    C. at least $2100 but less than $2200
    D. $2200 or over

18. Miss Gray is not a candidate for a degree. She registers for the following courses in the fall semester: History 3, 3 hours a week, 3 credits; English 5, 3 hours a week, 2 credits; Physics 5, 6 hours a week, 3 credits, laboratory fee $ 60; Mathematics 7, 4 hours a week, 3 credits. The TOTAL amount in fees that Miss Gray must pay is   18.____

    A. less than $3150
    B. at least $3150 but less than $3250
    C. at least $3250 but less than $3350
    D. $3350 or over

19. Mr. Wall is a candidate for the Bachelor of Arts degree and has completed 126 credits. He registers for the following courses in the spring semester, his final semester at college: French 4, 3 hours a week, 3 credits; Physics (G) 15, 6 hours a week, 3 credits, laboratory fee $80; History (G) 33, 4 hours a week, 3 credits. The TOTAL amount in fees that this candidate must pay is   19.____

    A. less than $2100
    B. at least $2100 but less than $2300
    C. at least $2300 but less than $2500
    D. $2500

20. Mr. Tindall, a candidate for the B.A. degree, has completed 122 credits of undergraduate courses. He registers for the following courses in his final semester: English 31, 3 hours a week, 3 credits; Philosophy 12, 4 hours a week, 4 credits; Anthropology 15, 3 hours a week, 3 credits; Economics (G) 68, 3 hours a week, 3 credits. The TOTAL amount in fees that Mr. Tindall must pay in his final semester is   20.____

    A. less than $1200
    B. at least $1200 but less than $1400
    C. at least $1400 but less than $1600
    D. $1600

21. Mr. Cantrell, who was graduated from the college a year ago, registers for graduate courses in the fall semester. Each course for which he registers carries the same number of credits as the number of hours a week it meets.
    If he pays a total of $1530; including a $100 laboratory fee, the number of credits for which he is registered is

    21.____

    A. 4   B. 5   C. 6   D. 7

22. Miss Jayson, who is not a candidate for a degree, has, registered for several courses including a lecture course in History. She withdraws from the course in History for which she had paid the required course fee of $690. The number of hours that this course is scheduled to meet is

    22.____

    A. 4   B. 5   C. 2   D. 3

23. Mr. Van Arsdale, a graduate of a college is Iowa, registers for the following courses in one semester: Chemistry 35, 5 hours a week, 3 credits; Biology 13, 4 hours a week, 3 credits, laboratory fee $150; Mathematics (G) 179, 3 hours a week, 3 credits.
    The TOTAL amount in fees that Mr. Van Arsdale must pay is

    23.____

    A. less than $2400
    B. at least $2400 but less than $2500
    C. at least $2500 but less than $2600
    D. at least $2600 or over

Questions 24-25.

DIRECTIONS: Questions 24 and 25 are to be answered SOLELY on the basis of the following passage.

A duplex envelope is an envelope composed of two sections securely fastened together so that they become one mailing piece. This type of envelope makes it possible for a first class letter to be delivered simultaneously with third or fourth class matter and yet not require payment of the much higher first class postage rate on the entire mailing. First class postage is paid only on the letter which goes in the small compartment, third or fourth class postage being paid on the contents of the larger compartment. The larger compartment generally has an ungummed flap or clasp for sealing. The first class or smaller compartment has a gummed flap for sealing. Postal regulations require that the exact amount of postage applicable to each compartment be separately attached to it.

24. On the basis of the above passage, it is MOST accurate to state that

    24.____

    A. the smaller compartment is placed inside the larger compartment before mailing
    B. the two compartments may be detached and mailed separately
    C. two classes of mailing matter may be mailed as a unit at two different postage rates
    D. the more expensive postage rate is paid on the matter in the larger compartment

25. When a duplex envelope is used, the   25._____

    A. first class compartment may be sealed with a clasp
    B. correct amount of postage must be placed on each compartment
    C. compartment containing third or fourth class mail requires a gummed flap for seal-ing
    D. full amount of postage for both compartments may be placed on the larger com-partment

———

KEY (CORRECT ANSWERS)

1.	A		11.	C
2.	D		12.	D
3.	B		13.	A
4.	B		14.	C
5.	C		15.	B
6.	A		16.	D
7.	C		17.	B
8.	B		18.	A
9.	C		19.	B
10.	D		20.	B

21.	C
22.	A
23.	C
24.	C
25.	B

———

CLERICAL ABILITIES TEST

EXAMINATION SECTION
TEST 1

DIRECTIONS: Each question or incomplete statement is followed by several suggested answers or completions. Select the one that *BEST* answers the question or completes the statement. *PRINT THE LETTER OF THE CORRECT ANSWER IN THE SPACE AT THE RIGHT.*

Questions 1-10.

DIRECTIONS: Questions 1 through 10 consist of lines of names, dates and numbers. For each question, you are to choose the option (A, B, C, or D) in Column II which *EXACTLY* matches the information in Column I. *PRINT THE LETTER OF THE CORRECT ANSWER IN THE SPACE AT THE RIGHT.*

SAMPLE QUESTION

Column I		Column II		
Schneider 11/16/75 581932	A.	Schneider	11/16/75	518932
	B.	Schneider	11/16/75	581932
	C.	Schnieder	11/16/75	581932
	D.	Shnieder	11/16/75	518932

The correct answer is B. Only option B shows the name, date and number exactly as they are in Column I. Option A has a mistake in the number. Option C has a mistake in the name. Option D has a mistake in the name and in the number. Now answer Questions 1 through 10 in the same manner.

Column I		Column II	
1. Johnston 12/26/74 659251	A.	Johnson 12/23/74 659251	1._____
	B.	Johston 12/26/74 659251	
	C.	Johnston 12/26/74 695251	
	D.	Johnston 12/26/74 659251	
2. Allison 1/26/75 9939256	A.	Allison 1/26/75 9939256	2._____
	B.	Alisson 1/26/75 9939256	
	C.	Allison 1/26/76 9399256	
	D.	Allison 1/26/75 9993256	
3. Farrell 2/12/75 361251	A.	Farell 2/21/75 361251	3._____
	B.	Farrell 2/12/75 361251	
	C.	Farrell 2/21/75 361251	
	D.	Farrell 2/12/75 361151	
4. Guerrero 4/28/72 105689	A.	Guerrero 4/28/72 105689	4._____
	B.	Guererro 4/28/72 105986	
	C.	Guerrero 4/28/72 105869	
	D.	Guerrero 4/28/72 105689	

5. McDonnell 6/05/73 478215

    A. McDonnell 6/15/73 478215
    B. McDonnell 6/05/73 478215
    C. McDonnell 6/05/73 472815
    D. MacDonell 6/05/73 478215

5._____

6. Shepard 3/31/71 075421

    A. Sheperd 3/31/71 075421
    B. Shepard 3/13/71 075421
    C. Shepard 3/31/71 075421
    D. Shepard 3/13/71 075241

6._____

7. Russell 4/01/69 031429

    A. Russell 4/01/69 031429
    B. Russell 4/10/69 034129
    C. Russell 4/10/69 031429
    D. Russell 4/01/69 034129

7._____

8. Phillips 10/16/68 961042

    A. Philipps 10/16/68 961042
    B. Phillips 10/16/68 960142
    C. Phillips 10/16/68 961042
    D. Philipps 10/16/68 916042

8._____

9. Campbell 11/21/72 624856

    A. Campbell 11/21/72 624856
    B. Campbell 11/21/72 624586
    C. Campbell 11/21/72 624686
    D. Campbel 11/21/72 624856

9._____

10. Patterson 9/18/71 76199176

    A. Patterson 9/18/72 76191976
    B. Patterson 9/18/71 76199176
    C. Patterson 9/18/72 76199176
    D. Patterson 9/18/71 76919176

10._____

Questions 11-15.

DIRECTIONS: Questions 11 through 15 consist of groups of numbers and letters which you are to compare. For each question, you are to choose the option (A, B, C, or D) in Column II which *EXACTLY* matches the group of numbers and letters given in Column I.

SAMPLE QUESTION

Column I	Column II
B92466	A. B92644
	B. B94266
	C. A92466
	D. B92466

The correct answer is D. Only option D in Column II shows the group of numbers and letters *EXACTLY* as it appears in Column I. Now answer Questions 11 through 15 in the same manner.

	Column I	Column II
11.	925AC5	A. 952CA5
		B. 925AC5
		C. 952AC5
		D. 925CA6

12.   Y006925

A. Y060925
B. Y006295
C. Y006529
D. Y006925

13.   J236956

A. J236956
B. J326965
C. J239656
D. J932656

14.   AB6952

A. AB6952
B. AB9625
C. AB9652
D. AB6925

15.   X259361

A. X529361
B. X259631
C. X523961
D. X259361

Questions 16-25.

DIRECTIONS: Each of Questions 16 through 25 consists of three lines of code letters and three lines of numbers. The numbers on each line should correspond with the code letters on the same line in accordance with the table below.

Code Letter	S	V	W	A	Q	M	X	E	G	K
Corresponding Number	0	1	2	3	4	5	6	7	8	9

On some of the lines, an error exists in the coding. Compare the letters and numbers in each question carefully. If you find an error or errors on:

only *one* of the lines in the question, mark your answer A;
any *two* lines in the question, mark your answer B;
all *three* lines in the question, mark your answer C;
none of the lines in the question, mark your answer D.

SAMPLE QUESTION

WQGKSXG   2489068
XEKVQMA   6591453
KMAESXV   9527061

In the above example, the first line is correct since each code letter listed has the correct corresponding number. On the second line, an error exists because code letter E should have the number 7 instead of the number 5. On the third line an error exists because the code letter A should have the number 3 instead of the number 2. Since there are errors in two of the three lines, the correct answer is B. Now answer Questions 16 through 25 in the same manner.

16.   SWQEKGA   0247983   16.____
       KEAVSXM   9731065
       SSAXGKQ   0036894

17.   QAMKMVS   4259510   17.____
       MGGEASX   5897306
       KSWMKWS   9125920

18.	WKXQWVE	2964217	18.____
	QKXXQVA	4966413	
	AWMXGVS	3253810	

19.	GMMKASE	8559307	19.____
	AWVSKSW	3210902	
	QAVSVGK	4310189	

20.	XGKQSMK	6894049	20.____
	QSVKEAS	4019730	
	GSMXKMV	8057951	

21.	AEKMWSG	3195208	21.____
	MKQSVQK	5940149	
	XGQAEVW	6843712	

22.	XGMKAVS	6858310	22.____
	SKMAWEQ	0953174	
	GVMEQSA	8167403	

23.	VQSKAVE	1489317	23.____
	WQGKAEM	2489375	
	MEGKAWQ	5689324	

24.	XMQVSKG	6541098	24.____
	QMEKEWS	4579720	
	KMEVKGA	9571983	

25.	GKVAMEW	8912572	25.____
	AXMVKAE	3651937	
	KWAGMAV	9238531	

Questions 26-35.

DIRECTIONS: Each of Questions 26 through 35 consists of a column of figures. For each question, add the column of figures and choose the correct answer from the four choices given.

26.   5,665.43   26.____
     2,356.69
     6,447.24
     <u>7,239.65</u>

    A. 20,698.01   B. 21,709.01
    C. 21,718.01   D. 22,609.01

27.   817,209.55   27.____
   264,354.29
    82,368.76
   <u>849,964.89</u>

    A. 1,893,997.49   B. 1,989,988.39
    C. 2,009,077.39   D. 2,013,897,49

28. 156,366.89
    249,973.23
    823,229.49
    <u>56,869.45</u>

    A. 1,286,439.06   B. 1,287,521.06
    C. 1,297,539.06   D. 1,296,421.06

28.____

29. 23,422.15
    149,696.24
    238,377.53
    86,289.79
    <u>505,544.63</u>

    A. 989,229.34   B. 999,879.34
    C. 1,003,330.34   D. 1,023,329.34

29.____

30. 2,468,926.70
    656,842.28
    49,723.15
    <u>832,369.59</u>

    A. 3,218,061.72   B. 3,808,092.72
    C. 4,007,861.72   D. 4,818,192.72

30.____

31. 524,201.52
    7,775,678.51
    8,345,299.63
    40,628,898.08
    <u>31,374,670.07</u>

    A. 88,646,647.81   B. 88,646,747.91
    C. 88,648,647.91   D. 88,648,747.81

31.____

32. 6,824,829.40
    682,482.94
    5,542,015.27
    775,678.51
    <u>7,732,507.25</u>

    A. 21,557,513.37   B. 21,567,513.37
    C. 22,567,503.37   D. 22,567,513.37

32.____

33. 22,109,405.58
    6,097,093.43
    5,050,073.99
    8,118,050.05
    <u>4,313,980.82</u>

    A. 45,688,593.87   B. 45,688,603.87
    C. 45,689,593.87   D. 45,689,603.87

33.____

34. 79,324,114.19
    99,848,129.74
    43,331,653.31
    <u>41,610,207.14</u>

34.____

A. 264,114,104.38   B. 264,114,114.38
C. 265,114,114.38   D. 265,214,104.38

35.   33,729,653.94   35.____
       5,959,342.58
    26,052,715.47
      4,452,669.52
      7,079,953.59

A. 76,374,334.10   B. 76,375,334.10
C. 77,274,335.10   D. 77,275,335.10

Questions 36-40.

DIRECTIONS: Each of Questions 36 through 40 consists of a single number in Column I and four options in Column II. For each question, you are to choose the option (A, B, C, or D) in Column II which *EXACTLY* matches the number in Column I.

SAMPLE QUESTION

Column I   Column II
5965121   A.   5956121
                         B.   5965121
                         C.   5966121
                         D.   5965211

The correct answer is B. Only option B shows the number *EXACTLY* as it appears in Column I. Now answer Questions 36 through 40 in the same manner.

	Column I	Column II
36.	9643242	A. 9643242
		B. 9462342
		C. 9642442
		D. 9463242
37.	3572477	A. 3752477
		B. 3725477
		C. 3572477
		D. 3574277
38.	5276101	A. 5267101
		B. 5726011
		C. 5271601
		D. 5276101
39.	4469329	A. 4496329
		B. 4469329
		C. 4496239
		D. 4469239
40.	2326308	A. 2236308
		B. 2233608
		C. 2326308
		D. 2323608

KEY (CORRECT ANSWERS)

1. D	11. B	21. A	31. D
2. A	12. D	22. C	32. A
3. B	13. A	23. B	33. B
4. D	14. A	24. D	34. A
5. B	15. D	25. A	35. C
6. C	16. D	26. B	36. A
7. A	17. C	27. D	37. C
8. C	18. A	28. A	38. D
9. A	19. D	29. C	39. B
10. B	20. B	30. C	40. C

———

TEST 2

Questions 1-5.

DIRECTIONS: Each of Questions 1 through 5 consists of a name and a dollar amount. In each question, the name and dollar amount in Column II should be an exact copy of the name and dollar amount in Column I. If there is:

a mistake only in the name, mark your answer A;

a mistake only in the dollar amount, mark your answer B;

a mistake in both the name and the dollar amount, mark your answer C;

no mistake in either the name or the dollar amount, mark your answer D.

SAMPLE QUESTION

Column I	Column II
George Peterson	George Petersson
$125.50	$125.50

Compare the name and dollar amount in Column II with the name and dollar amount in Column I. The name *Petersson* in Column II is spelled *Peterson* in Column I. The amount is the same in both columns. Since there is a mistake only in the name, the answer to the sample question is A.

Now answer Questions 1 through 5 in the same manner.

	Column I	Column II	
1.	Susanne Shultz $3440	Susanne Schultz $3440	1._____
2.	Anibal P. Contrucci $2121.61	Anibel P. Contrucci $2112.61	2._____
3.	Eugenio Mendoza $12.45	Eugenio Mendozza $12.45	3._____
4.	Maurice Gluckstadt $4297	Maurice Gluckstadt $4297	4._____
5.	John Pampellonne $4656.94	John Pammpellonne $4566.94	5._____

Questions 6-11.

DIRECTIONS: Each of Questions 6 through 11 consists of a set of names and addresses which you are to compare. In each question, the name and addresses in Column II should be an *EXACT* copy of the name and address in Column I. If there is:

a mistake only in the name, mark your answer A;

a mistake only in the address, mark your answer B;

a mistake in both the name and address, mark your answer C;

no mistake in either the name or address, mark your answer D.

SAMPLE QUESTION

Column I	Column II
Michael Filbert	Michael Filbert
456 Reade Street	645 Reade Street
New York, N.	New York, N . Y. 10013

Since there is a mistake only in the address (the street number should be 456 instead of 645), the answer to the sample question is B.

Now answer Questions 6 through 11 in the same manner.

	Column I	Column II	

6. Hilda Goettelmann
   55 Lenox Rd.
   Brooklyn, N. Y. 11226

   Hilda Goettelman
   55 Lenox Ave.
   Brooklyn, N. Y. 11226

   6.____

7. Arthur Sherman
   2522 Batchelder St.
   Brooklyn, N. Y. 11235

   Arthur Sharman
   2522 Batcheder St.
   Brooklyn, N. Y. 11253

   7.____

8. Ralph Barnett
   300 West 28 Street
   New York, New York 10001

   Ralph Barnett
   300 West 28 Street
   New York, New York 10001

   8.____

9. George Goodwin
   135 Palmer Avenue
   Staten Island, New York 10302

   George Godwin
   135 Palmer Avenue
   Staten Island, New York 10302

   9.____

10. Alonso Ramirez
    232 West 79 Street
    New York, N. Y. 10024

    Alonso Ramirez
    223 West 79 Street
    New York, N. Y. 10024

    10.____

11. Cynthia Graham
    149-35 83 Street
    Howard Beach, N. Y. 11414

    Cynthia Graham
    149-35 83 Street
    Howard Beach, N. Y. 11414

    11.____

Questions 12-20.

DIRECTIONS: Questions 12 through 20 are problems in subtraction. For each question do the subtraction and select your answer from the four choices given.

12. 232,921.85
    -179,587.68

    12.____

    A. 52,433.17   B. 52,434.17
    C. 53,334.17   D. 53,343.17

13. 5,531,876.29
    -3,897,158.36

    13.____

    A. 1,634,717.93   B. 1,644,718.93
    C. 1,734,717.93   D. 1,734,718.93

14. 1,482,658.22
    - 937,925.76

    14.____

    A. 544,633.46   B. 544,732.46
    C. 545,632.46   D. 545,732.46

15. 937,828.17
    -259,673.88

    15.____

    A. 678,154.29   B. 679,154.29
    C. 688,155.39   D. 699,155.39

16. 760,412.38
    -263,465.95

    A. 496,046.43   B. 496,946.43
    C. 496,956.43   D. 497,046.43

17. 3,203,902.26
    -2,933,087.96

    A. 260,814.30   B. 269,824.30
    C. 270,814.30   D. 270,824.30

18. 1,023,468.71
    - 934,678.88

    A. 88,780.83   B. 88,789.83
    C. 88,880.83   D. 88,889.83

19. 831,549.47
    -772,814.78

    A. 58,734.69   B. 58,834.69
    C. 59,735,69   D. 59,834.69

20. 6,306,281.74
    -3,617,376.75

    A. 2,687,904.99   B. 2,688,904.99
    C. 2,689,804.99   D. 2,799,905.99

Questions 21-30.

DIRECTIONS: Each of Questions 21 through 30 consists of three lines of code letters and three lines of numbers. The numbers on each line should correspond with the code letters on the same line in accordance with the table below.

Code Letter	J	U	B	T	Y	D	K	R	L	P
Corresponding Number	0	1	2	3	4	5	6	7	8	9

On some of the lines, an error exists in the coding. Compare the letters and numbers in each question carefully. If you find an error or errors on:

only *one* of the lines in the question, mark your answer A;
any *two* lines in the question, mark your answer B;
all *three* lines in the question, mark your answer C;
none of the lines in the question, mark your answer D.

SAMPLE QUESTION

BJRPYUR   2079417
DTBPYKJ   5328460
YKLDBLT   4685283

In the above sample the first line is correct since each code letter listed has the correct corresponding number. On the second line, an error exists because code letter P should have the number 9 instead of the number 8. The third line is correct since each code letter listed has the correct corresponding number. Since there is an error in *one* of the three lines, the correct answer is A.

Now answer Questions 21 through 30 in the same manner.

21. BYPDTJL   2495308   21._____
     PLRDTJU   9815301
     DTJRYLK   5207486

22. RPBYRJK   7934706   22._____
     PKTYLBU   9624821
     KDLPJYR   6489047

23. TPYBUJR   3942107   23._____
     BYRKPTU   2476931
     DUKPYDL   5169458

24. KBYDLPL   6345898   24._____
     BLRKBRU   2876261
     JTULDYB   0318542

25. LDPYDKR   8594567   25._____
     BDKDRJL   2565708
     BDRPLUJ   2679810

26. PLRLBPU   9858291   26._____
     LPYKRDJ   8936750
     TDKPDTR   3569527

27. RKURPBY   7617924   27._____
     RYUKPTJ   7426930
     RTKPTJD   7369305

28. DYKPBJT   5469203   28._____
     KLPJBTL   6890238
     TKPLBJP   3698209

29. BTPRJYL   2397148   29._____
     LDKUTYR   8561347
     YDBLRPJ   4528190

30. ULPBKYT   1892643   30._____
     KPDTRBJ   6953720
     YLKJPTB   4860932

KEY (CORRECT ANSWERS)

1.	A		16.	B
2.	C		17.	C
3.	A		18.	B
4.	D		19.	A
5.	C		20.	B
6.	C		21.	B
7.	C		22.	C
8.	D		23.	D
9.	A		24.	B
10.	B		25.	A
11.	D		26.	C
12.	C		27.	A
13.	A		28.	D
14.	B		29.	B
15.	A		30.	D

CLERICAL ABILITIES

EXAMINATION SECTION
TEST 1

DIRECTIONS: Each question or incomplete statement is followed by several suggested answers or completions. Select the one that BEST answers the question or completes the statement. *PRINT THE LETTER OF THE CORRECT ANSWER IN THE SPACE AT THE RIGHT.*

Questions 1-4.

DIRECTIONS: Questions 1 through 4 are to be answered on the basis of the information given below.

The most commonly used filing system and the one that is easiest to learn is alphabetical filing. This involves putting records in an A to Z order, according to the letters of the alphabet. The name of a person is filed by using the following order: first, the surname or last name; second, the first name; third, the middle name or middle initial. For example, *Henry C. Young* is filed under *Y* and thereafter under *Young, Henry C.* The name of a company is filed in the same way. For example, *Long Cabinet Co.* is filed under *L*, while *John T. Long Cabinet Co.* is filed under *L* and thereafter under *Long., John T. Cabinet Co.*

1. The one of the following which lists the names of persons in the CORRECT alphabetical order is: 1.____

   A. Mary Carrie, Helen Carrol, James Carson, John Carter
   B. James Carson, Mary Carrie, John Carter, Helen Carrol
   C. Helen Carrol, James Carson, John Carter, Mary Carrie
   D. John Carter, Helen Carrol, Mary Carrie, James Carson

2. The one of the following which lists the names of persons in the CORRECT alphabetical order is: 2.____

   A. Jones, John C.; Jones, John A.; Jones, John P.; Jones, John K.
   B. Jones, John P.; Jones, John K.; Jones, John C.; Jones, John A.
   C. Jones, John A.; Jones, John C.; Jones, John K.; Jones, John P.
   D. Jones, John K.; Jones, John C.; Jones, John A.; Jones, John P.

3. The one of the following which lists the names of the companies in the CORRECT alphabetical order is: 3.____

   A. Blane Co., Blake Co., Block Co., Blear Co.
   B. Blake Co., Blane Co., Blear Co., Block Co.
   C. Block Co., Blear Co., Blane Co., Blake Co.
   D. Blear Co., Blake Co., Blane Co., Block Co.

4. You are to return to the file an index card on *Barry C. Wayne Materials and Supplies Co.* 4.____
   Of the following, the CORRECT alphabetical group that you should return the index card to is

   A. A to G   B. H to M   C. N to S   D. T to Z

Questions 5-10.

DIRECTIONS: In each of Questions 5 through 10, the names of four people are given. For each question, choose as your answer the one of the four names given which should be filed FIRST according to the usual system of alphabetical filing of names, as described in the following paragraph.

In filing names, you must start with the last name. Names are filed in order of the first letter of the last name, then the second letter, etc. Therefore, BAILY would be filed before BROWN, which would be filed before COLT. A name with fewer letters of the same type comes first; i.e., Smith before Smithe. If the last names are the same, the names are filed alphabetically by the first name. If the first name is an initial, a name with an initial would come before a first name that starts with the same letter as the initial. Therefore, I. BROWN would come before IRA BROWN. Finally, if both last name and first name are the same, the name would be filed alphabetically by the middle name, once again an initial coming before a middle name which starts with the same letter as the initial. If there is no middle name at all, the name would come before those with middle initials or names.

Sample Question: A. Lester Daniels
                  B. William Dancer
                  C. Nathan Danzig
                  D. Dan Lester

The last names beginning with D are filed before the last name beginning with L. Since DANIELS, DANCER, and DANZIG all begin with the same three letters, you must look at the fourth letter of the last name to determine which name should be filed first. C comes before I or Z in the alphabet, so DANCER is filed before DANIELS or DANZIG. Therefore, the answer to the above sample question is B.

5.   A. Scott Biala   5.____
       B. Mary Byala
       C. Martin Baylor
       D. Francis Bauer

6.   A. Howard J. Black   6.____
       B. Howard Black
       C. J. Howard Black
       D. John H. Black

7.   A. Theodora Garth Kingston   7.____
       B. Theadore Barth Kingston
       C. Thomas Kingston
       D. Thomas T. Kingston

8.   A. Paulette Mary Huerta   8.____
       B. Paul M. Huerta
       C. Paulette L. Huerta
       D. Peter A. Huerta

9. A. Martha Hunt Morgan
    B. Martin Hunt Morgan
    C. Mary H. Morgan
    D. Martine H. Morgan

    9._____

10. A. James T. Meerschaum
    B. James M. Mershum
    C. James F. Mearshaum
    D. James N. Meshum

    10._____

Questions 11-14.

DIRECTIONS: Questions 11 through 14 are to be answered SOLELY on the basis of the following information.

You are required to file various documents in file drawers which are labeled according to the following pattern:

DOCUMENTS

MEMOS		LETTERS	
File	Subject	File	Subject
84PM1 - (A-L)		84PC1 - (A-L)	
84PM2 - (M-Z)		84PC2 - (M-Z)	

REPORTS		INQUIRIES	
File	Subject	File	Subject
84PR1 - (A-L)		84PQ1 - (A-L)	
84PR2 - (M-Z)		84PQ2 - (M-Z)	

11. A letter dealing with a burglary should be filed in the drawer labeled

    A. 84PM1   B. 84PC1   C. 84PR1   D. 84PQ2

    11._____

12. A report on Statistics should be found in the drawer labeled

    A. 84PM1   B. 84PC2   C. 84PR2   D. 84PQ2

    12._____

13. An inquiry is received about parade permit procedures. It should be filed in the drawer labeled

    A. 84PM2   B. 84PC1   C. 84PR1   D. 84PQ2

    13._____

14. A police officer has a question about a robbery report you filed.
    You should pull this file from the drawer labeled

    A. 84PM1   B. 84PM2   C. 84PR1   D. 84PR2

    14._____

Questions 15-22.

DIRECTIONS: Each of Questions 15 through 22 consists of four or six numbered names. For each question, choose the option (A, B, C, or D) which indicates the order in which the names should be filed in accordance with the following filing instructions:
- File alphabetically according to last name, then first name, then middle initial.
- File according to each successive letter within a name.

- When comparing two names in which, the letters in the longer name are identical to the corresponding letters in the shorter name, the shorter name is filed first.
- When the last names are the same, initials are always filed before names beginning with the same letter.

15.   I.   Ralph Robinson   15._____
           II. Alfred Ross
         III. Luis Robles
         IV. James Roberts

The CORRECT filing sequence for the above names should be

A. IV, II, I, III   B. I, IV, III, II
C. III, IV, I, II   D. IV, I, III, II

16.   I.   Irwin Goodwin   16._____
           II. Inez Gonzalez
         III. Irene Goodman
         IV. Ira S. Goodwin
          V. Ruth I. Goldstein
        VI. M.B. Goodman

The CORRECT filing sequence for the above names should be

A. V, II, I, IV, III, VI   B. V, II, VI, III, IV, I
C. V, II, III, VI, IV, I   D. V, II, III, VI, I, IV

17.   I.   George Allan   17._____
           II. Gregory Allen
         III. Gary Allen
         IV. George Allen

The CORRECT filing sequence for the above names should be

A. IV, III, I, II   B. I, IV, II, III
C. III, IV, I, II   D. I, III, IV, II

18.   I.   Simon Kauffman   18._____
           II. Leo Kaufman
         III. Robert Kaufmann
         IV. Paul Kauffmann

The CORRECT filing sequence for the above names should be

A. I, IV, II, III   B. II, IV, III, I
C. III, II, IV, I   D. I, II, III, IV

19.   I.   Roberta Williams   19._____
           II. Robin Wilson
         III. Roberta Wilson
         IV. Robin Williams

The CORRECT filing sequence for the above names should be

A. III, II, IV, I   B. I, IV, III, II
C. I, II, III, IV   D. III, I, II, IV

20.
    I. Lawrence Shultz
    II. Albert Schultz
    III. Theodore Schwartz
    IV. Thomas Schwarz
    V. Alvin Schultz
    VI. Leonard Shultz

20.____

The CORRECT filing sequence for the above names should be

  A. II, V, III, IV, I, VI
  C. II, V, I, VI, III, IV
  B. IV, III, V, I, II, VI
  D. I, VI, II, V, III, IV

21.
    I. McArdle
    II. Mayer
    III. Maletz
    IV. McNiff
    V. Meyer
    VI. MacMahon

21.____

The CORRECT filing sequence for the above names should be

  A. I, IV, VI, III, II, V
  C. VI, III, II, I, IV, V
  B. II, I, IV, VI, III, V
  D. VI, III, II, V, I, IV

22.
    I. Jack E. Johnson
    II. R.H. Jackson
    III. Bertha Jackson
    IV. J.T. Johnson
    V. Ann Johns
    VI. John Jacobs

22.____

The CORRECT filing sequence for the above names should be

  A. II, III, VI, V, IV, I
  C. VI, II, III, I, V, IV
  B. III, II, VI, V, IV, I
  D. III, II, VI, IV, V, I

Questions 23-30.

DIRECTIONS: The code table below shows 10 letters with matching numbers. For each question, there are three sets of letters. Each set of letters is followed by a set of numbers which may or may not match their correct letter according to the code table. For each question, check all three sets of letters and numbers and mark your answer:

    A. if no pairs are correctly matched
    B. if only one pair is correctly matched
    C. if only two pairs are correctly matched
    D. if all three pairs are correctly matched

CODE TABLE

T	M	V	D	S	P	R	G	B	H
1	2	3	4	5	6	7	8	9	0

Sample Question: TMVDSP - 123456
                       RGBHTM - 789011
                       DSPRGB - 256789

In the sample question above, the first set of numbers correctly matches its set of letters. But the second and third pairs contain mistakes. In the second pair, M is incorrectly matched with number 1. According to the code table, letter M should be correctly matched with number 2. In the third pair, the letter D is incorrectly matched with number 2. According to the code table, letter D should be correctly matched with number 4. Since only one of the pairs is correctly matched, the answer to this sample question is B.

23. RSBMRM 759262
    GDSRVH 845730
    VDBRTM 349713

23._____

24. TGVSDR 183247
    SMHRDP 520647
    TRMHSR 172057

24._____

25. DSPRGM 456782
    MVDBHT 234902
    HPMDBT 062491

25._____

26. BVPTRD 936184
    GDPHMB 807029
    GMRHMV 827032

26._____

27. MGVRSH 283750
    TRDMBS 174295
    SPRMGV 567283

27._____

28. SGBSDM 489542
    MGHPTM 290612
    MPBMHT 269301

28._____

29. TDPBHM 146902
    VPBMRS 369275
    GDMBHM 842902

29._____

30. MVPTBV 236194
    PDRTMB 647128
    BGTMSM 981232

30._____

KEY (CORRECT ANSWERS)

1.	A	11.	B	21.	C
2.	C	12.	C	22.	B
3.	B	13.	D	23.	B
4.	D	14.	D	24.	B
5.	D	15.	D	25.	C
6.	B	16.	C	26.	A
7.	B	17.	D	27.	D
8.	B	18.	A	28.	A
9.	A	19.	B	29.	D
10.	C	20.	A	30.	A

TEST 2

DIRECTIONS: Each question or incomplete statement is followed by several suggested answers or completions. Select the one that BEST answers the question or completes the statement. *PRINT THE LETTER OF THE CORRECT ANSWER IN THE SPACE AT THE RIGHT.*

Questions 1-10.

DIRECTIONS: Questions 1 through 10 each consists of two columns, each containing four lines of names, numbers and/or addresses. For each question, compare the lines in Column I with the lines in Column II to see if they match exactly, and mark your answer A, B, C, or D, according to the following instructions:
- A. all four lines match exactly
- B. only three lines match exactly
- C. only two lines match exactly
- D. only one line matches exactly

		COLUMN I	COLUMN II	
1.	I.	Earl Hodgson	Earl Hodgson	1.____
	II.	1409870	1408970	
	III.	Shore Ave.	Schore Ave.	
	IV.	Macon Rd.	Macon Rd.	
2.	I.	9671485	9671485	2.____
	II.	470 Astor Court	470 Astor Court	
	III.	Halprin, Phillip	Halperin, Phillip	
	IV.	Frank D. Poliseo	Frank D. Poliseo	
3.	I.	Tandem Associates	Tandom Associates	3.____
	II.	144-17 Northern Blvd.	144-17 Northern Blvd.	
	III.	Alberta Forchi	Albert Forchi	
	IV.	Kings Park, NY 10751	Kings Point, NY 10751	
4.	I.	Bertha C. McCormack	Bertha C. McCormack	4.____
	II.	Clayton, MO.	Clayton, MO.	
	III.	976-4242	976-4242	
	IV.	New City, NY 10951	New City, NY 10951	
5.	I.	George C. Morill	George C. Morrill	5.____
	II.	Columbia, SC 29201	Columbia, SD 29201	
	III.	Louis Ingham	Louis Ingham	
	IV.	3406 Forest Ave.	3406 Forest Ave.	
6.	I.	506 S. Elliott Pl.	506 S. Elliott Pl.	6.____
	II.	Herbert Hall	Hurbert Hall	
	III.	4712 Rockaway Pkway	4712 Rockaway Pkway	
	IV.	169 E. 7 St.	169 E. 7 St.	

	COLUMN I	COLUMN II	

7.
- I. 345 Park Ave.
- II. Colman Oven Corp.
- III. Robert Conte
- IV. 6179846

345 Park Pl.
Coleman Oven Corp.
Robert Conti
6179846

7._____

8.
- I. Grigori Schierber
- II. Des Moines, Iowa
- III. Gouverneur Hospital
- IV. 91-35 Cresskill Pl.

Grigori Schierber
Des Moines, Iowa
Gouverneur Hospital
91-35 Cresskill Pl.

8._____

9.
- I. Jeffery Janssen
- II. 8041071
- III. 40 Rockefeller Plaza
- IV. 407 6 St.

Jeffrey Janssen
8041071
40 Rockafeller Plaza
406 7 St.

9._____

10.
- I. 5971996
- II. 3113 Knickerbocker Ave.
- III. 8434 Boston Post Rd.
- IV. Penn Station

5871996
3113 Knickerbocker Ave.
8424 Boston Post Rd.
Penn Station

10._____

Questions 11-14.

DIRECTIONS: Questions 11 through 14 are to be answered by looking at the four groups of names and addresses listed below (I, II, III, and IV) and then finding out the number of groups that have their corresponding numbered lines exactly the same.

	GROUP I	GROUP II
Line 1.	Richmond General Hospital	Richman General Hospital
Line 2.	Geriatric Clinic	Geriatric Clinic
Line 3.	3975 Paerdegat St.	3975 Peardegat St.
Line 4	Loudonville, New York 11538	Londonville, New York 11538

	GROUP III	GROUP IV
Line 1.	Richmond General Hospital	Richmend General Hospital
Line 2.	Geriatric Clinic	Geriatric Clinic
Line 3.	3795 Paerdegat St.	3975 Paerdegat St.
Line 4.	Loudonville, New York 11358	Loudonville, New York 11538

11. In how many groups is line one exactly the same?   11._____

    A. Two   B. Three   C. Four   D. None

12. In how many groups is line two exactly the same?   12._____

    A. Two   B. Three   C. Four   D. None

13. In how many groups is line three exactly the same?   13._____

    A. Two   B. Three   C. Four   D. None

14. In how many groups is line four exactly the same? 14._____

 A. Two B. Three C. Four D. None

Questions 15-18.

DIRECTIONS: Each of Questions 15 through 18 has two lists of names and addresses. Each list contains three sets of names and addresses. Check each of the three sets in the list on the right to see if they are the same as the corresponding set in the list on the left. Mark your answers:
 A. if none of the sets in the right list are the same as those in the left list
 B. if only one of the sets in the right list is the same as those in the left list
 C. if only two of the sets in the right list are the same as those in the left list
 D. if all three sets in the right list are the same as those in the left list

15. Mary T. Berlinger   Mary T. Berlinger   15._____
     2351 Hampton St.   2351 Hampton St.
     Monsey, N.Y. 20117   Monsey, N.Y. 20117

     Eduardo Benes   Eduardo Benes
     473 Kingston Avenue   473 Kingston Avenue
     Central Islip, N.Y. 11734   Central Islip, N.Y. 11734

     Alan Carrington Fuchs   Alan Carrington Fuchs
     17 Gnarled Hollow Road 17 Gnarled Hollow Road
     Los Angeles, CA 91635   Los Angeles, CA 91685

16. David John Jacobson   David John Jacobson   16._____
     178 35 St. Apt. 4C   178 53 St. Apt. 4C
     New York, N.Y. 00927   New York, N.Y. 00927

     Ann-Marie Calonella   Ann-Marie Calonella
     7243 South Ridge Blvd. 7243 South Ridge Blvd.
     Bakersfield, CA 96714   Bakersfield, CA 96714

     Pauline M. Thompson   Pauline M. Thomson
     872 Linden Ave.   872 Linden Ave.
     Houston, Texas 70321   Houston, Texas 70321

17. Chester LeRoy Masterton Chester LeRoy Masterson   17._____
     152 Lacy Rd.   152 Lacy Rd.
     Kankakee, Ill. 54532   Kankakee, Ill. 54532

     William Maloney   William Maloney
     S. LaCrosse Pla.   S. LaCross Pla.
     Wausau, Wisconsin 52146 Wausau, Wisconsin 52146

     Cynthia V. Barnes   Cynthia V. Barnes
     16 Pines Rd.   16 Pines Rd.
     Greenpoint, Miss. 20376 Greenpoint, Miss. 20376

18.

Marcel Jean Frontenac	Marcel Jean Frontenac
8 Burton On The Water	6 Burton On The Water
Calender, Me. 01471	Calender, Me. 01471
J. Scott Marsden	J. Scott Marsden
174 S. Tipton St.	174 Tipton St.
Cleveland, Ohio	Cleveland, Ohio
Lawrence T. Haney	Lawrence T. Haney
171 McDonough St.	171 McDonough St.
Decatur, Ga. 31304	Decatur, Ga. 31304

18.____

Questions 19-26.

DIRECTIONS: Each of Questions 19 through 26 has two lists of numbers. Each list contains three sets of numbers. Check each of the three sets in the list on the right to see if they are the same as the corresponding set in the list on the left. Mark your answers:
- A. if none of the sets in the right list are the same as those in the left list
- B. if only one of the sets in the right list is the same as those in the left list
- C. if only two of the sets in the right list are the same as those in the left list
- D. if all three sets in the right list are the same as those in the left list

19. 7354183476   7354983476   19.____
     4474747744   4474747774
     57914302311   57914302311

20. 7143592185   7143892185   20.____
     8344517699   8344518699
     9178531263   9178531263

21. 2572114731   257214731   21.____
     8806835476   8806835476
     8255831246   8255831246

22. 331476853821   331476858621   22.____
     6976658532996   6976655832996
     3766042113715   3766042113745

23. 8806663315   8806663315   23.____
     74477138449   74477138449
     211756663666   211756663666

24. 990006966996   99000696996   24.____
     53022219743   53022219843
     4171171117717   4171171177717

25. 24400222433004   24400222433004   25.____
     5300030055000355   5300030055500355
     20000075532002022   20000075532002022

26. 611166640660001116   61116664066001116   26.____
     7111300117001100733   7111300117001100733
     26666446664476518   26666446664476518

Questions 27-30.

DIRECTIONS: Questions 27 through 30 are to be answered by picking the answer which is in the correct numerical order, from the lowest number to the highest number, in each question.

27. A. 44533, 44518, 44516, 44547   27.____
     B. 44516, 44518, 44533, 44547
     C. 44547, 44533, 44518, 44516
     D. 44518, 44516, 44547, 44533

28. A. 95587, 95593, 95601, 95620   28.____
     B. 95601, 95620, 95587, 95593
     C. 95593, 95587, 95601, 95620
     D. 95620, 95601, 95593, 95587

29. A. 232212, 232208, 232232, 232223   29.____
     B. 232208, 232223, 232212, 232232
     C. 232208, 232212, 232223, 232232
     D. 232223, 232232, 232208, 232212

30. A. 113419, 113521, 113462, 113588   30.____
     B. 113588, 113462, 113521, 113419
     C. 113521, 113588, 113419, 113462
     D. 113419, 113462, 113521, 113588

KEY (CORRECT ANSWERS)

1.	C	11.	A	21.	C
2.	B	12.	C	22.	A
3.	D	13.	A	23.	D
4.	A	14.	A	24.	A
5.	C	15.	C	25.	C
6.	B	16.	B	26.	C
7.	D	17.	B	27.	B
8.	A	18.	B	28.	A
9.	D	19.	B	29.	C
10.	C	20.	B	30.	D

EXAMINATION SECTION
TEST 1

DIRECTIONS: Each question or incomplete statement is followed by several suggested
answers or completions. Select the one that BEST answers the question or
completes the statement. *PRINT THE LETTER OF THE CORRECT ANSWER
IN THE SPACE AT THE RIGHT.*

Questions 1 -3
For questions 1 through 3, there is a name or code provided along with four other names or
codes listed in alphabetical/numerical order. Find the correct space for the given name or code
so that it will be in proper order with the rest of the list.

1. Roggen, Sam   1.____

    A. _
        Rogers, Arthur L
    B. _
        Roghani, Fada
    C. _
        Rogovin, H.T.
    D. _
        Rogowski, Marie R.
    E. _

2. 05076012   2.____

    A. _
        05076004
    B. _
        05076007
    C. _
        05076010
    D. _
        05076021
    E. _

3. CBA-1875   3.____

    A. _
        CAA-1720
    B. _
        CAB-1819
    C. _
        CAC-1804
    D. _
        CAD-1402
    E. _

Questions 4-8
Questions 4 through 8 require you to compare names, addresses or codes. In each line below
there are three items that are very much alike. Compare the three and answer as follows:

Answer "A" if all three are exactly alike;
Answer "B" if only the FIRST and SECOND items are exactly alike;
Answer "C" if only the FIRST and THIRD items are exactly alike;
Answer "D" if only the SECOND AND THIRD items are exactly alike;
Answer "E" if all three names are different.

4.	Helene Bedell	Helene Beddell	Helene Beddell	4._____
5.	FT. Wedemeyer	FT. Wedemeyer	FT. Wedmeyer	5._____
6.	3214 W. Beaumont St.	3214 W. Beaumount St.	3214 Beaumont St.	6._____
7.	BC3105T-5	BC3015T-5	BC3105T-5	7._____
8.	4460327	4460327	4460327	8._____

For questions 9 through 11, find the correct spelling of the word and write the correct letter in the space at the right.

9. A. accomodate B. acommodate 9._____
    C. accommadate D. none of the above

10. A. manageble B. manageable 10._____
    C. manegeable D. none of the above

11. A. reccommend B. recommend 11._____
    C. recammend D. none of the above

12. 32 + 26 = 12._____

    A. 69
    B. 59
    C. 58
    D. 54
    E. none of the above

13. 57-15 = 13._____

    A. 72
    B. 62
    C. 54
    D. 44
    E. none of the above

14. 23x7 = 14._____

    A. 164
    B. 161
    C. 154
    D. 141
    E. none of the above

15. 160/5 = 15._____

    A. 32

B. 30
C. 25
D. 21
E. none of the above

16. 17.8 + 13.3 =   16.____

    A. 30.1
    B. 31.0
    C. 31.1
    D. 33.3

Questions 17-19

Questions 17 through 19 test the ability to follow instructions. Following the directions in each item will lead you to identify or create a specific letter-number combination. Next, use the "Look-Up Table" to find the letter that corresponds with your letter-number combination. Mark this letter in the space at the right.

For example, if the combination is "P1," the answer would be "A" because this is the letter indicated in the box where "P" and "1" meet in the table.

LOOK-UP TABLE					
	P	Q	R	S	T
1	A	B	c ,	D	E
2	B	C	D	E	A
3	C	D	E	A	B
4	D	E	A	B	C
5	E	A	B	C	D
6-	A	B	C	D	E
7	B	C	D	E	A
8	C	D	E	A	B
9	D	E	A	B	C
10	E	A	B	C	D

17. Look at the letter-number combinations below. Draw a circle around the third combina-   17.____
    tion from the left. Write that letter-number combination in this space: _____
       T1   S5   P2   Q5   P5   R2

18. Draw a line under each letter that appears only once in the line. Write the letter "Q" and   18.____
    the number of lines you drew here: _____
       S T Q T Q P T Q

19. Look again at the line of letters in question 16. Draw a circle around each "Q." Write the   19.____
    letter that appears at the beginning of the line and the number of circles you drew here:

    _____

20. Select the sentence which is MOST APPROPRIATE with respect to grammar, usage and   20.____
    punctuation suitable for a formal letter or report:

    A. Major repairs has caused the cafeteria to be closed until late October.
    B. The cafeteria will be closed until late October on account of major repairs.

C. The cafeteria will be closed for major repairs until late October.
D. The closing of the cafeteria until late October due to the completion of major repairs.

In questions 21 through 23, identify the most similar meaning to the highlighted word:

21. The staff was **amazed** by the news.   21.____

A. pleased
B. surprised
C. saddened
D. relieved

22. Please **delete** the second paragraph.   22.____

A. retype
B. reread
C. revise
D. remove

23. Did you **duplicate** the information as written?   23.____

A. type
B. copy
C. remember
D. understand

24. "It is a simple matter to find and correct the errors made by a typist, but often a file clerk's   24.____
errors are not discovered until something which is needed cannot be found. For this reason, the work of every file clerk should be checked at regular intervals."
The paragraph BEST supports the statement that filing

A. may contain errors that are not immediately noticeable
B. should be organized by typists rather than file clerks
C. is a more difficult process than typing
D. should be checked for errors more frequently than typing

25. "The most efficient method for performing a task is not always easily determined. That   25.____
which is economical in terms of time must be carefully distinguished from that which is
economical in terms of expended energy. In short, the quickest method may require a
degree of physical effort that may be neither essential nor desirable." The paragraph
BEST supports the statement that

A. it is more efficient to perform a task slowly than rapidly
B. skill in performing a task should not be acquired at the expense of time
C. the most efficient execution of a task is not always the one done in the shortest time
D. energy and time cannot both be considered in the performance of a single task

KEY (CORRECT ANSWERS)

1.	B	11.	B
2.	D	12.	C
3.	E	13.	E
4.	D	14.	B
5.	B	15.	A
6.	E	16.	C
7.	C	17.	B
8.	A	18.	C
9.	D	19.	A
10.	B	20.	C

21.	B
22.	D
23.	B
24.	A
25.	C

NAME and NUMBER COMPARISONS

COMMENTARY

This test seeks to measure your ability and disposition to do a job carefully and accurately, your attention to exactness and preciseness of detail, your alertness and versatility in discerning similarities and differences between things, and your power in systematically handling written language symbols.

It is actually a test of your ability to do academic and/or clerical work, using the basic elements of verbal (qualitative) and mathematical (quantitative) learning – words and numbers.

EXAMINATION SECTION
TEST 1

Tests 1-2

DIRECTIONS: Questions 1 through 6 consist of sets of names and addresses. In each question, the name and address in Column II should be an exact copy of the name and address in Column I. *PRINT IN THE SPACE AT THE RIGHT THE LETTER:*
  A. if there is a mistake only in the name
  B. if there is a mistake only in the address
  C. if there is a mistake in both name and address
  D. if there is no mistake in either name or address

SAMPLE:

Michael Filbert	Michael Filbert
456 Reade Street	645 Reade Street
New York, N.Y. 10013	New York, N.Y. 10013

Since there is a mistake only in the address, the answer is B.

1. Esta Wong
   141 West 68 St.
   New York, N.Y. 10023

   Esta Wang
   141 West 68 St.
   New York, N.Y. 10023   1.____

2. Dr. Alberto Grosso
   3475 12th Avenue
   Brooklyn, N.Y. 11218

   Dr. Alberto Grosso
   3475 12th Avenue
   Brooklyn, N.Y. 11218   2.____

3. Mrs. Ruth Bortlas
   482 Theresa Ct.
   Far Rockaway, N.Y. 11691

   Ms. Ruth Bortlas
   482 Theresa Ct.
   Far Rockaway, N.Y. 11169   3.____

4. Mr. and Mrs. Howard Fox
   2301 Sedgwick Ave.
   Bronx, N.Y. 10468

   Mr. and Mrs. Howard Fox
   231 Sedgwick Ave.
   Bronx, N.Y. 10468   4.____

5. Miss Marjorie Black
   223 East 23 Street
   New York, N.Y. 10010

   Miss Margorie Black
   223 East 23 Street
   New York, N.Y. 10010   5.____

6. Michelle Herman
    806 Valley Rd.
    Old Tappan, N.J. 07675

Michelle Hermann
806 Valley Dr.
Old Tappan, N.J. 07675

6.____

KEY (CORRECT ANSWERS)

1. A
2. D
3. C
4. B
5. A
6. C

6.____

TEST 2

DIRECTIONS: Questions 1 through 6 consist of sets of names and addresses. In each question, the name and address in Column II should be an exact copy of the name and address in Column I. *PRINT IN THE SPACE AT THE RIGHT THE LETTER:*

    A. if there is a mistake only in the name
    B. if there is a mistake only in the address
    C. if there is a mistake in both name and address
    D. if there is no mistake in either name or address

1. Ms. Joan Kelly
   313 Franklin Ave.
   Brooklyn, N.Y. 11202

   Ms. Joan Kielly
   318 Franklin Ave.
   Brooklyn, N.Y. 11202

   1.____

2. Mrs. Eileen Engel
   47-24 86 Road
   Queens, N.Y. 11122

   Mrs. Ellen Engel
   47-24 86 Road
   Queens, N.Y. 11122

   2.____

3. Marcia Michaels
   213 E. 81 St.
   New York, N.Y. 10012

   Marcia Michaels
   213 E. 81 St.
   New York, N.Y. 10012

   3.____

4. Rev. Edward J. Smyth
   1401 Brandeis Street
   San Francisco, Calif. 96201

   Rev. Edward J. Smyth
   1401 Brandies Street
   San Francisco, Calif. 96201

   4.____

5. Alicia Rodriguez
   24-68 81 St.
   Elmhurst, N.Y. 11122

   Alicia Rodriquez
   2468 81 St.
   Elmhurst, N.Y. 11122

   5.____

6. Ernest Eisemann
   21 Columbia St.
   New York, N.Y. 10007

   Ernest Eisermann
   21 Columbia St.
   New York, N.Y. 10007

   6.____

KEY (CORRECT ANSWERS)

1. C
2. A
3. D
4. B
5. C
6. A

TEST 3

DIRECTIONS: Questions 1 through 8 consist of names, locations and telephone numbers. In each question, the name, location and number in Column II should be an exact copy of the name, location and number in Column I. *PRINT IN THE SPACE AT THE RIGHT THE LETTER:*
A. if there is a mistake in one line only
B. if there is a mistake in two lines only
C. if there is a mistake in three lines only
D. if there are no mistakes in any of the lines

1. Ruth Lang
EAM Bldg., Room C101
625-2000, ext. 765

Ruth Lang
EAM Bldg., Room C110
625-2000, ext. 765

1.____

2. Anne Marie Ionozzi
Investigations, Room 827
576-4000, ext. 832

Anna Marie Ionozzi
Investigation, Room 827
566-4000, ext. 832

2.____

3. Willard Jameson
Fm C Bldg. Room 687
454-3010

Willard Jamieson
Fm C Bldg. Room 687
454-3010

3.____

4. Joanne Zimmermann
Bldg. SW, Room 314
532-4601

Joanne Zimmermann
Bldg. SW, Room 314
532-4601

4.____

5. Carlyle Whetstone
Payroll Division-A, Room 212A
262-5000, ext. 471

Caryle Whetstone
Payroll Division-A, Room 212A
262-5000, ext. 417

5.____

6. Kenneth Chiang
Legal Council, Room 9745
(201) 416-9100, ext. 17

Kenneth Chiang
Legal Counsel, Room 9745
(201) 416-9100, ext. 17

6.____

7. Ethel Koenig
Personnel Services Div, Rm 433
635-7572

Ethel Hoenig
Personal Services Div, Rm 433
635-7527

7.____

8. Joyce Ehrhardt
Office of Administrator, Rm W56
387-8706

Joyce Ehrhart
Office of Administrator, Rm W56
387-7806

8.____

KEY (CORRECT ANSWERS)

1. A
2. C
3. A
4. D
5. B

6. A
7. C
8. B

———

TEST 4

DIRECTIONS: Each of questions 1 through 10 gives the identification number and name of a person who has received treatment at a certain hospital. You are to choose the option (A, B, C or D) which has EXACTLY the same number and name as those given in the question.

SAMPLE:

123765 Frank Y. Jones
- A.   123675 Frank Y. Jones
- B.   123765 Frank T. Jones
- C.   123765 Frank Y. Johns
- D.   123765 Frank Y. Jones

The correct answer is D, because it is the only option showing the identification number and name exactly as they are in the sample question.

1.   754898 Diane Malloy   1._____

- A.   745898 Diane Malloy
- B.   754898 Dion Malloy
- C.   754898 Diane Malloy
- D.   754898 Diane Maloy

2.   661818 Ferdinand Figueroa   2._____

- A.   661818 Ferdinand Figeuroa
- B.   661618 Ferdinand Figueroa
- C.   661818 Ferdnand Figueroa
- D.   661818 Ferdinand Figueroa

3.   100101 Norman D. Braustein   3._____

- A.   100101 Norman D. Braustein
- B.   101001 Norman D. Braustein
- C.   100101 Norman P. Braustien
- D.   100101 Norman D. Bruastein

4.   838696 Robert Kittredge   4._____

- A.   838969 Robert Kittredge
- B.   838696 Robert Kittredge
- C.   388696 Robert Kittredge
- D.   838696 Robert Kittridge

5.   243716 Abraham Soletsky   5._____

- A.   243716 Abrahm Soletsky
- B.   243716 Abraham Solestky
- C.   243176 Abraham Soletsky
- D.   243716 Abraham Soletsky

6. 981121 Phillip M. Maas   6.____

    A.   981121 Phillip M. Mass
    B.   981211 Phillip M. Maas
    C.   981121 Phillip M. Maas
    D.   981121 Phillip N. Maas

7. 786556 George Macalusso   7.____

    A.   785656 George Macalusso
    B.   786556 George Macalusso
    C.   786556 George Maculusso
    D.   786556 George Macluasso

8. 639472 Eugene Weber   8.____

    A.   639472 Eugene Weber
    B.   639472 Eugene Webre
    C.   693472 Eugene Weber
    D.   639742 Eugene Weber

9. 724936 John J. Lomonaco   9.____

    A.   724936 John J. Lomanoco
    B.   724396 John L. Lomonaco
    C.   724936 John J. Lomonaco
    D.   724936 John J. Lamonaco

10. 899868 Michael Schnitzer   10.____

    A.   899868 Micheal Schnitzer
    B.   898968 Michael Schnizter
    C.   899688 Michael Schnitzer
    D.   899868 Michael Schnitzer

KEY (CORRECT ANSWERS)

1.	C	6.	C
2.	D	7.	B
3.	A	8.	A
4.	B	9.	C
5.	D	10.	D

NAME AND NUMBER CHECKING
EXAMINATION SECTION
TEST 1

DIRECTIONS: Each question or incomplete statement is followed by several suggested answers or completions. Select the one that *BEST* answers the question or completes the statement. *PRINT THE LETTER OF THE CORRECT ANSWER IN THE SPACE AT THE RIGHT.*

Questions 1-10

DIRECTIONS: Questions 1 through 10 below present the identification numbers, initials, and last names of employees enrolled in a city retirement system. You are to choose the option (A, B, C, or D) that has the *identical* identification number, initials, and last name as those given in each question.

SAMPLE QUESTION
B145698 JL Jones
   A. B146798 JL Jones   B. B145698 JL Jonas
   C. P145698 JL Jones   D. B145698 JL Jones

The correct answer is D. Only option D shows the identification number, initials and last name exactly as they are in the sample question. Options A, B, and C have errors in the identification number or last name.

1.   J297483 PL Robinson   1._____

    A. J294783 PL Robinson   B. J297483 PL Robinson
    C. J297483 PI Robinson   D. J297843 PL Robinson

2.   S497662 JG Schwartz   2._____

    A. S497662 JG Schwarz   B. S497762 JG Schwartz
    C. S497662 JG Schwartz   D. S497663 JG Schwartz

3.   G696436 LN Alberton   3._____

    A. G696436 LM Alberton   B. G696436 LN Albertson
    C. G696346 LN Albertson   D. G696436 LN Alberton

4.   R774923 AD Aldrich   4._____

    A. R774923 AD Aldrich   B. R744923 AD Aldrich
    C. R774932 AP Aldrich   D. R774932 AD Allrich

5.   N239638 RP Hrynyk   5._____

    A. N236938 PR Hrynyk   B. N236938 RP Hrynyk
    C. N239638 PR Hrynyk   D. N239638 RP Hrynyk

6.   R156949 LT Carlson   6._____

    A. R156949 LT Carlton   B. R156494 LT Carlson
    C. R159649 LT Carlton   D. R156949 LT Carlson

7. T524697 MN Orenstein 7.____

    A. T524697 MN Orenstein   B. T524967 MN Orinstein
    C. T524697 NM Ornstein   D. T524967 NM Orenstein

8. L346239 JD Remsen 8.____

    A. L346239 JD Remson   B. L364239 JD Remsen
    C. L346329 JD Remsen   D. L346239 JD Remsen

9. P966438 SB Rieperson 9.____

    A. P996438 SB Reiperson   B. P966438 SB Reiperson
    C. R996438 SB Rieperson   D. P966438 SB Rieperson

10. D749382 CD Thompson 10.____

    A. P749382 CD Thompson   B. D749832 CD Thomsonn
    C. D749382 CD Thompson   D. D749823 CD Thomspon

Questions 11 - 20

DIRECTIONS: Each of Questions 11 through 20 gives the identification number and name of a person who has received treatment at a certain hospital. You are to choose the option (A, B, C, or D) which has *EXACTLY* the same identification number and name as those given in the question.

SAMPLE QUESTION

123765 Frank Y. Jones

    A.   123675 Frank Y. Jones
    B.   123765 Frank T. Jones
    C.   123765 Frank Y. Johns
    D.   123765 Frank Y. Jones

    The correct answer is D. Only option D shows the identification number and name exactly as they are in the sample question. Option A has a mistake in the identification number. Option B has a mistake in the middle initial of the name. Option C has a mistake in the last name.

    Now answer Questions 11 through 20 in the same manner.

11. 754898 Diane Malloy   A. 745898 Diane Malloy   11.____
                                      B. 754898 Dion Malloy
                                      C. 754898 Diane Malloy
                                      D. 754898 Diane Maloy

12. 661818 Ferdinand Figueroa   A. 661818 Ferdinand Figeuroa   12.____
                                      B. 661618 Ferdinand Figueroa
                                      C. 661818 Ferdnand Figueroa
                                      D. 661818 Ferdinand Figueroa

13. 100101 Norman D. Braustein   A. 100101 Norman D. Braustein   13.____
                                        B. 101001 Norman D. Braustein
                                        C. 100101 Norman P. Braustien
                                        D. 100101 Norman D. Bruastein

14. 838696 Robert Kittredge

    A. 838969 Robert Kittredge
    B. 838696 Robert Kittredge
    C. 388696 Robert Kittredge
    D. 838696 Robert Kittridge

14._____

15. 243716 Abraham Soletsky

    A. 243716 Abrahm Soletsky
    B. 243716 Abraham Solestky
    C. 243176 Abraham Soletsky
    D. 243716 Abraham Soletsky

15._____

16. 981121 Phillip M. Maas

    A. 981121 Phillip M. Mass
    B. 981211 Phillip M. Maas
    C. 981121 Phillip M. Maas
    D. 981121 Phillip N. Maas

16._____

17. 786556 George Macalusso

    A. 785656 George Macalusso
    B. 786556 George Macalusso
    C. 786556 George Maculasso
    D. 786556 George Macluasso

17._____

18. 639472 Eugene Weber

    A. 639472 Eugene Weber
    B. 639472 Eugene Webre
    C. 693472 Eugene Weber
    D. 639742 Eugene Weber

18._____

19. 724936 John J. Lomonaco

    A. 724936 John J. Lomanoco
    B. 724396 John J. Lomonaco
    C. 724936 John J. Lomonaco
    D. 724936 John J. Lamonaco

19._____

20. 899868 Michael Schnitzer

    A. 899868 Micheal Schnitzer
    B. 898968 Michael Schnizter
    C. 899688 Michael Schnitzer
    D. 899868 Michael Schnitzer

20._____

Questions: 21 - 28

DIRECTIONS: Questions 21 through 28 consist of lines of names, dates, and numbers which represent the names. membership dates, social security numbers, and members of the retirement system.For each question you are to choose the option (A, B, C, or D) in Column II which *EXACTLY* matches the information in Column I.

SAMPLE QUESTION

Column I	Column II
Crossen 12/23/56 173568929 253492	A. Crossen 2/23/56 173568929 253492
	B. Crossen 12/23/56 173568729 253492
	C. Crossen 12/23/56 173568929 253492
	D. Crossan 12/23/56 173568929 258492

The correct answer is C. Only option C shows the name, date, and numbers exactly as they are in Column I. Option A has a mistake in the date. Option B has a mistake in the social security number. Option D has a mistake in the name and in the membership number.

21. Figueroa 1/15/64 119295386 147563   21._____

A.	Figueroa	1/5/64	119295386	147563
B.	Figueroa	1/15/64	119295386	147563
C.	Figueroa	1/15/64	119295836	147563
D.	Figueroa	1/15/64	119295886	147563

22. Goodridge 6/19/59 106237869 128352   22._____

A.	Goodridge	6/19/59	106287869	128332
B.	Goodrigde	6/19/59	106237869	128352
C.	Goodridge	6/9/59	106237869	128352
D.	Goodridge	6/19/59	106237869	128352

23. Balsam 9/13/57 109652382 116938   23._____

A.	Balsan	9/13/57	109652382	116938
B.	Balsam	9/13/57	109652382	116938
C.	Balsom	9/13/57	109652382	116938
D.	Balsalm	9/13/57	109652382	116938

24. Mackenzie 2/16/49 127362513 101917   24._____

A.	Makenzie	2/16/49	127362513	101917
B.	Mackenzie	2/16/49	127362513	101917
C.	Mackenzie	2/16/49	127362513	101977
D.	Mackenzie	2/16/49	127862513	101917

25. Halpern 12/2/73 115206359 286070   25._____

A.	Halpern	12/2/73	115206359	286070
B.	Halpern	12/2/73	113206359	286070
C.	Halpern	12/2/73	115206359	206870
D.	Halpern	12/2/73	115206359	286870

26. Phillips 4/8/66 137125516 192612   26._____

A.	Phillips	4/8/66	137125516	196212
B.	Philipps	4/8/66	137125516	192612
C.	Phillips	4/8/66	137125516	192612
D.	Phillips	4/8/66	137122516	192612

27. Francisce 11/9/63 123926037 152210   27._____

A.	Francisce	11/9/63	123826837	152210
B.	Francisce	11/9/63	123926037	152210
C.	Francisce	11/9/63	123936037	152210
D.	Franscice	11/9/63	123926037	152210

28. Silbert 7/28/54 118421999 178514   28._____

	A.	Silbert	7/28/54	118421999	178544
	B.	Silbert	7/28/54	184421999	178514
	C.	Silbert	7/28/54	118421999	178514
	D.	Siblert	7/28/54	118421999	178514

_____

KEY (CORRECT ANSWERS)

1.	B	16.	C
2.	C	17.	B
3.	D	18.	A
4.	A	19.	C
5.	D	20.	D
6.	D	21.	B
7.	A	22.	D
8.	D	23.	B
9.	D	24.	B
10.	C	25.	A
11.	C	26.	C
12.	D	27.	B
13.	A	28.	C
14.	B		
15.	D		

_____

TEST 2

Questions 1-3

DIRECTIONS: Items 1 to 3 are a test of your proofreading ability. Each item consists of Copy I and Copy II. You are to assume that Copy I in each item is correct. Copy II, which is meant to be a duplicate of Copy I, may contain some typographical errors. In each item, compare Copy II with Copy I and determine the number of errors in Copy II. If there are:
> no errors, mark your answer A;
> 1 or 2 errors, mark your answer B;
> 3 or 4 errors, mark your answer C;
> 5 or 6 errors, mark your answer D;
> 7 errors or more, mark your answer E.

1.   1.____

COPY I

The Commissioner, before issuing any such license, shall cause an investigation to be made of the premises named and described in such application, to determine whether all the provisions of the sanitary code, building code, state industrial code, state minimum wage law, local laws, regulations of municipal agencies, and other requirements of this article are fully observed. (Section B32-169.0 of Article 23.)

COPY II

The Commissioner, before issuing any such license shall cause an investigation to be made of the premises named and described in such applecation, to determine whether all the provisions of the sanitary code, bilding code, state industrial code, state minimum wage laws, local laws, regulations of municipal agencies, and other requirements of this article are fully observed. (Section E32-169.0 of Article 23.)

2.   2.____

COPY I

Among the persons who have been appointed to various agencies are John Queen, 9 West 55th Street, Brooklyn; Joseph Blount, 2497 Durward Road, Bronx: Lawrence K. Eberhardt, 3194 Bedford Street, Manhattan; Reginald L. Darcy, 1476 Allerton Drive, Bronx; and Benjamin Ledwith, 177 Greene Street, Manhattan.

COPY II

Among the persons who have been appointed to various agencies are John Queen, 9 West 56th Street, Brooklyn, Joseph Blount, 2497 Dureward Road, Bronx: Lawrence K. Eberhart , 3194 Belford Street, Manhattan; Reginald L. Barcey, 1476 Allerton drive, Bronx; and Benjamin Ledwith, 177 Green Street, Manhattan.

3.   3.____

COPY I

Except as hereinafter provided, it shall be unlawful to use, store or have on hand any inflammable motion picture film in quantities greater than one standard or two sub-standard reels, or aggregating more than two thousand feet in length, or more than ten pounds in weight without the permit required by this section.

COPY II

Except as herinafter provided, it shall be unlawfull to use, store or have on hand any inflamable motion picture film, in quantities greater than one standard or two substandard reels or aggregating more than two thousand feet in length, or more then ten pounds in weight without the permit required by this section.

Questions 4-6

Questions 4 to 6 are a test of your proofreading ability. Each question consists of Copy I and Copy II. You are to assume that Copy I in each question is correct. Copy II, which is meant to be a duplicate of Copy I, may contain some typographical errors. In each question, compare Copy II with Copy I and determine the number of errors in Copy II. If there are

no errors, mark your answer A;
1 or 2 errors, mark your answer B;
3 or 4 errors, mark your answer C;
5 errors or more, mark your answer D.

4.   4.____

COPY I

It shall be unlawful to install wires or appliances for electric light, heat or power, operating at a potential in excess of seven hundred fifty volts, in or on any part of a building, with the exception of a central station, sub-station, transformer, or switching vault, or motor room; provided, however, that the Commissioner may authorize the use of radio transmitting apparatus under special conditions.

COPY II

It shall be unlawful to install wires or appliances for electric light, heat or power, operating at a potential in excess of seven hundred fifty volts, in or on any part of a building, with the exception of a central station, sub-station, transformer, or switching vault, or motor room, provided, however, that the Commissioner may authorize the use of radio transmitting apperatus under special conditions.

5.   5.____

COPY I

The grand total debt service for the fiscal year 2006-07 amounts to $350,563,718.63, as compared with $309,561,347.27 for the current fiscal year, or an increase of $41,002,371.36. The amount payable from other sources in 2006-07 shows an increase of $13,264,165.47, resulting in an increase of $27,733,205.89 payable from tax levy funds.

COPY II

The grand total debt service for the fiscal year 2006-07 amounts to $350,568,718.63, as compared with $309,561,347.27 for the current fiscel year, or an increase of $41,002,371.36. The amount payable from other sources in 2006-07 show an increase of $13,264,165.47 resulting in an increase of $27,733,295.89 payable from tax levy funds.

6.   6.____

<u>COPY I</u>

The following site proposed for the new building is approximately rectangular in shape
and comprises an entire block, having frontages of about 721 feet on 16th Road, 200 feet
on 157th Street, 721 feet on 17th Avenue and 200 feet on 154th Street, with a gross area
of about 144,350 square feet. The 2006-07 assessed valuation is $28,700,000 of which
$6,000,000 is for improvements.

<u>COPY II</u>

The following site proposed for the new building is approximately rectangular in shape
and comprises an entire block, having frontage of about 721 feet on 16th Road, 200 feet
on 157th Street, 721 feet on 17th Avenue, and 200 feet on 134th Street, with a gross
area of about 114,350 square feet. The 2006-07 assessed valuation is $28,700,000 of which
$6,000,000 is for improvements.

KEY (CORRECT ANSWERS)

1. D
2. E
3. E
4. B
5. D
6. C

TEST 3

DIRECTIONS: Each of the Questions numbered 1 through 8 consists of three sets of names and name codes. In each question, the two names and name codes on the same line are supposed to be exactly the same.

Look carefully at each set of names and codes and mark your answer

  A.   if there are mistakes in all three sets
  B.   if there are mistakes in two of the sets
  C.   if there is a mistake in only one set
  D.   if there are no mistakes in any of the sets

SAMPLE QUESTION

The following sample question is given to help you understand the procedure

Macabe, John N. - V 53162	Macade, John N. - V 53162
Howard, Joan S. - J 24791	Howard, Joan S. - J 24791
Ware, Susan B. - A 45068	Ware, Susan B. - A 45968

In the above sample question, the names and name codes of the first set are not exactly the same because of the spelling of the last name (Macabe - Macade). The names and name codes of the second set are exactly the same. The names and name codes of the third set are not exactly the same because the two name codes are different (A 45068 - A 45968). Since there are mistakes in only 2 of the sets, the answer to the sample question is B.

1.   Powell, Michael C. - 78537 F   Powell, Michael C. - 78537 F   1.____
     Martinez, Pablo J. - 24435 P   Martinez, Pablo J. - 24435 P
     MacBane, Eliot M. - 98674 E   MacBane, Eliot M. - 98674 E

2.   Fitz-Kramer Machines Inc.   Fitz-Kramer Machines Inc.   2.____
                  - 259090   - 259090
     Marvel Cleaning Service   Marvel Cleaning Service
                  - 482657   - 482657
     Donato, Carl G. - 637418   Danato, Carl G. - 687418

3.   Martin Davison Trading Corp.   Martin Davidson Trading Corp.   3.____
                  - 43108 T   - 43108 T
     Cotwald Lighting Fixtures   Cotwald Lighting Fixtures
                  - 76065 L   - 70056 L
     R. Crawford Plumbers   R. Crawford Plumbers
                  - 23157 C   - 23157 G

4.   Fraiman Engineering Corp.
              - M4773
    Neuman, Walter B. - N7745
    Pierce, Eric M.   - W6304

Friaman Engineering Corp.
              - M4773
Neumen, Walter B. - N7745
Pierce, Eric M.   - W6304

4.____

5.   Constable, Eugene - B 64837
    Derrick, Paul - H 27119
    Heller, Karen - S 49606

Comstable, Eugene - B 64837
Derrik, Paul - H 27119
Heller, Karen - S 46906

5.____

6.   Hernando Delivery Service Co.
              - D 7456
    Barettz Electrical Supplies
              - N 5392
    Tanner, Abraham - M 4798

Hernando Delivery Service Co.
              - D 7456
Barettz Electrical Supplies
              - N 5392
Tanner, Abraham - M 4798

6.____

7.   Kalin Associates - R 38641
    Sealey, Robert E. - P 63533
    Seals! Office Furniture
              - R36742

Kaline Associates - R 38641
Sealey, Robert E. - P 63553
Seals! Office Furniture
              - R36742

7.____

8.   Janowsky, Philip M.- 742213
    Hansen, Thomas H. - 934816
    L. Lester and Son Inc.
              – 294568

Janowsky, Philip M.- 742213
Hanson, Thomas H. - 934816
L. Lester and Son Inc.
              - 294568

8.____

Questions 9-13

DIRECTIONS: Each of the questions number 9 through 13 consists of three sets of names and building codes. In each question, the two names and building codes on the same line are supposed to be exactly the same.

If you find an error or errors on only *one* of the sets in the question, mark your answer A; any *two* of the sets in the question, mark your answer B; all *three* of the sets in the question, mark your answer C; *none* of the sets in the question, mark your answer D.

Column I
Duvivier, Anne P. - X52714
Dyrborg, Alfred - B4217
Dymnick, JoAnne - P482596

Column II
Duviver, Anne P. - X52714
Dyrborg, Alfred - B4267
Dymnick, JoAnne - P482596

In the above sample question, the first set of names and building codes is not exactly the same because the last names are spelled differently (Duvivier - Duviver). The second set of names and building codes is not exactly the same because the building codes are different (B4217 - B4267). The third set of names and building codes is exactly the same. Since there are mistakes in two of the sets of names and building codes, the answer to the sample question is B.

Now answer the questions on the following page using, the same procedure.

Column I	Column II	
9. Lautmann, Gerald G. - C2483 Lawlor, Michael - W44639 Lawrence, John J. - H1358	Lautmann, Gerald C. - C2483 Lawler, Michael - W44639 Lawrence, John J. - H1358	9.____
10. Mittmann, Howard - J4113 Mitchell, William T.- M75271 Milan, T. Thomas - Q67533	Mittmann, Howard - J4113 Mitchell, William T.- M75271 Milan, T. Thomas - Q67553	10.____
11. Quarles, Vincent - J34760 Quinn, Alan N. - S38813 Quinones, Peter W. - B87467	Quarles, Vincent - J34760 Quinn, Alan N. - S38813 Quinones, Peter W. - B87467	11.____
12. Daniels, Harold H. - A26554 Dantzler, Richard - C35780 Davidson, Martina - E62901	Daniels, Harold H - A26544 Dantzler, Richard - 035780 Davidson, Martin - E62901	12.____
13. Graham, Cecil J. - I20244 Granger, Deborah - T86211 Grant, Charles L. - G5788	Graham, Cecil J. - I20244 Granger, Deborah - T86211 Grant, Charles L. - G5788	13.____

KEY (CORRECT ANSWERS)

1.	D	8.	C
2.	C	9.	B
3.	A	10.	A
4.	B	11.	D
5.	A	12.	C
6.	D	13.	D
7.	B		

TEST 4

DIRECTIONS: In questions 1 to 10 there are five pairs of numbers or letters and numbers. Compare each pair and decide how many pairs are *EXACTLY ALIKE*. PRINT *THE LETTER OF THE CORRECT ANSWER IN THE SPACE AT THE RIGHT.*

     A. if only one pair is exactly alike
     B. if only two pairs are exactly alike
     C. if only three pairs are exactly alike
     D. if only four pairs are exactly alike
     E. if all five pairs are exactly alike

1.   73-F......F-73   FF-73. . . .FF-73   1.____
       F-7373....F-7373   373-FF...337-FF
       F-733.....337-F

2.   0-17158. . ..0-17158   0-71518 ... 0-71518   2.____
       0-11758....0-11758   0-15817... 0-15817
       0-51178....0-51178

3.   1A-7908....1A-7908   7A-8901....7A-8091   3.____
       7A-891.....7A-891   1A-9078....1A-9708.
       9A-7018....9A-7081

4.   2V-6426....2V-6246   2N-6246....2N-6246   4.____
       2V-6426....2N-6426   2N-6624....2N-6624
       2V-6462....2V-6462

5.   3NY-56......3ny-65   5NY-356.....3NY-356   5.____
       6NY-3566....3ny-3566   5NY-6536....5NY-6536
       3NY-5663....5ny-3663

6.   COB-065....COB-065   BCL-506....BCL-506   6.____
       LBC-650....LBC-650   DLB-560....DLB-560
       CDB-056....COB-065

7.   4KQ-9130....4KQ-9130   4KQ-9310....4KQ-9130   7.____
       4KQ-9031....4KQ-9031   4KQ-9301....4KQ-9301
       4KQ-9013....4KQ-9013

8.   MK-89......MK-98   98-MK......89-MK   8.____
       MSK-998........MSK-998 MOSK.......MOKS
       SMK-899....SMK-899

9.   8MD-2104....SMD-2014 2MD-8140....2MD-8140   9.____
       814-MD......814-MD   4MD-8201. . . .4MD-8201
       MD-281......MD-481

10.   161-035. .. .161-035   150-316.... 150-316   10.____
       315-160....315-160   131-650....131-650
       165-301....165-301

KEY (CORRECT ANSWERS)

1.	B		6.	D
2.	E		7.	D
3.	B		8.	B
4.	C		9.	C
5.	A		10.	E

———

TEST 5

DIRECTIONS: Each question or incomplete statement is followed by several suggested answers or completions. Select the one that *BEST* answers the question or completes the statement. *PRINT THE LETTER OF THE CORRECT ANSWER IN THE SPACE AT THE RIGHT.*

Questions 1-5

DIRECTIONS: Questions 1 through 5, inclusive, consist of groups of four displays representing license identification plates. Examine each group of plates and determine the number of plates in each group which are identical. Mark your answer sheets as follows:

If only two plates are identical, mark answer A.
If only three plates are identical, mark answer B.
If all four plates are identical, mark answer C.
If the plates are all different, mark answer D

EXAMPLE

ABC123   BCD123   ABC123   BCD235

Since only two plates are identical, the first and the third, the correct answer is A.

1. PBV839	PVB839	PVB839	PVB839	1.____
2. WTX083	WTX083	WTX083	WTX083	2.____
3. B73609	D73906	BD7396	BD7906	3.____
4. AK7423	AK7423	AK1423	A81324	4.____
5. 583Y10	683Y10	583Y01	583Y10	5.____

Questions 6-10

DIRECTIONS: Questions 6 through 10 consist of groups of numbers and letters similar to those which might appear on license plates. Each group of numbers and letters will be called a license identification. Choose the license identification lettered A, B, C, or D that *EXACTLY* matches the license identification shown next to the question number.

SAMPLE
NY 1977
ABC-123

A. NY 1976   B. NY 1977   C. NY 1977   D. NY 1977
    ABC-123   ABC-132   CBA-123   ABC-123

The license identification given is NY 1977. The only choice
                    ABC-123.
that exactly matches it is the license identification next to the letter D. The correct answer is therefore D.

6.   NY 1976   6._____
                                  QLT-781

    A. NJ 1976   B. NY 1975   C. NY 1976   D. NY 1977
        QLT-781   QLT-781   QLT-781   QLT-781

7.   FLA 1977   7._____
                                  2-7LT58J

    A. FLA 1977   B. FLA 1977   C. FLA 1977   D. LA 1977
        2-7TL58J   2-7LTJ58   2-7LT58J   2-7LT58J

8.   NY 1975   8._____
                                  OQC383

    A. NY 1975   B. NY 1975   C. NY 1975   D. NY 1977
        OQC383   OQC833   QCQ383   OCQ383

9.   MASS 1977   9._____
                                  B-8DK02

    A. MISS 1977   B. MASS 1977   C. MASS 1976   D. MASS 1977
        B-8DK02   B-8DK02   B-8DK02   B-80KD2

10.   NY 1976   10._____
                                  ZV0586

    A. NY 1976   B. NY 1977   C. NY 1976   D. NY 1976
        2V0586   ZV0586   ZV0586   ZU0586

KEY (CORRECT ANSWERS)

1.	B	6.	C
2.	C	7.	C
3.	D	8.	A
4.	A	9.	B
5.	A	10.	C

TEST 6

DIRECTIONS: Assume that each of the capital letters in the table below represents the name of an employee enrolled in the city employees' retirement system. The number directly beneath the letter represents the agency for which the employee works, and the small letter directly beneath represents the code for the employee's account.

Name of Employee	L	O	T	Q	A	M	R	N	C
Agency	3	4	5	9	8	7	2	1	6
Account Code	r	f	b	i	d	t	g	e	n

In each of the following questions 1 through 3, the agency code numbers and the account code letters in Columns 2 and 3 should correspond to the capital letters in Column 1 and should be in the same consecutive order. For each question, look at each column carefully and mark your answer as follows:

If there are one or more errors *in Column 2 only*, mark your answer A.
If there are one or more errors *in Column 3 only*, mark your answer B.
If there are one or more errors in Column 2 and one or more errors in Column 3, mark your answer C.
If there are *NO* errors in either column, mark your answer D.
The following sample question is given to help you understand the procedure.

Column I	Column 2	Column 3
TQLMOC	583746	birtfn

In Column 2, the second agency code number (corresponding to letter Q) should be "9", not "8". Column 3 is coded correctly to Column 1. Since there is an error only in Column 2, the correct answer is A.

	Column 1	Column 2	Column 3	
1.	QLNRCA	931268	iregnd	1._____
2.	NRMOTC	127546	egftbn	2._____
3.	RCTALM	265837	gndbrt	3._____

KEY (CORRECT ANSWERS)

1. D
2. C
3. B

CODING

COMMENTARY

An ingenious question-type called coding, involving elements of alphabetizing, filing, name and number comparison, and evaluative judgment and application, has currently won wide acceptance in testing circles for measuring clerical aptitude and general ability, particularly on the senior (middle) grades (levels).

While the directions for this question-type usually vary in detail, the candidate is generally asked to consider groups of names, codes, and numbers, and, then, according to a given plan, to arrange codes in alphabetic order; to arrange these in numerical sequence; to re-arrange columns of names and numbers in correct order; to espy errors in coding; to choose the correct coding arrangement in consonance with the given directions and examples, etc.

This question-type appears to have few parameters in respect to form, substance, or degree of difficulty.

Accordingly, acquaintance with, and practice in the coding question is recommended for the serious candidate.

EXAMINATION SECTION
TEST 1

DIRECTIONS: Questions 1 through 10 are to be answered on the basis of the following Code Table. In this table every letter has a corresponding code number to be punched. Each question contains three lines of letters and code numbers. In each line, the code numbers should correspond with the letters in accordance with the table.

Letter	M	X	R	T	W	A	E	Q	Z	C
Code	1	2	3	4	5	6	7	8	9	0

On some of the lines, an error exists in the coding. Compare the letters and numbers in each question carefully. If you find an error or errors on
  only *one* of the lines in the question, mark your answer A;
  any *two* lines in the question, mark your answer B;
  all *three* lines in the question, mark your answer C;
  none of the lines in the question, mark your answer D.

SAMPLE QUESTION

XAQMZMRQ   -   26819138
RAERQEX   -   3573872
TMZCMTZA   -   46901496

In the above sample, the first line is correct since each letter, as listed, has the correct corresponding code number.
In the second line, an error exists because the letter A should have the code number 6 instead of 5.
In the third line, an error exists because the letter W should have the code number 5 instead of 6.
Since there are errors in two of the three lines, your answer should be B.

1. EQRMATTR   -   78316443   1.____
   MACWXRQW   -   16052385
   XZEMCAR   -   2971063

2. CZEMRXQ   -   0971238   2.____
   XMTARET   -   2146374
   WCEARWEC   -   50863570

3. CEXAWRQZ   -   07265389   3.____
   RCRMMZQT   -   33011984
   ACMZWTEX   -   60195472

4. XRCZQZWR   -   23089953   4.____
   CMRQCAET   -   01389574
   ZXRWTECM   -   92345701

5.	AXMTRAWR	-	62134653		5.____
	EQQCZCEW	-	77809075		
	MAZQARTM	-	16086341		
6.	WRWQCTRM	-	53580431		6.____
	CXMWAERZ	-	02156739		
	RCQEWWME	-	30865517		
7.	CRMECEAX	-	03170762		7.____
	MZCTRXRQ	-	19043238		
	XXZREMEW	-	22937175		
8.	MRCXQEAX	-	13928762		8.____
	WAMZTRMZ	-	65194319		
	ECXARWXC	-	70263520		
9.	MAWXECRQ	-	16527038		9.____
	RXQEAETM	-	32876741		
	RXEWMCZQ	-	32751098		
10.	MRQZCATE	-	13890647		10.____
	WCETRXAW	-	50743625		
	CZWMCERT	-	09510734		

KEY (CORRECT ANSWERS)

1. D
2. B
3. A
4. C
5. C

6. A
7. D
8. B
9. D
10. A

TEST 2

DIRECTIONS: Questions 1 through 6 consist of three lines of code letters and numbers. The numbers on each, line should correspond with the code letters on the same line in accordance with the table below.

Code Letter	F	X	L	M	R	W	T	S	B	H
Corresponding Number	0	1	2	3	4	5	6	7	8	9

On some of the lines, an error exists in the coding. Compare the letters and numbers in each question carefully. If you find an error or errors on

   only *one* of the lines in the question, mark your answer A;
   any *two* lines in the question, mark your answer B;
   all *three* lines in the question, mark your answer C;
   none of the lines in the question, mark your answer D.

SAMPLE QUESTION

LTSXHMF	2671930
TBRWHLM	6845913
SXLBFMR	5128034

In the above sample, the first line is correct since each code letter listed has the correct corresponding number.

   On the second line, an error exists because code letter L should have the number 2 instead of the number 1.

   On the third line, an error exists because the code letter S should have the number 7 instead of the number 5.

   Since there are errors on two of the three lines, the correct answer is B.

1. XMWBHLR   1358924   1._____
    FWSLRHX   0572491
    MTXBLTS   3618267

2. XTLSMRF   1627340   2._____
    BMHRFLT   8394026
    HLTSWRX   9267451

3. LMBSFXS   2387016   3._____
    RWLMBSX   4532871
    SMFXBHW   7301894

4. RSTWTSML   47657632   4._____
    LXRMHFBS   21439087
    FTLBMRWX   06273451

5. XSRSBWFM   17478603   5._____
    BRMXRMXT   84314216
    XSTFBWRL   17609542

6. TMSBXHLS   63781927   6.____
    RBSFLFWM   48702053
    MHFXWTRS   39015647

KEY (CORRECT ANSWERS)

1. D
2. A
3. C
4. B
5. C
6. D

TEST 3

DIRECTIONS: Questions 1 through 5 consist of three lines of code letters and numbers. The numbers on each line should correspond with the code letters on the same line in accordance with the table below.

Code Letter	P	L	I	J	B	O	H	U	C	G
Corresponding Number	0	1	2	3	4	5	6	7	8	9

On some of the lines, an error exists in the coding. Compare the letters and numbers in each question carefully. If you find an error or errors on
  only *one* of the lines in the question, mark your answer A;
  any *two* lines in the question, mark your answer B;
  all *three* lines in the question, mark your answer C;
  none of the lines in the question, mark your answer D.

SAMPLE QUESTION

JHOILCP   3652180
BICLGUP   4286970
UCIBHLJ   5824613

In the above sample, the first line is correct since each code letter listed has the correct corresponding number.
On the second line, an error exists because code letter L should have the number 1 instead of the number 6.
On the third line an error exists because the code letter U should have the number 7 instead of the number 5.
Since there are errors on two of the three lines, the correct answer is B.

7. BULJCIP   4713920   7.____
        HIGPOUL   6290571
        OCUHJBI   5876342

8. CUBLOIJ   8741023   8.____
        LCLGCLB   1818914
        JPUHIOC   3076158

9. OIJGCBPO   52398405   9.____
        UHPBLIOP   76041250
        CLUIPGPC   81720908

10. BPCOUOJI   40875732   10.____
        UOHCIPLB   75682014
        GLHUUCBJ   92677843

11. HOIOHJLH   65256361   11.____
        IOJJHHBP   25536640
        OJHBJOPI   53642502

KEY (CORRECT ANSWERS)

1. A
2. C
3. D
4. B
5. C

_____

TEST 4

DIRECTIONS: Questions 1 through 5 consist of three lines of code letters and numbers. The numbers on each line should correspond with the code letters on the same line in accordance with the table below.

Code Letters	Q	S	L	Y	M	0	U	N	W	Z
Corresponding Numbers	1	2	3	4	5	6	7	8	9	0

On some of the lines, an error exists in the coding. Compare the letters and numbers in each question carefully. If you find an error on

only *one* of the lines in the question, mark your answer A;
any *two* lines in the question, mark your answer B;
all *three* lines in the question, mark your answer C;
none of the lines in the question, mark your answer D.

SAMPLE QUESTION
MOQNWZQS   56189012
QWNMOLYU   19865347
LONLMYWN   36835489

In the above sample, the first line is correct since each code letter, as listed, has the correct corresponding number.
On the second line, an error exists because code letter M should have the number 5 instead of the number 6.
On the third line an error exists because the code letter W should have the number 9 instead of the number 8.
Since there are errors on two of the three lines, the correct answer is B.

1.   SMUWOLQN   25796318   1._____
     ULSQNMZL   73218503
     NMYQZUSL   85410723

2.   YUWWMYQZ   47995410   2._____
     SOSOSQSO   26262126
     ZUNLWMYW   07839549

3.   QULSWZYN   17329045   3._____
     ZYLQWOYF   04319639
     QLUYWZSO   13749026

4.   NLQZOYUM   83106475   4._____
     SQMUWZOM   21579065
     MMYWMZSQ   55498021

5.   NQLOWZZU   81319007   5._____
     SMYLUNZO   25347806
     UWMSNZOL   79528013

KEY (CORRECT ANSWERS)

1. D
2. D
3. B
4. A
5. C

———

TEST 5

DIRECTIONS: Answer Questions 1 through 6 *SOLELY* on the basis of the chart and the instructions given below.

Toll Rate	$.25	$.30	$.45	$.60	$.75	$8.90	$1.20	$2.50
Classification Number of Vehicle	1	2	3	4	5	6	7	8

Assume that each of the amounts of money on the above chart is a toll rate charged for a type of vehicle and that the number immediately below each amount is the classification number for that type of vehicle. For instance, "1" is the classification number for a vehicle paying a $.25 toll; "2" is the classification number for a vehicle paying a $.30 toll; and so forth.

In each question, a series of tolls is given in Column I. Column II gives four different arrangements of classification numbers. You are to pick the answer (A, B, C, or D) in Column II that gives the classification numbers that match the tolls in Column I and are in the same order as the tolls in Column I.

SAMPLE QUESTION

Column I	Column II
$.30, $.90, $2.50, $.45	A. 2, 6, 8, 2
	B. 2, 8, 6, 3
	C. 2, 6, 8, 3
	D. 1, 6, 8, 3

According to the chart, the classification numbers that correspond to these toll rates are as follows: $.30 - 2, $.90 - 6, $2.50 - 8, $.45 -3. Therefore, the right answer is 2, 6, 8, 3. The answer is C in Column II.

Do the following questions in the same way.

	Column I		Column II	
1.	$.60, $.30, $.90, $1.20, $.60	A.	4, 6, 2, 8, 4	1.____
		B.	4, 2, 6, 7, 4	
		C.	2, 4, 7, 6, 2	
		D.	2, 4, 6, 7, 4	
2.	$.90, $.45, $.25, $.45, $2.50, $.75	A.	6, 3, 1, 3, 8, 3	2.____
		B.	6, 3, 3, 1, 8, 5	
		C.	6, 1, 3, 3, 8, 5	
		D.	6, 3, 1, 3, 8, 5	
3.	$.45, $.75, $1.20, $.25, $.25, $.30, $.45	A.	3, 5, 7, 1, 1, 2, 3	3.____
		B.	5, 3, 7, 1, 1, 2, 3	
		C.	3, 5, 7, 1, 2, 1, 3	
		D.	3, 7, 5, 1, 1, 2, 3	
4.	$1.20, $2.50, $.45, $.90, $1.20, $.75, $.25	A.	7, 8, 5, 6, 7, 5, 1	4.____
		B.	7, 8, 3, 7, 6, 5, 1	
		C.	7, 8, 3, 6, 7, 5, 1	
		D.	7, 8, 3, 6, 7, 1, 5	

5. $2.50, $1.20, $.90, $.25, $.60, $.45, $.30   A. 8, 6, 7, 1, 4, 3, 2   5.____
                                                    B. 8, 7, 5, 1, 4, 3, 2
                                                    C. 8, 7, 6, 2, 4, 3, 2
                                                    D. 8, 7, 6, 1, 4, 3, 2

6. $.75, $.25, $.45, $.60, $.90, $.30, $2.50   A. 5, 1, 3, 2, 4, 6, 8   6.____
                                                    B. 5, 1, 3, 4, 2, 6, 8
                                                    C. 5, 1, 3, 4, 6, 2, 8
                                                    D. 5, 3, 1, 4, 6, 2, 8

_____

KEY (CORRECT ANSWERS)

1. B
2. D
3. A
4. C
5. D
6. C

_____

TEST 6

DIRECTIONS: Answer Questions 1 through 10 on the basis of the following information:
A code number for any item is obtained by combining the date of delivery, number of units received, and number of units used. The first two digits represent the day of the month, the third and fourth digits represent the month, and the fifth and sixth digits represent the year.
The number following the letter R represents the number of units received and the number following the letter U represents the number of units used.
For example, the code number 120603-R5690-U1001 indicates that a delivery of 5,690 units was made on June 12, 2003 of which 1,001 units were used.

Questions 1-6.

DIRECTIONS: Using the chart below, answer Questions 1 through 6 by choosing the letter (A, B, C, or D) in which the supplier and stock number correspond to the code number given.

Supplier	Stock Number	Number of Units Received	Delivery Date	Number of Units Used
Stony	38390	8300	May 11, 2002	3800
Stoney	39803	1780	September 15, 2003	1703
Nievo	21220	5527	October 10, 2003	5007
Nieve	38903	1733	August 5, 2003	1703
Monte	39213	5527	October 10, 2002	5007
Stony	38890	3308	December 9, 2002	3300
Stony	83930	3880	September 12, 2002	380
Nevo	47101	485	June 11, 2002	231
Nievo	12122	5725	May 11, 2003	5201
Neve	47101	9721	August 15, 2003	8207
Nievo	21120	2275	January 7, 2002	2175
Rosa	41210	3821	March 3, 2003	2710
Stony	38890	3308	September 12, 2002	3300
Dinal	54921	1711	April 2, 2003	1117
Stony	33890	8038	March 5, 2003	3300
Dinal	54721	1171	March 2, 2002	717
Claridge	81927	3308	April 5, 2003	3088
Nievo	21122	4878	June 7, 2002	3492
Haley	39670	8300	December 23, 2003	5300

1. Code No. 120902-R3308-U3300   1._____

    A. Nievo - 12122   B. Stony - 83930
    C. Nievo - 21220   D. Stony -38890

2. Code No. 101002-R5527-U5007   2._____

    A. Nievo - 21220   B. Haley - 39670
    C. Monte - 39213   D. Claridge - 81927

3. Code No. 101003-R5527-U5007   3._____

    A. Nievo - 21220   B. Monte - 39213
    C. Nievo - 12122   D. Nievo - 21120

188

4. Code No. 110503-R5725-U5201   4.____

   A. Nievo - 12122   B. Nievo - 21220
   C. Haley - 39670   D. Stony - 38390

5. Code No. 070102-R2275-U2175   5.____

   A. Stony - 33890   B. Stony - 83930
   C. Stony - 38390   D. Nievo - 21120

6. Code No. 120902-R3880-U380   6.____

   A. Stony - 83930   B. Stony - 38890
   C. Stony - 33890   D. Monte - 39213

Questions 7-10.

DIRECTIONS: Using the same chart, answer Questions 7 through 10 by choosing the letter
               (A, B, C, or D) in which the code number corresponds to the supplier and stock
               number given.

7. Nieve - 38903   7.____

   A. 851903-R1733-U1703   B. 080502-R1733-U1703
   C. 080503-R1733-U1703   D. 050803-R1733-U1703

8. Nevo - 47101   8.____

   A. 081503-R9721-U8207   B. 091503-R9721-U8207
   C. 110602-R485-U231   D. 061102-R485-U231

9. Dinal - 54921   9.____

   A. 020403-R1711-U1117   B. 030202-R1171-U717
   C. 020302-R1171-U717   D. 421903-R1711-U1117

10. Nievo - 21122   10.____

   A. 070602-R4878-U3492   B. 060702-R4878-U349
   C. 761902-R4878-U3492   D. 060702-R4878-U3492

KEY (CORRECT ANSWERS)

1. D
2. C
3. A
4. A
5. D

6. A
7. D
8. C
9. A
10. A

———

FILING

EXAMINATION SECTION
TEST 1

Questions 1-15

DIRECTIONS: Questions 1 through 15 contain fifteen (15) groups of names. For each group four different filing arrangements of the names are given, each arrangement being identified by the letters A B, C and D. In ONE and only one of the arrangements of each group are the names in correct filing order as compared with the arrangement in the local Telephone Company Directory. Indicate the ONE correct arrangement for each group.

	ARRANGEMENT A	ARRANGEMENT B	ARRANGEMENT C	ARRANGEMENT D
1.	Smithe, Alice Stone, Fred G. St. Albans Knit Co. Smith, Chas.	Stone, Fred G. St. Albans Knit Co. Smith, Chas. Smithe, Alice	St. Albans Knit Co. Smith, Chas. Smithe, Alice Stone, Fred G.	Smith, Chas. Smithe, Alice St. Albans Knit Co. Stone, Fred G.
2.	Brower, George Brown, Frank Brown and Stone Brown's Sandwich Shop	Brown, Frank Brown's Sandwich Shop Brower, George Brown and Stone	Brown and Stone Brown, Frank Brown's Sandwich Shop Brower, George	Brown, Frank Brower, George Brown's Sandwich Shop Brown and Stone
3.	McClellen, BenJamin Maclellen, Hattie MacClellen. Beatrice McClelland, Walter	Maclellen, Hattie MacClellen, Beatrice McClelland, Walter McClellen, Benjamin	McClelland, Walter McClellen, Benjamin MacClellen, Beatrice Maclellen, Hattie	MacClellen, Beatrice Maclellen, Hattie McClelland,Walter McClellen, Benjamin
4.	Des-Art Inc. de Sasso, Irving De Sanctis, V.J. Desantis, Vin-cenzo	Des-Art Inc. de Sasso, Irving De Sanctis, V.J. Desantis, Vincenzo	Desantis, Vincenzo de Sasso, Irving Des-Art Inc. De Sanctis, V.J.	de Sasso, Irving De Sanctis, V.J. Desantis, Vincenzo Des-Art Inc.
5.	Abbott Sons Abbott High School Abbott, Harry Abbott, H.J.	Abbott, Harry Abbott, H. J. Abbott High School Abbott Sons	Abbott, H. J. Abbott, Harry Abbott High School Abbott Sons	Abbott, Harry Abbott High School Abbott, H.J. Abbott Sons
6.	Helman, E. Helman-Grant Co. Helman, Ltd. Helman's Clothing Co.	Helman's Clothing Co. Helman, E. Helman-Grant Co. Helman, Ltd.	Helman, E. Helman's Clothing Co. Helman, Ltd. Helman-Grant Co.	Helman's Clothing Co. Helman-Grant Co. Helman, E. Helman, Ltd.

7.
Five East Twelfth Restaurant	Five Fifteen Madison Ave, Bldg.	Five Hundred Fifth Ave. Apts.	Five Boro Tea & Coffee Co.
Five Boro Tea & Coffee Co.	Five Hundred Fifth Ave. Apts.	Five Fifteen Madison Ave. Bldg.	Five East Twelfth Restaurant
Five Hundred Fifth Ave. Apts.	Five East Twelfth Restaurant	Five Boro Tea & Coffee Co.	Five Fifteen Madison Ave. Bldg.
Five Fifteen Madison Ave. Bldg.	Five Boro Tea & Coffee Co.	Five East Twelfth Restaurant	Five Hundred Fifth Ave. Apts.

8.
R K China Co.	R & K Camera Corp.	RKO Corp.	R K China Co.
R & K Camera Corp.	R K China Co.	R K Cut Rate Stores	R K Cut Rate Stores
RKO Corp.	R K Cut Rate Stores	R & K Camera Corp.	R & K Camera Corp.
R K Cut Rate Store	RKO Corp.	R K China Co.	RKO Corporation

9.
Thomas, John	Thomas, J. C.	Thomas & Jones Co.	Thomas & Jones Co.
Thomas, J. C.	Thomas, John	Thomas, John	Thomas, J.C.
Thomas' Jaunty Hats	Thomas' Jaunty Hats	Thomas, J.C.	Thomas' Jaunty Hats
Thomas & Jones Co.	Thomas & Jones Co.	Thomas' Jaunty Hats	Thomas, John

10.
Von Heyde Saylor	Vanderbergh, Sol	Vandenburgh, S.	Van Heyden, Silas
Vandenburgh, S.	Vandenburgh, S.	Vanderbergh, Sol	Vandenburgh, S.
Van Heyden, Silas	Von Heyde, Saylor	Van Heyden, Silas	Vanderbergh, Sol Von
Vanderbergh, Sol	Van Heyden, Silas	Von Heyde, Saylor	Heyde, Saylor

11.
Lafayette Sales Co.	La Clere, Thomas	L. B. K. Lines	La Clere, Thomas
La Clere, Thomas	Le Clair, A.M.	La Clere, Thom--as	Lafayette Sales Co.
L.B.K. Lines	L. B. K. Lines	Lafayette Sales Co.	Le Clair, A.M.
Le Clair, A.M.	Lafayette Sales Co.	Le Clair, A.M.	L.B.K. Lines

12.
Warner Bros.	Warner, Chas.	Warner Bros.	Warner Charity Bazaar
Warner Charity Bazaar	Warner Charity Bazaar	Warner, Chas.	Warner, Chas.
Warner, Chas.	Warner Home for the Aged	Warner Home for the Aged	Warner Home for the Aged
Warner Home for the Aged	Warner Bros.	Warner Charity Bazaar	Warner Bros.

13.
Fidelity Loan Co.	Film Bd. of Trade	Ft. Orange Garage	Fidelity Loan Co.
Film Bd. of	Ft. Orange Garage	Fidelity Loan Co.	Film Bd. of Trade
Fort Orange Grill	Fort Orange Grill	Fort Orange Grill	Ft. Orange Garage
Ft. Orange Garage	Fidelity Loan Co.	Film Bd. of Trade	Fort Orange Grill

14.
Re-Vi-Vo Mfg. Co.	R & W Food Stores	Roebling, John	Re-Vi-Vo Mfg. Co.
Roebling, John	Re-Vi-Vo Mfg. Co.	Robbins and Johnson	R & W Food Stores
R & W Food Stores	Robbins and Johnson	R & W Food Stores	Roebling, John
Robbins and Johnson	Roebling, John	Re-Vi-Vo Mfg. Co.	Robbins and Johnson

15. Hillton, Ernest V.   Hill-Harris John   Hill-Harris, John   Hilton Memorial Fund
    Hilton, Inc.   Hilton, Inc.   Hillton, Ernest V.   Hill-Harris, John
    Hill-Harris John   Hilton, Memorial Fund   Hilton, Inc.   Hillton, Ernest v.
    Hilton Memorial Fund Hillton, Ernest V.   Hilton Memorial Fund Hilton, Inc.

Questions 16 - 19

DIRECTIONS: In Questions 16 through 19, choose the option which lists names in the alphabetical order used in telephone directories.

16.   A.   Maclay, R.; MacGuiness, J.; McKay, C,; McKinley, D.
     B.   MacLeod, S.; McPherson, T.; MacRae, G.; McVeigh, E.
     C.   Mackintosh, P.; MacKintosh, R.; Maclin, F.; Macnee, P.
     D.   D. MacIntyre, J.; MacIver, C.; Machlin, M.; Mack, L.

17.   A.   ABC Camera Corp.; A & B Auto Parts Co.; ABA Testing Corp.; A & B Wool Corp.
     B.   A & B Auto Parts Co.; ABA Testing Corp.; ABC Camera Corp.; A & B Wool Corp.
     C.   ABC Camera Corp.; ABA Testing Corp.; A & B Wool Corp.; A & B Auto Parts Co.
     D.   ABA Testing Corp.; A & B Auto Parts Co.; ABC Camera Corp.; A & B Wool Corp.

18.   A.   O'Dwyer and Bernstein; Oduro, E. S.; O'Driscoll, Michael; Odyssey House Inc.
     B.   O'Driscoll, Michael; Oduro, E. S.; O'Dwyer and Bernstein; Odyssey House Inc.
     C.   Oduro, E. S.; O'Driscoll, Michael; Odyssey House Inc.; O'Dwyer and Bernstein
     D.   O'Driscoll, Michael; O'Dwyer and Bernstein; Oduro, E. S.; Odyssey House Inc.

19.   A.   F & A Beauty Salon; FAJ Co.; F & A Polishing Co.; Faaland Pharmacy
     B.   Faaland Pharmacy; F & A Beauty Salon; FAJ Co.; F & A Polishing Co.
     C.   Faaland Pharmacy; FAJ Co.; F A Beauty Salon; F & A Polishing Co.
     D.   FAJ Co.; Faaland Pharmacy; F & A Beauty Salon; F & A Polishing Co.

KEY (CORRECT ANSWERS)

1. C	6. A	11. C	16. C
2. A	7. D	12. A	17. D
3. D	8. B	13. D	18. B
4. B	9. B	14. B	19. A
5. C	10. C	15. C	

TEST 2

Questions 1-6

DIRECTIONS: Questions 1 through 6 consist of descriptions of material to which a filing designation must be assigned.

Assume that the matters and cases described in the questions were referred for handling to a government legal office which has its files set up according to these file designations. The file designation consists of a number of characters and punctuations marks as described below.

The first character refers to agencies whose legal work is handled by this office. These agencies are numbered consecutively in the order in which they first submit a matter for attention, and are identified in an alphabetical card index. To date numbers have been assigned to agencies as follows:

Department of Correction	1
Police Department	2
Department of Traffic	3
Department of Consumer Affairs	4
Commission on Human Rights	5
Board of Elections	6
Department of Personnel	7
Board of Estimate	8

The second character is separated from the first character by a dash. The second character is the last digit of the year in which a particular lawsuit or matter is referred to the legal office.

The third character is separated from the second character by a colon and may consist of either of the following:

I. A sub-number assigned to each lawsuit to which the agency is a party. Lawsuits are numbered consecutively regardless of year. (Lawsuits are brought by or against agency heads rather than agencies themselves, but references are made to agencies for the purpose of simplification.)

or II. A capital letter assigned to each matter other than a lawsuit according to subject, the subject being identified in an alphabetical index. To date, letters have been assigned to subjects as follows:

Citizenship	A
Discrimination	B
Residence Requirements	C
Civil Service Examinations	D
Housing	E
Gambling	F
Freedom of Religion	G

These referrals are numbered consecutively regardless of year. The first referral by a particular agency on citizenship, for example, would be desginated A1, followed by A2, A3, etc.

If no reference is made in a question as to how many letters involving a certain subject or how many lawsuits have been referred by an agency, assume that it is the first.

For each question, choose the file designation which is most appropriate for filing the material described in the question.

1. In January, 2010, two candidates in a 2009 civil service examination for positions with the Department of Correction filed a suit against the Department of Personnel seeking to set aside an educational requirement for the title. The Department of Personnel immediately referred the lawsuit to the legal office for handling.

    A. 1-9:1   B. 1-0:D1   C. 7-9:D1   D. 7-0:1

    1.____

2. In 2004, the Police Department made its sixth request for an opinion on whether an employee assignment proposed for 2005 could be considered discriminatory

    A. 2-5:1-B6   B. 2-4:6   C. 2-4:1-B6   D. 2-4:B6

    2.____

3. In 2005, a lawsuit was brought by the Bay Island Action Committee against the Board of Estimate in which the plaintiff sought withdrawal of approval of housing for the elderly in the Bay Island area given by the Board in 2005.

    A. 8-3:1   B. 8-5:1   C. 8-3:B1   D. 8-5:E1

    3.____

4. In December, 2004, community leaders asked the Police Department to ban outdoor meetings of a religious group on the grounds that the meetings were disrupting the area. Such meetings had been held from time to time during 2004. On January 31, 2005, the Police Department asked the government legal office for an opinion on whether granting this request would violate the worshippers' right to freedom of religion.

    A. 2-4:G-1   B. 2-5:G1   C. 2-5:B-1   D. 2-4:B1

    4.____

5. In 2004, a woman filed suit against the Board of Elections. She alleged that she had not been permitted to vote at her usual polling place in the 2003 election and had been told she was not registered there. She claimed that she had always voted there and that her record card had been lost. This was the fourth case of its type for this agency.

    A. 6-4:4   B. 6-3:C4   C. 3-4:6   D. 6-3:4

    5.____

6. A lawsuit was brought in 2001 by the Ace Pinball Machine Company against the Commissioner of Consumer Affairs.
The lawsuit contested an ordinance which banned the use of pinball machines on the ground that they are gambling devices. This was the third lawsuit to which the Department of Consumer Affairs was a party.

    A. 4-1:1   B. 4-3:F1   C. 4-1:3   D. 3F-4:1

    6.____

KEY (CORRECT ANSWERS)

1. D
2. D
3. B
4. B
5. A
6. C

———

TEST 3

DIRECTIONS: In each of the following questions on filing, three groups of names are arranged correctly and one group is arranged INCORRECTLY. Indicate the group that is arranged INCORRECTLY.

1.   A.   Emory & Sons; Emory, Steuart: Emory, Stewart; Emory, T.E.   1._____
     B.   Erdlund, Edward; Erdlunda, Mary; Erdlunds, Arnold; Erdlundton, Albert
     C.   Allan-Jones, Sylvia; The Allan-Jones Tire Corp.; Allan, Robert; Allan, Roberta
     D.   Frank, Peter; Frank & Peters; Franks, George; Franks, George N.

2.   A.   Harris, Harriet; Harris, Harriette; Harriss, Harold; Harriss, Hyme   2._____
     B.   St. George, Vivian; St. George, Vivyan; St. George, Vivyenne; Saint, George W.
     C.   Gorman, Esmond; Gorman, Esmonda; Gorman, Lila; O'Gorman, Linda
     D.   German, Norbert; Germans, Norbert Germansky, Nilda; Germansky, Norman

3.   A.   Murtagh, Muriel; Murtagh, Norton; Murtagh & Nortons; Murtagh & Sons   3._____
     B.   Nestor, G.C.; Nestor & George; Nestor, George C.; Nestoris, Alan
     C.   Hinton, Leslie; Hinton, Lester; Hinton, Lester A.; Hinton Linda
     D.   Hilton, Harry: Hilton, A. Harry; Hilton, Harry G.; Hiltons, Mary

4.   A.   Church, George; Church, Georgine; Church & Gibbons; Churchly, Bette   4._____
     B.   Edwards, A. Maxwell; Edwards, Martin A,; Edwardes, Peter; Edwards, S.
     C.   Danton, Daniel; Danton & Edwards; The Danton Shoe Co.: D'Antun, P.
     D.   Darcy, Thomas; Darcy, Walter: D'Arcy, William; Darcy, Worth

5.   A.   Oster, Vernon; Oster & Weed; Ostera, Nancy; Ostera, P,T.   5._____
     B.   Peter, Lyman; Perter, Nelson; Peters, William; Peters, William T.
     C.   Wilson, Martin; Wilson and Morton; Wilson Weaving Co.; Wilson, Wilbert
     D.   Wood, Charles; Woods, Chalmers; Woods, Melvin; Woods, Melvin C.

6.   A.   Pierce, Harold; Pierce, H. Lowell; Pierce, Lowel; Pierce, Lowell H.   6._____
     B.   Maston, G. ; Maston, G.H.; Maston, G. Harold; Maston, George H.
     C.   Boyce, Jonathan; Boyce, Joseph; Boyce, Jos, H.; Boyse, J.H.
     D.   Burne-Jones, Arthur; Burne-Jones, Arthur E,; Burns, A.E,; Burns,
          Arthur

7.   A.   Liberty Furniture Co.; Liberty, G.H.; Liberty and Jacobs; Liberty and Jacoby, Inc.   7._____
     B.   Fien, Mrs. Charles; Fein, Mrs. Dora; Fein, Mrs. Martha; Fein, Susan
     C.   Destry, M.N,; Destry Oil Co.; Destry and Putnam; Destry-Jones, G.
     D.   Douglas, Norman; Douglass and Norman; Douglass, Capt. Philip;
          Douglass Woodworking Corp,

8.   A.   Linton Steel Corp.; Steele and Linton; Stiles, Norma; Stiles Parking Company   8._____
     B.   Stern and Lyons; Stern, Matthew; Sterne, Alfred; Sterns, A. N.
     C.   Rodriguez, Jose; Rodriguez, Joseph; Rodstein, M.M.; Roth-stein,
          David
     D.   16 Park Avenue Building; Parke and Baker; Parke, Charles; Parker,
          Abner

9.	A.	Baker, John R., Jr.; Baker, John S.; Baker, Jonathan; Baker, Mrs. Julia
	B.	Vitality Grocery Co.; Vitalus, Grace; Vitaluso, Gerald; Vitaluso, Martin
	C.	Paige-Smith, Norma; Paigero, Patricia; Pelton, Sylvia; Peluso, John
	D.	Emett, Patrick; Emmett,John; Emmett, Karl; Emmetts, Carl

9.____

10.	A.	Associated Industries; Industrial Associates, Inc.; Howard Jones Associates; Alfred Kahn, Inc.
	B.	Inter-Continental Aircraft; Intercontinental Lumber; Inter-Continental Welfare Committee; Inter-Coastal Shipping
	C.	Lodge of the Astor; Lodge, Bernard: Lodge, Bertram A.; Lodges, Albert
	D.	Nieman Brothers; Nieman, Charles; Nieman, Dora A.; Niemann, Delbert

10.____

11.	A.	Delicato, Nemo; Delicate, Norman; Delicate, N,S.; Delicator, G.E.
	B.	ABC Corp.; Allied Battery Co.; Allied Bridges, Ltd.; Allied Cheese Co.
	C.	Nostrom, David; Nostrom, David J.; Nostromo, Anna; Nostromor, Ara
	D.	Nielsen, Mitchel; Nielsen, Nils; Nielson, Morris; Nielson, Moss

11.____

12.	A.	Gorgeous Frocks Co.; Gorgon, M.C.; Gorgon, Nathan; Gorgona, Cynthia
	B.	Boathe and Davis; Booth and Black; Boothe and Alamac; Boothe, May
	C.	Cantor Boat Co.; Canovis and Long; Canovis, Miriam; Canovis, Sam
	D.	Walton Watch Corp.; Walton, William; Walton, William B.; Waltons, Morris

12.____

13.	A.	Shepard, Vardis; Sheppard and Klein; Sheppard Moving Corp.; Sheppards, Ceil
	B.	Blivin, Bernard; Blivin, Capt. Bernard S.; Blivin, Bert; Blivins, Alicia
	C.	Yates Furniture Co.; Yates Furniture Corp.; Yates and Fynch; Yates, Harlow
	D.	Wooseter, B.C.; Wooster, C. Ian; Woostein, Ivan; Woosten, Mary

13.____

14.	A.	Lunt, Lindsay; Lunt Literary Agents, Inc.; Lunt Literacy Tests; Lunt, Marvin
	B.	Hunter, Lucy; Hunter and Lyttle; Hunter Moving Vans; Hunter and Vann
	C.	Pimental, George; Pimental, George A.; Pimentel, Donald; Pimentel, Dora
	D.	Nanton and Jones; Nanton, Joseph; Nanton Linens, Inc.; Nanton Printing Co.

14.____

15.	A.	Peters, Linda; Peters & Linden; Peterson, Charles; Peterson and Charleston
	B.	Jarry, Christopher; Jarry, C. David; Jarry and Davis; Jarry and Devons
	C.	Milton, Martha; Milton, Mona; Milton, Myrna; Milton Novelty Corp.
	D.	MacLean, Esther; Maclean and Evans; McHeath, George; McManus, Edith

15.____

16. A. Platt & Waters; Wilton O. Platt; Woodley Platt; Woodley & Parker
     B. Gerber Service Station; Gerber & Stevens; Steven O. Gerbers; S.O. Gerbert
     C. Alton Joly; A. Milton Joly; Mary Joly; Marian Juley
     D. John A. Lantern & Co.; Lantern & Jones; Lantern Steel Corp.; L.C. Steele

16.____

17. A. Liberty Beef Corp.; Mortola & Liberty; John Mortyn; M.O. Mortyn
     B. Church Street Corp.; Peter E, Church; Peters & Church; Lawrence Peterson
     C. Mimi La Touche; Miriam Latow; Myriam A. Latow; Milton Latows
     D. P.C. Johnson; Peter Johnson; Johnson & Royce; Steven Johnson

17.____

18. A. Buick Motors Corp.; Parker & Buick; Charles Parker ; Charles A. Parker
     B. Boston Savings Bank; First National Bank of Boston; Furst & Boston; Jason Furst
     C. M.C. Patton: Milton Patton; Milton A. Patton; Mary Pattone
     D. Denholm Elliot; D.C. Elliott; Dylan Elliott; Dylane Elliot

18.____

19. A. Capt. John Parker; Prof. Jacob Parkington; Parkins & Gates; Gabriel Parkins
     B. Curtis The Clothier; Clinton E. Curtiss; Curtiss & Jones; Peter Curtiss
     C. Mexican Trade Corp.; Vincent Mextico; Warren & Maxon; Walter Warren
     D. Denver Steel, Ltd.; William Denver; Yetta Denver; Y.C. Denver

19.____

20. A. Boston University; Boston Woodworking Co.; Boston & Yardley; University of Akron
     B. Durango Sales Corp.; Durango Wool Co.; Durango & Zenith; Mrs. Alice Durangow
     C. John La Beach; James Lachaise; James Levieu; James and Levin
     D. Morton Meat Corp.; Milton Morton; Mrs. Mary E. Mortona; M.E. Mortonia

20.____

KEY (CORRECT ANSWERS)

1.	C	11.	A
2.	B	12.	C
3.	D	13.	D
4.	B	14.	A
5.	B	15.	B
6.	A	16.	C
7.	B	17.	B
8.	D	18.	B
9.	C	19.	A
10.	B	20.	A

TEST 4

DIRECTIONS: In each of the following questions on filing, three groups of names are arranged correctly and one group is arranged incorrectly. Indicate the group that is arranged INCORRECTLY.

1. A. Walter Mack; James E. Mackey; R.W. MacGregor; James McGregor
   B. Charles D'Antonio; Arthur du Bois; Charles A. Du Bois; Philip A. Dubois
   C. Adolph Ochs; Thomas O'Day; John C. Odell; Herman Ogleby
   D. Herbert Van; Albert Van der Veer; James C. Vanderveer; James C. Vanderveer, Jr.

   1.____

2. A. Aberdeen Trading Co.; Adams Hats; Adams Health Foods; Adams Historical Society
   B. Gross Bakery; Grosse Plumbers; Grossman's Inc.; Grossman & Son
   C. T.R. Simmons, Jr.; T.R. Simmons, Sr.; James Smith Co.; James C. Smith Co.
   D. J.C. Dithers; Jos. Dithers & Son; Joseph Dithers; Ditto Company

   2.____

3. A. Albert Browning; Albert A. Browning; Albert Browning, M.D.; Dr. Albert Browning
   B. Major John V. Lind; Col. Walter M. Lundy; Gen M.W. Lutting-ham; Eric Luytens, Esq.
   C. Brother Walter; Lady Anne; Princess Margaret Rose; Sister Maria Theresa
   D. Daniel A, Pope; Danielle R. Popeau; Alexander Poppington; Alexandra C. Poppo

   3.____

4. A. Boy's Life Magazine; Boys' Books, Inc.; Child's Restaurant; Children's World
   B. New Jersey Scrap Co.; N.Y. Pipe Co.; New York Tire Corp.; New Zealand Importers
   C. University of California; Colorado University; Denver National Savings; Savings Bank of Denver
   D. West Shore Raincoat Co.; West Shore Ry.; Western Reserve Corp.; Western Travel, Inc.

   4.____

5. A. Gun Supplies Shop; Gunn Printing Co.; P.L. Gunne; Gunnell Radio Shop
   B. Irwin Shoe Mgfrs.; Irwin Shoe Mart; The Tom Irwin Co.; R.W. Irwine
   C. H.B. Anderson; Andrew's Inn; Andrews and Breen; The Andrew Brook Co.
   D. The Half Moon Inn; Haft Construction Co.; Harry the Hatter; The Hart Co.

   5.____

6. A. Jas. Johnson; James A. Johnson; John Jonsen; John A. Jonson
   B. Queen Victoria; Victoria A. Queen; Thomas Quill; Thomas J. Quill, Jr.
   C. Lillian Bernstein; Lillian A. Byrnes; Lillian A. Byrn-ville; Mrs. Lillian A. Byrnville
   D. Jane Willa Smythe; Jane Wilsonworth; Jane W. Wilkinson; Janet Woolworth

   6.____

7. 	A. 	J. David; J.A. David; James David; James David Eastlake 7.____
	B. 	Gregory P. Eck; Joseph Fullerton; Francis Greene; Frances A, Greene
	C. 	Jerome C. St. Cloud; Jeremy C. Starkey; Allen Stechel; Francis A. Stickland, Jr.
	D. 	Louis B. Ryan; Louise A. Ryon; Elizabeth Ryoneck; Betty R. Ryontorg

8. 	A. 	Las Vegas Machine Co.; La Traviata Opera Co.; Los Angeles Chamber of Commerce; The Los Angeles Daily Star 8.____
	B. 	Madame Mimi's Hats; Mademoiselle Marie Dresses; I. Maid-man Enterprises; Maidman's Club
	C. 	St. Louis Shops; San Diego Drug Co.; San Francisco Products; Santa Barbara Hotel
	D. 	40 Winks Motel; 400 Park Avenue Club; One Fifth Avenue Hotel; The Two Park Row Hotel

9. 	A. 	F. Scott Hemingway; Francis Scott Key; Frank A. Keystone; F.A. Keyting 9.____
	B. 	Algernon Blaisdell; Andrew Blaithwaite, Sr.; Ernesto de Cesare; Eleanor D'Ortiz
	C. 	Paul St. James; Paul E. Sperling; Gretchen Springer; Amanda Sprunzmeyer
	D. 	Geraldine Martin; Wilhelmina McAndrew; Ella Santangelo; Florence St. George

10. 	A. 	Thos. Peters Co.; Thor Peters, Inc.; Jas. Pool, Inc.; Jane Pool Dresses 10.____
	B. 	Harold Gannon, Inc.; John T. Gannon Associates; L.E. Gannon Co.; L.O. Gannon, Sr.
	C. 	The Jones Co.; Jones and Howell; Jones of the Plaza; Jones the Plumber
	D. 	J.C. Gorden; James Gordon Co.; Gordon, Inc.; J.R. Gordon, Ltd.

11. 	A. 	J. Williams; John Williams; John A. Williams; John A Williamson 11.____
	B. 	Allan Danieli Music Company; Arthur Davis Photo Studio; Amy Vanderbilt Courtesy Club; Frank C. Weil Bakery
	C. 	Ann Jackson; A. Ann Jackson; Anne Jackson; Annie Jackson
	D. 	Greta L. LaRoy: Gretta M. Larue; Gene Losey; Lotito Insurance Company

12. 	A. 	Edward Santos; Alberto Santujo; Salvatore St. John; Sister Loretta 12.____
	B. 	Percy St. Pierre; Perry Senior; Percy A. Sommers, Jr.; Percy Sonnenschein
	C. 	Rome Opera Company; Rome Plastering Co., Inc.; Robert L. Rome; Roy Romeo, Jr.
	D. 	Ivan MacCarthy; Ivan C. McCarthy; Ivor Melnick; 17th Street Association

13.   A.   Sister Grace; Sister Theresa; Brother Walter; Mrs. Wendy C. Sister   13.____
        B.   Dr. John's Cough Syrup; Lady Edith's Hat Shoppe; Mr. Richard of
Carnaby Street; Sir Edward Cigars
        C.   Alan Miller Rug Co.; Allan Mills Concert Bureau; Allen Milton Muller
Investment Co.; Alice Myers Consulting Service
        D.   Ideal, Inc.; Ideal Ink Co.; Ideal Inking Company; Ideal Toys

14.   A.   Bernardo A. Rodriguez; C. Arturo Rodriguez; Charles Antonio Rodriguez; F.A.   14.____
Rodriguez
        B.   Seneca Falls Moving Company; Seneca Falls Plumbing Company;
Seneca Falls Restaurant; Sam Snedeker-Smithwick
        C.   Margaret Santa Rosa; Margaretta Scanlon; Mary Sue Spalato; Mar-
tha Van Axel
        D.   Thomas O'Brien; OCA Corporation; Thomas A. O'Hara; Tim O'Hara

15.   A.   902 Corporation; Northwest Paper Company; 1400 Northwest Street; Northwest   15.____
Travel Agency
        B.   First National Bank, Columbus, Georgia; First National Bank,
Columbus, Ohio; First National Bank, Dayton, Ohio; First National
Bank, Poughkeepsie, N.Y.
        C.   The Club 97; 8th Street Theater; 400 Fifth Avenue Corporation; 3
Washington Square Club
        D.   Brother William; Father Walter; Sister Mary Louise; Sister Maryann

16.   A.   D'Andrea Art Supplies Co.; Leonardo da Vinci; Leonard Davins; Lorenzo De la   16.____
Robles
        B.   Lowell-McCann Book Co.; Lurie-Moyers Advertising Agency; Lur-
yea-Madison Stamp Co.; Lycoming Pet Shops
        C.   Morton Richardson Tire Company; Morton Robinson Auto Com-
pany; Paulette Robins Hat Shoppe; Samuel Robertson, Inc.
        D.   C B S Publishers; Canton Supply Co.; Consolidated Edison; Crown
Heights Delivery Co.

17.   A.   Peter Rabinow; Kenneth R. Rabinow-Alliota; Nancy M. Rabinowitz; Edith Rabinow-   17.____
Wilson
        B.   New Grocery Company; New Orleans Acting Company; The New
York Times; Selma Newton
        C.   Department of Housing, State of Montana; Department of Gas and
Electricity, City of St. Louis; Town of Tonowanda, Police Dept.; Vil-
lage of Westwood, Fire Department
        D.   Used Car Corporation; U.S. Rubber Company; Vincent Health
Foods; Western Supplies, Ltd.

18.   A.   Dicken's Trucks; Abraham Dickens; Charles Dickens; Dickens' Yacht Club   18.____
        B.   David Gordon-Fox Mfg. Co.; Pauline Gordon-Fox Dress Shop;
Steven Gordoni; Robert Guenther
        C.   The New Deal Restaurant; The Newton Shipping Co.; North Shore
Press; The PEN Club
        D.   Thomas J. Grace; Thos. A. Grace; Grace Zoo Supplies, Inc.; Gracie
Mfg. Co.

19.   A. U.S. Department of Defense; U.S. Dept, of the Interior; U.S. Department of the   19.____
           Treasury; U.S. Editing Co., Inc.
      B. Jas. A. Craig; James C. Craig; Jay D. Cray; Jerrold A. Craymore
      C. Benjamin Hicks; Hicks & Co., Salem, Mass.; Hicks & Co., Salem,
           Ore.; Martin Hicks
      D. Dominion of Canada, Ministry of Fisheries; U.S. Dept. of Agriculture; U.S. Dept. of Justice; United States Housing Corporation Inc.

20.   A. Southeast Supply Co.; South East Trading Co.; South- East Trading Co., Inc.;   20.____
           Southeast University
      B. Thurston the Magician; Norman E. Thurston; Thurstone Oil Company; Thurstone Paint Company
      C. BBB Clothes; Canes Corp.; CTF Corporation; Candy Shops, Inc.
      D. Pedro Roldan-Rodriguez; Paul Roldano-Rodriguez; Carlos Santana; Carlotta Santana

KEY (CORRECT ANSWERS)

1.	A	11.	C
2.	D	12.	A
3.	A	13.	A
4.	D	14.	D
5.	D	15.	A
6.	D	16.	C
7.	B	17.	D
8.	B	18.	D
9.	D	19.	A
10.	D	20.	C

TEST 5

DIRECTIONS: Questions 1 through 8 each show in Column I the information written on five cards (lettered j, k, l, m, n) which have to be filed. You are to choose the option (lettered A, B, C, or D) in Column II which *BEST* represents the *proper* order of filing according to the information, rules, and sample question given below.

A file card record is kept of the work assignments for all the employees in a certain bureau. On each card is the employee's name, the date of work assignment, and the work assignment code number. The cards are to be filed according to the following rules:

FIRST: File in alphabetical order according to employee's name

SECOND: When two or more cards have the same employee's name, file according to the assignment date beginning with the earliest date.

THIRD: When two or more cards have the same employee's name and the same date, file according to the work assignment number beginning with the lowest number.

Column II shows the cards arranged in four different orders. Pick the option (A, B, C, or D) in Column II which shows the correct arrangement of the cards according to the above filing rules.

SAMPLE QUESTION

Column I				Column II
(j)	Cluney	4/ 8/72	(486503)	A. k, l, m, j, n
(k)	Roster	5/ 10/71	(246611)	B. k, n, j, l, m
(l)	Altool	10/ 15/72	(711433)	C. l, k, j, m, n
(m)	Cluney	12/ 18/72	(527610)	D. l, n, j, m, k
(n)	Cluney	4/ 8/72	(486500)	

The correct way to file the cards is:

(l)	Altool	10/15/72	(711433)
(n)	Cluney	4/8/72	(486500)
(j)	Cluney	4/8/72	(486503)
(m)	Cluney	12/18/72	(527610)
(k)	Roster	5/10/71	(246611)

The correct filing order is shown by the letters l, n, j, m, k. The answer to the sample question is the letter D, which appears in front of the letters l, n, j, m, k in Column II.

Now answer the following questions using the same procedure.

<u>Column I</u>				<u>Column II</u>	
1. (j) Smith	3/19/73	(662118)	A. j, m, l, n, k	1.____
(k) Turner	4/16/69	(481349)	B. j, l, n, m, k	
(l) Terman	3/20/72	(210229)	C. k, n, m, l, j	
(m) Smyth	3/20/72	(481359)	D. j, n, k, l, m	
(n) Terry	5/11/71	(672128)		
2. (j) Ross	5/29/72	(396118)	A. l, m, k, n, j	2.____
(k) Rosner	5/29/72	(439281)	B. m, l, k, n, j	
(l) Rose	7/19/72	(723456)	C. l, m, k, j, n	
(m) Rosen	5/29/73	(829692)	D. m, l, j, n, k	
(n) Ross	5/29/72	(399118)		
3. (j) Sherd	10/12/69	(552368)	A. n, m, k, j, l	3.____
(k) Snyder	11/12/69	(539286)	B. j, m, l, k, n	
(l) Shindler	10/13/68	(426798)	C. m, k, n, j, l	
(m) Scherld	10/12/69	(552386)	D. m, n, j, l, k	
(n) Schneider	11/12/69	(798213)		
4. (j) Carter	1/16/72	(489636)	A. k, n, j, l, m	4.____
(k) Carson	2/16/71	(392671)	B. n, k, m, l, j	
(l) Carter	1/16/71	(486936)	C. n, k, l, j, m	
(m) Carton	3/15/70	(489639)	D. k, n, l, j, m	
(n) Carson	2/16/71	(392617)		
5. (j) Thomas	3/18/69	(763182)	A. m, l, j, k, n	5.____
(k) Tompkins	3/19/70	(928439)	B. j, m, l, k, n	
(l) Thomson	3/21/70	(763812)	C. j, l, n, m, k	
m) Thompson	3/18/69	(924893)	D. l, m, j, n, k	
(n) Tompson	3/19/69	(928793)		
6. (j) Breit	8/10/73	(345612)	A. m, j, n, k, l	6.____
(k) Briet	5/21/70	(837543)	B. n, m, j, k, l	
(l) Bright	9/18/69	(931827)	C. m, j, k, l, n	
(m) Breit	3/7/68	(553984)	D. j, m, k, l, n	
(n) Brent	6/14/74	(682731)		
7. (j) Roberts	10/19/72	(581932)	A. n, k, l, m, j	7.____
(k) Rogers	8/9/70	(638763)	B. n, k, l, j, m	
(l) Rogerts	7/15/67	(105689)	C. k, n, l, m, j	
(m) Robin	3/8/62	(287915)	D. j, m, k, n, l	
(n) Rogers	4/2/74	(736921)		
8. (j) Hebert	4/28/72	(719468)	A. n, k, j, m, l	8.____
(k) Herbert	5/8/71	(938432)	B. j, l, n, k, m	
(1) Helbert	9/23/74	(832912)	C. l, j, k, n, m	
(m) Herbst	7/10/73	(648599)	D. l, j, n, k, m	
(n) Herbert	5/8/71	(487627)		

KEY (CORRECT ANSWERS)

1. A
2. C
3. D
4. C
5. B

6. A
7. D
8. B

———————

ARITHMETIC

EXAMINATION SECTION
TEST 1

DIRECTIONS: Each question or incomplete statement is followed by several suggested answers or completions. Select the one that BEST answers the question or completes the statement. *PRINT THE LETTER OF THE CORRECT ANSWER IN THE SPACE AT THE RIGHT.*

1. From 30983 subtract 29998. The answer should be
   A. 985   B. 995   C. 1005   D. 1015   1._____

2. From $2537.75 subtract $1764.28. The answer should be
   A. $763.58   B. $773.47   C. $774.48   D. $873.58   2._____

3. From 254211 subtract 76348. The answer should be
   A. 177863   B. 177963   C. 187963   D. 188973   3._____

4. Divide 4025 by 35. The answer should be
   A. 105   B. 109   C. 115   D. 125   4._____

5. Multiply 0.35 by 2764. The answer should be
   A. 997.50   B. 967.40   C. 957.40   D. 834.40   5._____

6. Multiply 1367 by 0.50. The answer should be
   A. 6.8350   B. 68.350   C. 683.50   D. 6835.0   6._____

7. Multiply 841 by 0.01. The answer should be
   A. 0.841   B. 8.41   C. 84.1   D. 841   7._____

8. Multiply 1962 by 25. The answer should be
   A. 47740   B. 48460   C. 48950   D. 49050   8._____

9. Multiply 905 by 0.05. The answer should be
   A. 452.5   B. 45.25   C. 4.525   D. 0.4525   9._____

10. Multiply 8.93 by 4.7. The answer should be
    A. 41.971   B. 40.871   C. 4.1971   D. 4.0871   10._____

11. Multiply 25 by 763. The answer should be
    A. 18075   B. 18875   C. 19075   D. 20965   11._____

12. Multiply 2530 by 0.10. The answer should be
    A. 2.5300   B. 25.300   C. 253.00   D. 2530.0   12._____

13. Multiply 3053 by 0.25. The answer should be   13.____

    A. 76.325   B. 86.315   C. 763.25   D. 863.15

14. Multiply 6204 by 0.35. The answer should be   14.____

    A. 2282.40   B. 2171.40   C. 228.24   D. 217.14

15. Multiply $.35 by 7619. The answer should be   15.____

    A. $2324.75   B. $2565.65   C. $2666.65   D. $2756.75

16. Multiply 6513 by 45. The answer should be   16.____

    A. 293185   B. 293085   C. 292185   D. 270975

17. Multiply 3579 by 70. The answer should be   17.____

    A. 25053.0   B. 240530   C. 250530   D. 259530

18. A class had an average of 24 words correct on a spelling test. The class average on this   18.____
spelling test was 80%.
The AVERAGE number of words missed on this test was

    A. 2   B. 4   C. 6   D. 8

19. In which one of the following is 24 renamed as a product of primes?   19.____

    A. 2 x 6 x 2   B. 8 x 3 x 1
    C. 2 x 2 x 3 x 2   D. 3 x 4 x 2

Questions 20-23.

DIRECTIONS: In answering Questions 20 through 23, perform the indicated operation. Select
the BEST answer from the choices below.

20. Add: 7068   20.____
           2807
           9434
           6179

    A. 26,488   B. 24,588   C. 25,488   D. 25,478

21. Divide: $75\sqrt{45555}$ 21.____

    A. 674   B. 607.4   C. 6074   D. 60.74

22. Multiply: 907   22.____
             x806

    A. 73,142   B. 13,202   C. 721,042   D. 731,042

23. Subtract: 60085   23.____
             -47194

    A. 12,891   B. 13,891   C. 12,991   D. 12,871

24. A librarian reported that 1/5% of all books taken out last school year had not been returned.
If 85,000 books were borrowed from the library, how many were not returned?

    A. 170   B. 425   C. 1,700   D. 4,250

    24.____

25. At 40 miles per hour, how many minutes would it take to travel 12 miles?

    A. 30   B. 18   C. 15   D. 20

    25.____

KEY (CORRECT ANSWERS)

1.	A	11.	C
2.	B	12.	C
3.	A	13.	C
4.	C	14.	B
5.	B	15.	C
6.	C	16.	B
7.	B	17.	C
8.	D	18.	C
9.	B	19.	C
10.	A	20.	C

21.	B
22.	D
23.	A
24.	A
25.	B

SOLUTIONS TO PROBLEMS

1. 30,983 - 29,998 = 985

2. $2537.75 - $1764.28 = $773.47

3. 254,211 - 76,348 = 177,863

4. 4025 ÷ 35 = 115

5. (.35)(2764) = 967.4

6. (1367)(.50) = 683.5

7. (841)(.01) = 8.41

8. (1962)(25) = 49,050

9. (905)(.05) = 45.25

10. (8.93)(4.7) = 41.971

11. (25)(763) = 19,075

12. (2530)(.10) = 253

13. (3053)(.25) = 763.25

14. (6204)(.35) = 2171.4

15. ($.35)(7619) = $2666.65

16. (6513)(45) = 293,085

17. (3579)(70) = 250,530

18. 24 ÷ .80 = 30. Then, 30 - 24 = 6 words

19. 24 = 2 x 2 x 3 x 2, where each number is a prime.

20. 7068 ÷ 2807 + 9434 + 6179 = 25,488

21. 45,555 ÷ 75 = 607.4

22. (907)(806) = 731,042

23. 60,085 - 47,194 = 12,891

24. (1/5%)(85,000) = (.002)(85,000) = 170 books

25. Let x = number of minutes. Then, $\dfrac{40}{60} = \dfrac{12}{x}$. Solving, x = 18

TEST 2

DIRECTIONS: Each question or incomplete statement is followed by several suggested answers or completions. Select the one that BEST answers the question or completes the statement. *PRINT THE LETTER OF THE CORRECT ANSWER IN THE SPACE AT THE RIGHT.*

1. The sum of 57901 + 34762 is   1._____
    A. 81663   B. 82663   C. 91663   D. 92663

2. The sum of 559 + 448 + 362 + 662 is   2._____
    A. 2121   B. 2031   C. 2021   D. 1931

3. The sum of 36153 + 28624 + 81379 is   3._____
    A. 136156   B. 146046   C. 146146   D. 146156

4. The sum of 742 + 9197 + 8972 is   4._____
    A. 19901   B. 18911   C. 18801   D. 17921

5. The sum of 7989 + 8759 + 2726 is   5._____
    A. 18455   B. 18475   C. 19464   D. 19474

6. The sum of $111.55 + $95.05 + $38.80 is   6._____
    A. $234.40   B. $235.30   C. $245.40   D. $254.50

7. The sum of 1302 + 46187 + 92610 + 4522 is   7._____
    A. 144621   B. 143511   C. 134621   D. 134521

8. The sum of 47953 + 58041 + 63022 + 22333 is   8._____
    A. 170248   B. 181349   C. 191349   D. 200359

9. The sum of 76563 + 43693 + 38521 + 50987 + 72723 is   9._____
    A. 271378   B. 282386   C. 282487   D. 292597

10. The sum of 85923 + 97211 + 11333 + 4412 + 22533 is   10._____
    A. 209302   B. 212422   C. 221412   D. 221533

11. The sum of 4299 + 54163 + 89765 + 1012 + 38962 is   11._____
    A. 188201   B. 188300   C. 188301   D. 189311

12. The sum of 48526 + 709 + 11534 + 80432 + 6096 is   12._____
    A. 135177   B. 139297   C. 147297   D. 149197

13. The sum of $407.62 + $109.01 + $68.44 + $378.68 is   13._____
    A. $963.75   B. $964.85   C. $973.65   D. $974.85

14. From 40614 subtract 4697. The answer should be   14.____

    A.   35917   B.   35927   C.   36023   D.   36027

15. From 81773 subtract 5717. The answer should be   15.____

    A.   75964   B.   76056   C.   76066   D.   76956

16. From $1755.35 subtract $1201.75. The answer should be   16.____

    A. $542.50   B. $544.50   C. $553.60   D. $554.60

17. From $2402.10 subtract $998.85. The answer should be   17.____

    A. $1514.35   B. $1504.25   C. $1413.25   D. $1403.25

18. Add: 12 1/2   18.____
             2 1/2
             3 1/2

    A.   17   B.   17 1/4   C.   17 3/4   D.   18

19. Subtract: 150   19.____
             -80

    A.   70   B.   80   C.   130   D.   150

20. After cleaning up some lots in the city dump, five cleanup crews loaded the following   20.____
amounts of garbage on trucks:
        Crew No. 1 loaded 2 1/4 tons
        Crew No. 2 loaded 3 tons
        Crew No. 3 loaded 1 1/4 tons
        Crew No. 4 loaded 2 1/4tons
        Crew No. 5 loaded 1/2 ton.
The TOTAL number of tons of garbage loaded was

    A.   8 1/4   B.   8 3/4   C.   9   D.   9 1/4

21. Subtract: 17 3/4   21.____
           -7 1/4

    A.   7 1/2   B.   10 1/2   C.   14 1/4   D.   17 3/4

22. Yesterday, Tom and Bill each received 10 leaflets about rat control. They were supposed   22.____
to distribute one leaflet to each supermarket in the neighborhood. When the day was
over, Tom had 8 leaflets left. Bill had no leaflets left.
How many supermarkets got leaflets yesterday?

    A.   8   B.   10   C.   12   D.   18

23. What is 2/3 of 1 1/8?   23.____

    A.   1 11/16   B.   3/4   C.   3/8   D.   4 1/3

24. A farmer bought a load of 120 bushels of corn.   24.____
After he fed 45 bushels to his hogs, what fraction of his supply remained?

    A.   5/8   B.   3/5   C.   3/8   D.   4/7

25. In the numeral 3,159,217, the 2 is in the _____ column.

    A. hundreds   B. units   C. thousands   D. tens

25._____

KEY (CORRECT ANSWERS)

1.	D		11.	A
2.	B		12.	C
3.	D		13.	A
4.	B		14.	A
5.	D		15.	B
6.	C		16.	C
7.	A		17.	D
8.	C		18.	D
9.	C		19.	A
10.	C		20.	D

21.	B
22.	C
23.	B
24.	A
25.	A

SOLUTIONS TO PROBLEMS

1. $57,901 + 34,762 = 92,663$

2. $559 + 448 + 362 + 662 = 2031$

3. $36,153 + 28,624 + 81,379 = 146,156$

4. $742 + 9197 + 8972 = 18,911$

5. $7989 + 8759 + 2726 = 19,474$

6. $\$111.55 + \$95.05 + \$38.80 = \$245.40$

7. $1302 + 46,187 + 92,610 + 4522 = 144,621$

8. $47,953 + 58,041 + 63,022 + 22,333 = 191,349$

9. $76,563 + 45,693 + 38,521 + 50,987 + 72,723 = 282,487$

10. $85,923 + 97,211 + 11,333 + 4412 + 22,533 = 221,412$

11. $4299 + 54,163 + 89,765 + 1012 + 38,962 = 188,201$

12. $48,526 + 709 + 11,534 + 80,432 + 6096 = 147,297$

13. $\$407.62 + \$109.01 + \$68.44 + \$378.68 = \$963.75$

14. $40,614 - 4697 = 35,917$

15. $81,773 - 5717 = 76,056$

16. $\$1755.35 - \$1201.75 = \$553.60$

17. $\$2402.10 - \$998.85 = \$1403.25$

18. $12 \ 1/2 + 2 \ 1/4 + 3 \ 1/4 = 17 \ 4/4 = 18$

19. $150 - 80 = 70$

20. $2 \ 1/4 + 3 + 1 \ 1/4 + 2 \ 1/4 + 1/2 = 8 \ 5/4 = 9 \ 1/4$ tons

21. $17 \ 3/4 - 7 \ 1/4 = 10 \ 2/4 = 10 \ 1/2$

22. $10 + 10 - 8 - 0 = 12$ supermarkets

23. $(\frac{2}{3})(1\frac{1}{8}) = (\frac{2}{3})(\frac{9}{8}) = \frac{18}{24} = \frac{3}{4}$

24. $120 - 45 = 75$. Then, $\frac{75}{120} = \frac{5}{8}$

25. The number 2 is in the hundreds column of 3,159,217

TEST 3

DIRECTIONS: Each question or incomplete statement is followed by several suggested answers or completions. Select the one that BEST answers the question or completes the statement. *PRINT THE LETTER OF THE CORRECT ANSWER IN THE SPACE AT THE RIGHT.*

1. The distance covered in three minutes by a subway train traveling at 30 mph is _____ mile(s). 1.____

   A. 3　　　　　B. 2　　　　　C. 1 1/2　　　　　D. 1

2. A crate contains 3 pieces of equipment weighing 73, 84, and 47 pounds, respectively. The empty crate weighs 16 pounds. 2.____
   If the crate is lifted by 4 trackmen, each trackman lifting one corner of the crate, the AVERAGE number of pounds lifted by each of the trackmen is

   A. 68　　　　　B. 61　　　　　C. 55　　　　　D. 51

3. The weight per foot of a length of square-bar 4" x 4" in cross-section, as compared with one 2" x 2" in cross-section, is _____ as much. 3.____

   A. twice　　　　　　　　　B. 2 1/2 times
   C. 3 times　　　　　　　　D. 4 times

4. An order for 360 feet of 2" x 8" lumber is shipped in 20-foot lengths. 4.____
   The MAXIMUM number of 9-foot pieces that can be cut from this shipment is

   A. 54　　　　　B. 40　　　　　C. 36　　　　　D. 18

5. If a trackman gets $10.40 per hour and time and one-half for working over 40 hours, his gross salary for a week in which he worked 44 hours should be 5.____

   A. $457.60　　　　B. $478.40　　　　C. $499.20　　　　D. $514.80

6. If a section of ballast 6'-0" wide, 8'-0" long, and 2'-6" deep is excavated, the amount of ballast removed is _____ cu. feet. 6.____

   A. 96　　　　　B. 104　　　　　C. 120　　　　　D. 144

7. The sum of 7'2 3/4", 0'-2 7/8", 3'-0", 4'-6 3/8", and 1'-9 1/4" is 7.____

   A. 16'-8 1/4"　　　B. 16'-8 3/4"　　　C. 16'-9 1/4"　　　D. 16' -9 3/4"

8. The sum of 3 1/16", 4 1/4", 2 5/8", and 5 7/16" is 8.____

   A. 15 3/16"　　　B. 15 1/4"　　　C. 15 3/8"　　　D. 15 1/2"

9. Add: $51.79, $29.39, and $8.98. 9.____
   The CORRECT answer is

   A. $78.97　　　　B. $88.96　　　　C. $89.06　　　　D. $90.16

10. Add: $72.07 and $31.54. Then subtract $25.75. 10.____
    The CORRECT answer is

    A. $77.86　　　　B. $82.14　　　　C. $88.96　　　　D. $129.36

11. Start with $82.47. Then subtract $25.50, $4.75, and 35¢.
The CORRECT answer is   11.____

    A. $30.60   B. $51.87   C. $52.22   D. $65.25

12. Add: $19.35 and $37.75. Then subtract $9.90 and $19.80.
The CORRECT answer is   12.____

    A. $27.40   B. $37.00   C. $37.30   D. $47.20

13. Add: $153   13.____
           114
           210
         +186

    A. $657   B. $663   C. $713   D. $757

14. Add: $64.91   14.____
          13.53
          19.27
         20.00
        +72.84

    A. $170.25   B. $178.35   C. $180.45   D. $190.55

15. Add: 1963   15.____
         1742
       +2497

    A.   6202   B.   6022   C.   5212   D.   5102

16. Add: 206   16.____
         709
       1342
     +2076

    A.   3432   B.   3443   C.   4312   D.   4333

17. Subtract: $190.76   17.____
         -   .99

    A. $189.97   B. $189.87   C. $189.77   D. $189.67

18. From 99876 subtract 85397. The answer should be   18.____

    A.   14589   B.   14521   C.   14479   D.   13589

19. From $876.51 subtract $92.89. The answer should be   19.____

    A. $773.52   B. $774.72   C. $783.62   D. $784.72

20. From 70935 subtract 49489. The answer should be   20.____

    A.   20436   B.   21446   C.   21536   D.   21546

21. From $391.55 subtract $273.45. The answer should be   21.____

    A. $118.10   B. $128.20   C. $178.10   D. $218.20

22. When 119 is subtracted from the sum of 2016 + 1634, the answer is   22.____

    A. 2460   B. 3531   C. 3650   D. 3769

23. Multiply 35 x 65 x 15. The answer should be   23.____

    A. 2275   B. 24265   C. 31145   D. 34125

24. Multiply: 4.06   24.____
             x.031

    A. 1.2586   B. .12586   C. .02586   D. .1786

25. When 65 is added to the result of 14 multiplied by 13, the answer is   25.____

    A. 92   B. 182   C. 247   D. 16055

KEY (CORRECT ANSWERS)

1.	C	11.	B
2.	C	12.	A
3.	D	13.	B
4.	C	14.	D
5.	B	15.	A
6.	C	16.	D
7.	C	17.	C
8.	C	18.	C
9.	D	19.	C
10.	A	20.	B

21.	A
22.	B
23.	D
24.	B
25.	C

SOLUTIONS TO PROBLEMS

1. Let x = distance. Then, $\dfrac{30}{60} = \dfrac{x}{3}$ Solving, x = 1 1/2 miles

2. $(73 + 84 + 47 + 16) \div 4 = 55$ pounds

3. $(4 \times 4) \div (2 \times 2) =$ a ratio of 4 to 1.

4. $20 \div 9 = 2\ 2/9$, rounded down to 2 pieces. Then, $(360 \div 20)(2) = 36$

5. Salary $=(\$10.40)(40) + (\$15.60)(4) = \$478.40$

6. $(6)(8)(2\ 1/2) = 120$ cu.ft.

7. $7'2\dfrac{3}{4}"+0'2\dfrac{7}{8}"+3'0"+4'6\dfrac{3}{8}"+1'9\dfrac{1}{4}"=15'19\dfrac{18}{8}"=15'21\dfrac{1}{4}"=16'9\dfrac{1}{4}"$

8. $3\dfrac{1}{16}"+4\dfrac{1}{4}"+2\dfrac{5}{8}"+5\dfrac{7}{16}"=14\dfrac{22}{16}"=15\dfrac{3}{8}"$

9. $\$51.79 + \$29.39 + \$8.98 = \$90.16$

10. $\$72.07 + \$31.54 = \$103.61$. Then, $\$103.61 - \$25.75 = \$77.86$

11. $\$82.47 - \$25.50 - \$4.75 - \$0.35 = \$51.87$

12. $\$19.35 + \$37.75 = \$57.10$. Then, $\$57.10 - \$9.90 - \$19.80 = \$27.40$

13. $\$153 + \$114 + \$210 + \$186 = \$663$

14. $\$64.91 + \$13.53 + \$19.27 + \$20.00 + \$72.84 = \$190.55$

15. $1963 + 1742 + 2497 = 6202$

16. $206 + 709 + 1342 + 2076 = 4333$

17. $\$190.76 - .99 = \$189.77$

18. $99,876 - 85,397 = 14,479$

19. $\$876.51 - \$92.89 = \$783.62$

20. $70,935 - 49,489 = 21,446$

21. $\$391.55 - \$273.45 = \$118.10$

22. $(2016 + 1634) - 119 = 3650 - 119 = 3531$

23. $(35)(65)(15) = 34,125$

24. $(4.06)(.031) = .12586$

25. $65 + (14)(13) = 65 + 182 = 247$
